CHRISTUS PRAESENS

Christus Praesens

A Reconsideration
of Rudolf Bultmann's Christology

James F. Kay

WILLIAM B. EERDMANS PUBLISHING COMPANY
GRAND RAPIDS, MICHIGAN

Copyright © 1994 by Wm. B. Eerdmans Publishing Co.
255 Jefferson Ave. S.E., Grand Rapids, Michigan 49503

Printed in the United States of America

Library of Congress Cataloging-in-Publication Data

Kay, James F., 1948-
Christus praesens: a reconsideration of Rudolf Bultmann's Christology / James F. Kay.
p.   cm.
Includes bibliographical references and index.
ISBN 0-8028-0131-5
1. Bultmann, Rudolf Karl, 1884-1976. 2. Bible. N.T. — Theology — History of
doctrines — 20th century. 3. Jesus Christ — Presence — History of
doctrines — 20th century. I. Title.
BX4827.B78K38   1993
225 — dc20   93-38658
                                                        CIP

Contents

Abbreviations

AdT	*Anfänge der dialektischen Theologie*
BDT	*The Beginnings of Dialectic Theology*
BK	*Der zweite Brief an die Korinther*
CC	*The Second Letter to the Corinthians*
CD	*Church Dogmatics*
EaF	*Existence and Faith*
EJ	*Das Evangelium des Johannes*
EPT	*Essays Philosophical and Theological*
ET	English translation
FaU 1	*Faith and Understanding*
GST	*Die Geschichte der synoptischen Tradition*
GuV	*Glauben und Verstehen: Gesammelte Aufsätze*
HJKC	*The Historical Jesus and the Kerygmatic Christ: Essays on the New Quest of the Historical Jesus*
HST	*The History of the Synoptic Tradition*
IJC	*The Identity of Jesus Christ: The Hermeneutical Bases of Dogmatic Theology*
JB	*Die drei Johannesbriefe*
JCaM	*Jesus Christ and Mythology*
JE	*The Johannine Epistles: A Commentary on the Johannine Epistles*
JG	*The Gospel of John: A Commentary*
JTS	*The Journal of Theological Studies*
KaM 1	*Kerygma and Myth: A Theological Debate*
KaM 2	*Kergyma and Myth*, vol. 2
KuM 1	*Kerygma und Mythos: Ein theologisches Gespräch*

KuM 2	*Kerygma und Mythos: Diskussionen und Stimmen zum Problem der Entmythologisierung*
NRSV	New Revised Standard Version
NTaM	*New Testament and Mythology and Other Basic Writings*
"NTaM"	"New Testament and Mythology: The Problem of Demythologizing the New Testament Proclamation"
NTQT	*New Testament Questions of Today*
NTS	*New Testament Studies*
"NTuM"	"Neues Testament und Mythologie: Das Problem der Entmythologisierung der neutestamentlichen Verkündigung"
OTaCF	*The Old Testament and Christian Faith: A Theological Discussion*
"PdE"	"Zum Problem der Entmythologisierung"
PT	*Political Theology*
RGG²	*Die Religion in Geschichte und Gegenwart: Handwörterbuch für Theologie und Religions-wissenschaft,* 2nd edition
RGG³	*Die Religion in Geschichte und Gegenwart: Handwörterbuch für Theologie und Religionswissenschaft,* 3rd edition
TdNT	*Theologie des Neuen Testaments*
TDNT	*Theological Dictionary of the New Testament*
TH	*Theology of Hope: On the Ground and the Implications of a Christian Eschatology*
TLZ	*Theologische Literaturzeitung*
TNT	*Theology of the New Testament*
TWNT	*Theologisches Wörterbuch zum Neuen Testament*

Acknowledgments

RESEARCH for this book began at Union Theological Seminary, New York, in 1984, the centennial of Rudolf Bultmann's birth. Since then a number of my teachers and colleagues have read drafts either of all or of several chapters. I wish to acknowledge each of them by name with sincere appreciation for their helpful comments and criticisms, some of which I actually heeded: J. Christiaan Beker, James H. Cone, Steven J. Kraftchick, Joel Marcus, J. Louis Martyn, Christopher Morse, Richard A. Norris, Jr., and Geoffrey Wainwright. I also benefited from an exchange of views with William C. Placher regarding the late Hans W. Frei. In addition, I was assisted by the bibliographical research of Patricia Howery Davis, the word processing of Joseph Herman, the technical Word Perfect wizardry of Jerry L. Gorham, and the administrative efficiency of Lois F. Haydu. I remain continually grateful for the personal encouragement of William B. Eerdmans, Jr., Paul S. Soule, and Alan R. Stenberg.

My colleagues at Princeton Theological Seminary have been unfailingly supportive in my teaching and research. I welcome this opportunity to thank my students who have heard some of this material over the years in courses in homiletics and theology, and I thank the Board of Trustees, President Thomas W. Gillespie, and Dean Conrad H. Massa for facilitating a generous research leave that enabled me to complete this book. To Thomas G. Long also goes my sincere appreciation for assuming an extra burden of teaching during my research leave.

A word of special thanks is owed Schubert M. Ogden of Southern Methodist University, Dallas, for generously making available to me a copy of *Protokoll der Tagung 'Alter Marburger' 2.-5. Januar 1979 in Hofgeismar*. Citations from Adolf von Harnack, *Das Christentum und die Ge-*

schichte: Ein Vortrag, 4th ed. (Leipzig: J. C. Hinrichs'sche Buchhandlung, 1897), are made possible courtesy of Burke Library of Union Theological Seminary, New York.

I gratefully acknowledge permission granted by the editors of *Theology Today* to make use of material contained in my article "Myth or Narrative? Bultmann's 'New Testament and Mythology' Turns Fifty," 48 (October, 1991): 326-32.

Unless otherwise indicated, I am responsible for the English translations of the cited German texts. The one exception is the excerpt from Bultmann's letter to Martin Rade, which John Jay Hughes of St. Louis kindly rendered into English.

Again, unless otherwise indicated, biblical citations in English are from the Revised Standard Version.

The students who have been both spellbound and welcomed by his teaching at Union know firsthand our common debt to Christopher Morse. This book is dedicated to him.

Introduction

WHEN I remarked to an American theologian that I was preparing a book on Bultmann, he asked me with astonishment, "Why?"

Clearly, as my questioner rightly assumed, we are in a post-Bultmann period. As one seminary dean has commented, "Students today do not even go *through* Bultmann; they go *around* him." The reasons for Rudolf Bultmann's eclipse have little to do with opposition to his program of demythologizing, which provoked such partisanship in the 1950s, and more to do with what are widely perceived in the 1990s as insurmountable difficulties with his theology as a whole.

In this book, I argue that Bultmann's exegesis and theology advance the claim of the Reformation that Christ is present "in the pulpit," in and through the proclamation of the gospel.[1] This persisting claim finds its way into dogmatics under the rubric of the *Christus praesens,* the "Christ who is present."[2] Bultmann's adoption of this very term takes place only

---

1. "Calvin was fond of saying that in the pulpit Christ must preside. The verb is significant, reminding us of the 'president' of the Eucharist in the early Church." T. H. L. Parker, *John Calvin: A Biography* (Philadelphia: Westminster, 1975), p. 95.

2. See, e.g., Otto Weber, *Foundations of Dogmatics,* 2 vols., ed. and trans. Darrell L. Guder (Grand Rapids: Wm. B. Eerdmans, 1983), 2:514-15. The following are also noteworthy: The fragmentary 1933 Christology lectures of Dietrich Bonhoeffer, *Christ the Center,* trans. Edwin H. Robinson (New York: Harper & Row, 1978); the dogmatics of Otto A. Dilschneider, *Gegenwart Christi (Christus praesens): Grundriss einer Dogmatik der Offenbarung,* 2 vols. (Gütersloh: C. Bertelsmann Verlag, 1948); the hermeneutical study of Peter Hodgson, *Jesus — Word and Promise: An Essay in Christology* (Philadelphia: Fortress, 1971); and the Roman Catholic perspectives in Lothar Lies, ed., *Praesentia Christi: Festschrift Johannes Betz zum 70 Geburtstag dargebracht von Kollegen, Freunden, Schülern* (Düsseldorf: Patmos Verlag, 1984).

by way of a reformulation that continues to challenge customary under-standings. To discover what Bultmann means by the *Christus praesens*, I reconsider his formative liberal heritage, reexamine his interpretations of Paul and John, and then systematically set forth his own constructive position.[3] Only then do I proceed to confront Bultmann's critics directly.

In conversation with the work of Hans W. Frei, I examine the renewed claim for the narrative character of the gospel in contrast to Bultmann's punctiliar kerygma; with Dorothee Sölle, I take account of the social and political scope of salvation over against Bultmann's existentialist constrictions; and, with Jürgen Moltmann, I attend to the future orienta-tion of New Testament eschatology as opposed to Bultmann's kerygmatic "presence of eternity."

I show that Bultmann's work can largely withstand the criticisms of Frei, Sölle, and Moltmann, and I venture replies to them based on a fuller examination of Bultmann's writings than is frequently found. The result is to uncover in Bultmann's critics assumptions that stem from the older liberalism. As both the heir and the critic of liberalism, Bultmann thus remains an indispensable conversation partner for theology today.

---

3. In seeking for Bultmann a new hearing, I rely chiefly on primary sources. For those wishing to test my own hearing or who need an introduction to Bultmann's thought, the following provide the best surveys in English of Bultmann's overall theology: Robert Morgan, "Rudolf Bultmann," in *The Modern Theologians: An Introduction to Christian Theology in the Twentieth Century,* 2 vols., ed. David F. Ford (Oxford: Basil Blackwell, 1989), 1:109-33; Roger A. Johnson, ed., Introduction to *Rudolf Bultmann: Interpreting Faith for the Modern Era* (London: Collins, 1987), pp. 9-43; John Painter, *Theology as Hermeneutics: Rudolf Bultmann's Interpretation of the History of Jesus* (Sheffield: The Almond Press, 1987); Norman Perrin, *The Promise of Bultmann* (Philadelphia: J. B. Lippincott, 1969); Walter Schmithals, *An Introduction to the Theology of Rudolf Bultmann,* 2nd ed., trans. John Bowden (London: SCM, 1967); Günther Bornkamm, "The Theology of Rudolf Bultmann," trans. Arne Unhjem, in *The Theology of Rudolf Bultmann,* ed. Charles W. Kegley (New York: Harper & Row, 1966), pp. 3-20; Robert W. Funk, ed., Introduction to *Faith and Understanding,* trans. Louise Pettibone Smith (New York: Harper & Row, 1966; reprint ed., Philadelphia: Fortress, 1987; hereafter cited as *FaU* 1), pp. 9-27; John Cobb, *Living Options in Protestant Theology: A Survey of Methods* (Philadelphia: Westminster, 1962), pp. 227-45; and Schubert M. Ogden, ed. and trans., Introduction to *Existence and Faith: Shorter Writings of Rudolf Bultmann* (New York: Meridian Books, 1960; hereafter cited as *EaF*), pp. 9-21.

CHAPTER 1

Rudolf Bultmann and "the *Christus Praesens*": Background for Reconsideration

Recent Scholarly Assessments

"REVISITING" *Theology of the New Testament* during the 1984 centennial of Rudolf Bultmann's birth, Dieter Georgi highlighted its kerygmatic Christology:

> In his *Theology* Bultmann does not use the pointed formulation made elsewhere that Jesus is risen into the kerygma of the early church, but his outline and discussion present something like that de facto. The eschatological experience of the early church Bultmann sees described most of all in christological terms centered in the experience of the presence of Jesus as eschatological functionary communicated by the kerygma.[1]

For Bultmann, the christological formulations of the New Testament express the church's encounter with "the presence of Jesus" as mediated by the kerygma.

This characterization by Georgi stands in contrast to some recent trends in Bultmann interpretation. Beginning in the late 1960s, the theological world was served notice from several quarters that, whatever else

---

1. "Rudolf Bultmann's *Theology of the New Testament* Revisited," in *Bultmann, Retrospect and Prospect: The Centenary Symposium at Wellesley*, ed. Edward C. Hobbs, Harvard Theological Studies, no. 35 (Philadelphia: Fortress, 1985), p. 79. See *Theology of the New Testament*, 2 vols., trans. Kendrick Grobel (New York: Charles Scribner's Sons, 1951-1955; hereafter cited as *TNT*); pub. in Ger. as *Theologie des Neuen Testaments*, 9th ed., ed. Otto Merk (Tübingen: J. C. B. Mohr [Paul Siebeck], 1984; hereafter cited as *TdNT*).

Bultmann had achieved, he had failed to deliver on the presence of Jesus Christ.

For example, Dietrich Ritschl's *Memory and Hope,* published in 1967 with the subtitle *An Inquiry Concerning the Presence of Christ,* acknowledges Bultmann's "concept of the *Christus praesens*" as the presence of the eschatological event in the life of the believer. Nevertheless, Ritschl sees Bultmann's "eschatological event" as only a version of Augustine's "eternal now."[2]

According to Ritschl, Augustine's God as the Creator stands outside and above the time which issues from creation. Therefore, unlike a creature, God is a timeless, unchangeable, trans-historical, and omnipresent Spirit. For God, there is no past and no future, only the present. Hence, only by centering in the present can the creature commune with God. Through this communion, the past events of the birth, passion, death, and resurrection of Christ, which for God are ever present, now become present for the creature as well. If Ritschl is right, then in Bultmann's view we reach Christ through the omnipresence of the timeless God; we do not reach God through the timely presence of the Risen Lord. So despite Bultmann's christological concentration, Ritschl finds it all betrayed by a controlling "deism" traceable to Augustine.[3]

While Dietrich Ritschl lamented Bultmann's Augustinianism, Charles David Barrett, in his 1968 Drew dissertation, questioned Bultmann's Lutheranism. Barrett observes in Bultmann that Luther's language of the "real presence" gives way to that of "the eschatological event."[4] Barrett then analyzes this event in terms of the Heideggerian categories it allegedly presupposes and concludes there is no real reason why "the eschatological event should be essentially and continually connected" to Jesus and "formally limited by him."[5] Thus, for all of its soteriological stress, Bultmann's Christology does not represent an interpretation of Luther's doctrine of the real presence, but, on the contrary, represents its transformation into a self-understanding bound to Heidegger — but not to Jesus.

---

2. (New York: Macmillan, 1967; London: Collier-Macmillan, 1967), pp. 40-41.

3. Ibid., pp. 125-26.

4. "The Lutheranism of Bultmann: An Analysis of His Doctrine of Pre-understanding and Eschatological Event, with Special Reference to the Question of Their Similarity to and Variance from Luther's Concepts of Theological Conscience and the Real Presence of Christ" (Ph.D. dissertation, Drew University), p. 4.

5. Ibid., p. 208.

In yet a third criticism of Bultmann from this same period, we note J. Louis Martyn's survey of "Attitudes Ancient and Modern toward Tradition about Jesus." Bultmann's classic formulation that after Easter the proclaimer became the proclaimed Martyn labels "a disastrous half-truth. For it is precisely one of the central aspects of the Easter faith that Jesus Christ remains the proclaimer."[6] Here Martyn underscores that for the primitive church Jesus Christ is the rendering agent, and not simply the rendered object, of Christian proclamation. Thus, the eschatological function of Jesus is to communicate the kerygma and not just be communicated by it.

What binds these criticisms of Ritschl, Barrett, and Martyn into a consensus is their common contention that for whatever reason — theological, philosophical, or exegetical — Bultmann passes over the presence of Jesus Christ, the contemporary agent of salvation.

A similar conclusion informs David H. Kelsey's subsequent characterization of Bultmann in *The Uses of Scripture in Recent Theology.*[7] Kelsey holds that whereas Karl Barth construes God's presence among the faithful "in the mode of a *concrete actuality,* e.g., the presence of the Risen Christ," Bultmann construes "God's presence in the mode of an *ideal possibility,* . . . for transformation of 'inauthentic existence' into 'authentic existence'."[8] While Kelsey neither intends nor constructs a definitive typology of how Bultmann and Barth use scripture, he certainly does type the way they construe the divine presence. On the basis of this unacknowledged typology, Barth — rather than Bultmann — emerges as the one who construes the divine presence in terms of the Risen Christ. Kelsey's characterization of Bultmann actually echoes that of Barth.[9] Nevertheless, in taking Barth's line on Bultmann, Kelsey neglects to mention Bultmann's reply to Barth: "Is my doctrine of the Christ event really only a doctrine of the 'event of transition'? Is it not rather the doctrine of the Word of God in which Christ is present [*in dem Christus präsent ist*]?"[10] Thus, Barth and

---

6. *Union Seminary Quarterly Review* 23 (Winter 1968): 143-44, n. 21.

7. (Philadelphia: Fortress, 1975).

8. Ibid., p. 162. See also pp. 161 and 168-69.

9. See Barth, "Rudolf Bultmann — An Attempt to Understand Him," in *Kerygma and Myth,* vol. 2, ed. Hans Werner Bartsch, trans. Reginald H. Fuller (London: SPCK, 1962; hereafter cited as *KaM* 2), pp. 95-97.

10. Bultmann to Barth, 11-15 November 1952, in *Karl Barth — Rudolf Bultmann Letters 1922-1966,* ed. Bernd Jaspert and Geoffrey Bromiley, trans. Geoffrey Bromiley (Grand Rapids: Wm. B. Eerdmans, 1981), p. 93; pub. in Ger. as Karl Barth, *Gesamtausgabe,*

Kelsey notwithstanding, Bultmann does claim to construe the divine presence in terms of Jesus Christ. For Bultmann, only the present actuality of Jesus Christ procures the possibility for our "authentic existence."

Remarkably, each of the negative verdicts we have surveyed on the significance of the *Christus praesens* for Bultmann is based on a narrow choice of admissible evidence. Ritschl's allegation of Bultmann's "deism" derives solely, if footnotes are indicative, from *History and Eschatology*.[11] Barrett's exclusively Heideggerian analysis of "the eschatological event" proceeds without one mention of Bultmann's exegetical work and without a single citation from Bultmann's frequent references to the presence of Christ. Martyn's attack on Bultmann for failing to see that, after Easter, "Jesus Christ remains the proclaimer" overlooks Bultmann's claim that in Christian preaching "the proclaimed is simultaneously present as the proclaimer."[12] Kelsey's description of Bultmann's "theological position" admittedly draws only from "the sum total of Bultmann's brief essays on individual theological topics."[13] To have used such selective sources in denying "the presence of Jesus" a place in Bultmann's thought raises new doubts about this collective judgment, especially in light of Georgi's more recent retrieval of this very theme as central to *Theology of the New Testament*.

---

vol. 5, pt. 1: *Karl Barth — Rudolf Bultmann Briefwechsel 1922-1966,* ed. Bernd Jaspert (Zürich: Theologischer Verlag, 1971) p. 178.

11. (Edinburgh: The University Press, 1957); pub. in Ger. as *Geschichte und Eschatologie* (Tübingen: J. C. B. Mohr [Paul Siebeck], 1958). Moreover, Ritschl ties Bultmann to a method Bultmann himself decries when he chastises Fritz Buri for "trying to sketch christology on the basis of theology, instead of going about it the other way round." See "The Christological Confession of the World Council of Churches [1951-52]," in *Essays Philosophical and Theological,* trans. James C. G. Grieg (London: SCM, 1955; hereafter cited as *EPT*), p. 288; pub. in Ger. as "Das christologische Bekenntnis des Ökumenischen Rates," in *Glauben und Verstehen: Gesammelte Aufsätze,* 4 vols. (Tübingen: J. C. B. Mohr [Paul Siebeck], 1933-65; hereafter cited as *GuV*), 2:259.

12. "Der Verkündigte zugleich als der Verkünder präsent ist." "Allgemeine Wahrheiten und christliche Verkündigung [1957]," in *GuV* 3:169. Cf. ET: "General Truths and Christian Proclamation," in *History and Hermeneutic,* ed. Robert W. Funk, *Journal for Theology and the Church,* no. 4 (Tübingen: J. C. B. Mohr [Paul Siebeck], 1967; New York: Harper & Row, 1967), p. 154.

13. *Uses of Scripture,* p. 4. In fact, about half of Kelsey's footnotes to Bultmann refer to *TNT*; the remaining notes refer to about a half-dozen other writings. Kelsey's own imaginative construal of Bultmann appears dependent on Barth and John Macquarrie. See p. 87, n. 46 and n. 53.

The *Christus Praesens:*
An Approach to Bultmann's Formulation

Since Bultmann produced both exegetical and theological treatises, and since his exegetical treatises venture theological judgments while his theological writings usually make appeals to scripture, grasping Bultmann's *Christus praesens* requires coming to grips with "the uses of scripture" in Bultmann's theology. To put the issue succinctly, should we approach Bultmann's positions primarily through his exegetical writings as Erich Dinkler, John Painter, and Robert Morgan insist;[14] or should we attend primarily, if not exclusively, to Bultmann's theological writings as in the case of Charles David Barrett and David Kelsey, since Bultmann's readings of scripture are actually determined by a pre-set theological understanding or what Kelsey calls a "pre-text."[15]

On the basis of his comparative study of how Bultmann and six other twentieth-century theologians actually employ scripture, Kelsey concludes that when a theologian takes a biblical text "as Christian scripture" then certain judgments are entailed in exegesis; for example, decisions pertaining to nurturing or reforming the church's identity, guiding the church's task and common life, and determining "which of several patterns in scripture are normative for doing theology and ought therefore to be the principal subject of the exegesis." Kelsey's thesis is that these kinds of judgments "are decisively shaped by an imaginative judgment about the mode in which God makes himself present in and through those uses of scripture, a judgment that is logically prior to any exegetical judgments about the text." If Kelsey is right, then Bultmann's imaginative construal of the divine presence as formulated in the concept of the *Christus praesens* — that is, Jesus Christ as the kerygmatic eschatological salvation event — is actually determining Bultmann's reading of scripture rather than emerging from it.[16]

One need not deny Kelsey's thesis on the role of what Bultmann would term "preunderstanding" to suggest (with Bultmann) that it is only

---

14. Dinkler, Editor's Foreword to *The Second Letter to the Corinthians,* by Rudolf Bultmann, trans. Roy A. Harrisville (Minneapolis: Augsburg Publishing House, 1985; hereafter cited as *CC*), p. 7; pub. in Ger. as Vorwort to *Der zweite Brief an die Korinther* (Göttingen: Vandenhoeck & Ruprecht, 1976; hereafter cited as *BK*), p. 11; Painter, *Theology as Hermeneutics,* pp. 4-5; and Morgan, "Bultmann," in *Modern Theologians,* 1:113.

15. *Uses of Scripture,* p. 170.

16. *Ibid.,* pp. 198-99. See also pp. 170 and 205.

part of the hermeneutical equation. Not only are the uses of scripture shaped by one's theological preunderstanding, but one's theological preunderstanding is also shaped by scripture and its uses. Where Kelsey sees only a one-way street, Bultmann discovers an interchange. Scripture not only awaits imaginative construals; it actively informs them. Given the interplay between the interpreter and the interpreted, the examination of Bultmann's exegetical work as a source of his theological perspectives is justified. Its omission leads, as we have seen, to distortions of his views.[17]

Nevertheless, as we attend to Bultmann's exegetical writings, how do we distinguish the voice of the scriptures from that of their Marburg commentator? Only occasionally, as when Bultmann criticizes Paul for 1 Corinthians 15, in accordance with the apostle's better lights, do we become immediately aware of an audible difference between the interpreter and the interpreted.[18] How, then, in less dramatic cases, do we decide whether Bultmann is giving us the view of the biblical writer, or, by contrast, simply his own?

Unfortunately, one of the more recent full-scale studies of Bultmann in English falters on this very question. Robert Campbell Roberts, a student of Kelsey, in *Rudolf Bultmann's Theology: A Critical Interpretation*, argues that what Paul and John say is not always what Bultmann says by means of them. Only "a raving fundamentalist," we are told, ever claims a one-to-one correspondence between the meanings of a biblical text and those assigned by its modern commentator. On the other hand, Roberts professes no ready way to ferret out the presumed differences. "Therefore, it would seem intrinsically overcomplicated and uncertain to execute an interpretation which took as its point of departure Bultmann's exegesis."

17. For Bultmann's discussion of the role of "preunderstanding" *(Vorverständnis)*, see "The Significance of 'Dialectical Theology' for the Scientific Study of the New Testament [1928]," in *FaU* 1:155-59; pub. in Ger. as "Die Bedeutung der 'dialektischen Theologie' für die neutestamentliche Wissenschaft," in *GuV* 1:124-28; "Church and Teaching in the New Testament [1929]," in *FaU* 1:184-93; pub. in Ger. as "Kirche und Lehre im Neuen Testament," in *GuV* 1:153-62; "The Problem of 'Natural Theology' [1933]," in *FaU* 1:315-18; pub. in Ger. as "Das Problem der 'natürlichen Theologie,'" in *GuV* 1:295-98; "The Problem of Hermeneutics [1950]," in Schubert M. Ogden, ed. and trans., *New Testament and Mythology and Other Basic Writings* (Philadelphia: Fortress, 1984; hereafter cited as *NTaM*), pp. 69-93; pub. in Ger. as "Das Problem der Hermeneutik," in *GuV* 2:211-35; and "Is Exegesis without Presuppositions Possible? [1957]," in *NTaM*, pp. 145-53; pub. in Ger. as "Ist voraussetzunglose Exegese möglich?," in *GuV* 3:142-50.

18. See, e.g., "Karl Barth, *The Resurrection of the Dead* [1926]," in *FaU* 1:83-84 and 92-93; pub. in Ger. as "Karl Barth, 'Die Auferstehung der Toten,'" in *GuV* 1:54.

In so concluding, Roberts justifies interpreting Bultmann solely on the basis of those passages where Bultmann is speaking for himself alone, in what Roberts calls the "less exegetical essays." Thus, we are urged to accept as a scholarly virtue the widespread practice of ignoring much, if not most, of Bultmann's work![19]

Roberts' stumble at the starting gate does not occur because of his recognition that Bultmann sometimes speaks as an exegete, but rather in his dismissal of exegetical work as bearing in any way on Bultmann's theological perspectives. Roberts apparently believes we can understand the citations of, and allusions to, scripture in Bultmann's theological writings without reference to his exegetical treatments. Such speciousness ignores the fact that Bultmann's shorthand references to scriptural passages in his theological writings are often illumined by his discussion of these texts in more strictly exegetical contexts.

As for Roberts' claim that it is virtually impossible to distinguish the views of a biblical text from those held by its modern commentator, the point with respect to interpreting *Bultmann* is not what Paul and John say in distinction from what Bultmann says they say. Rather, the point is to uncover similarities and differences between Bultmann's own views and Bultmann's own views of Paul and John. Once the hermeneutical issue is recast in these terms, there remains no justification for joining Roberts in shunning Bultmann the exegete — especially when attempting "a critical interpretation."

Nevertheless, neither Kelsey nor Roberts can be faulted for formally distinguishing between "the more" and "the less" exegetical and theological writings in the Bultmann corpus. On the more exegetical side we would group the treatises on New Testament texts and concepts, works of reference and form criticism, and commentaries on the Johannine books and 2 Corinthians. The unity of these various writings is accorded by their common acceptance of historical investigation as "the first requisite."[20] On the less exegetical side belong those occasional theological essays and lectures, of which any number collected in the four volumes of *Glauben und Verstehen* could be taken as representative. These writings are characterized by a more direct expression of Bultmann's own views, with some

19. (Grand Rapids: Wm. B. Eerdmans, 1976), p. 16.
20. "The Concept of the Word of God in the New Testament [1933]," in *FaU* 1:286, n. 2; pub. in Ger. as "Der Begriff des Wortes Gottes im Neuen Testament," in *GuV* 1:268, n. 1.

allusions and appeals to concepts and themes elaborated at greater length
in the more exegetical writings. Between the exegetical and the theological
works stand the hybrids, of which *Theology of the New Testament* is the
eminent example. Here the aim is to interpret the New Testament, teaching
what it teaches, by "translating" its categories into the language and conceptuality of the present.[21] Similarly, this translating, to which Bultmann's
entire theology aims, reaches its fulfillment in church proclamation, ordi-
narily through preaching. Thus, Bultmann's sermons illumine both his
exegetical decisions and theological positions. As such, they too serve as
sources for reconstructing his views. Therefore, a full-orbed examination
of Bultmann's works — both exegetical and theological — is required for
our study, especially since those who criticize Bultmann on "the presence
of Jesus" typically select only snippets from his work.

Kelsey does prove helpful in his insistence that theological positions
are actually the result of imaginative construals about the divine presence,
or, if you will, about the way in which God and humanity are related, or,
to employ the language of the older liberalism, about the "essence of
Christianity." For Bultmann, the *Christus praesens,* or Jesus Christ as the
kerygmatic eschatological salvation event, comprises the subject matter of
the scriptures in the light of which the scriptures are interpreted and church
tradition is tested.

In addition to the scriptures, what are the sources of Bultmann's
imaginative construal of the divine presence? There are many strands of
Christian tradition woven into his conceptual fabric, as his references to
Augustine, Luther, Melanchthon, and Herrmann indicate. Furthermore,
Bultmann adopted the Kierkegaardian conceptuality of the early Barth's
dialectical theology and, subsequently, the existentialist terminology of the
early Martin Heidegger.[22] No doubt, when the definitive account of Bult-

---

21. Bultmann, "Theology as Science [1941]," in *NTaM,* p. 59; pub. in Ger. as
"Theologie als Wissenschaft," in *Protokoll der Tagung 'Alter Marburger' 2.-5. Januar 1979
in Hofgeismar,* pp. 14-15. See also *NTaM,* pp. 146-48. Kelsey, *Uses of Scripture,* pp. 185-92,
argues for theology as "redescription" and not "translation."

22. See Heidegger, *Being and Time,* trans. John Macquarrie and Edward Robinson
(New York: Harper & Row, 1962); pub. in Ger. as *Sein und Zeit,* 6th ed. (Tübingen:
Neomarius Verlag, 1949); John Macquarrie, *An Existentialist Theology: A Comparison of
Heidegger and Bultmann,* with a Foreword by Rudolf Bultmann (London: SCM, 1955;
reprint ed., New York: Harper & Row, 1965); and Herbert C. Wolf, *Kierkegaard and
Bultmann: The Quest of the Historical Jesus* (Minneapolis: Augsburg, 1965).

mann's theology is written, it will have as one of its principal tasks the weighing and weighting of these and other sources in shaping his account of the Christian faith.[23]

What is undisputed is that Bultmann's work as a New Testament scholar began within the ranks of German liberal theology.[24] These ranks were decimated not only by the calamity of World War I but also by the rediscovery of New Testament eschatology. This rediscovery, itself the achievement of liberalism's historical interest and methods, completely out-flanked the liberals' own theological positions and assumptions. After examining in this chapter the role of liberalism and its crisis in framing Bultmann's starting point for his reformulation of the presence of Christ, we turn to his respective expositions of Paul and John in chapters two and three. The intention here is to reconstruct the exegetical arguments for the *Christus praesens* in those canonical writings which Bultmann sees as expressing most clearly the eschatological essence or subject matter of the New Testament.[25] Footnotes will indicate where "outside" philosophical or theological views correlate with Bultmann's exegetical decisions. In chapter four, we turn more directly to Bultmann the theologian. Chapter five then proceeds to question Bultmann about the presence of Jesus by way of the newer, but now mature,

23. Roger A. Johnson argues that Bultmann is more indebted to Marburg neo-Kantianism than to Heidegger. See *The Origins of Demythologizing: Philosophy and Historiography in the Theology of Rudolf Bultmann*, Studies in the History of Religion (Supplements to Numen), no. 28 (Leiden: E. J. Brill, 1974). More recently, David Fergusson claims Herrmann as "the central influence upon Bultmann" (and precisely over against neo-Kantianism) in "Meaning, Truth, and Realism in Bultmann and Lindbeck," *Religious Studies* 26 (June 1990): 191-95.

24. For Bultmann's education and intellectual development, see Martin Evang, *Rudolf Bultmann in seiner Frühzeit, beiträge zur historischen Theologie*, no. 74 (Tübingen: J. C. B. Mohr [Paul Siebeck], 1988). Following Bultmann's lead, we use the term "liberal" to refer to that tradition of theology deriving from Albrecht Ritschl. See "Liberal Theology and the Latest Theological Movement [1924]," in *FaU* 1:36; pub. in Ger. as "Die liberale Theologie und die jüngste theologische Bewegung," in *GuV* 1:9. For an overview of the Ritschlian School, including its intramural tensions, see George Rupp, *Culture Protestantism: German Liberal Theology at the Turn of the Twentieth Century*, American Academy of Religion Series, no. 15 (Missoula, Mont.: Scholars Press, 1977), esp. pp. 15-20.

25. Bultmann holds that among the New Testament writings only those of Paul and John sufficiently grasp the paradoxical relation between history and eschatology with respect to the salvation event. See *TNT* 2:119-27. Cf. *Primitive Christianity in Its Contemporary Setting*, trans. Reginald H. Fuller (Cleveland: Collins, 1956; reprint ed., Philadelphia: Fortress, 1980), p. 179; pub. in Ger. as *Das Urchristentum im Rahmen der antiken Religionen* (Zürich: Artemis-Verlag, 1949), p. 195.

theologies of narration (Hans Frei), political transformation (Dorothee Sölle), and eschatological expectation (Jürgen Moltmann).

In reopening the question of Rudolf Bultmann and the *Christus praesens,* we begin where he began — with German liberal theology. To that end, we draw synoptically upon Albrecht Ritschl (1822-89), and three of his theological heirs, each of whom became a teacher of Bultmann: Adolf von Harnack (1851-1930), Wilhelm Herrmann (1846-1922), and Johannes Weiss (1863-1914). Each of these liberal thinkers understood the presence of Jesus as the continuing influence of his incomparable personality.

The Personality of Jesus: Bultmann's Liberal Heritage

Reporting to the Prussian Academy of Sciences in 1927, Adolf von Harnack attempts to fill a gap in scholarship by surveying "how the church has experienced and grasped the 'Christus praesens.'" Harnack claims that virtually all ecclesial formulations regarding the presence of Christ are rooted in the farewell words of Matthew 28:20: "Lo, I am with you always, to the close of the age." From this starting point, which "presupposes a still definite impression of the nearness of Jesus and his continuing influence," Harnack goes on to sketch eight "types" of the presence of Christ known to church history. He begins with the "presence of Christ as a spiritual one," the oldest understanding in the New Testament (cf. Acts 2), and ends with the claim of Pope Innocent III to be the Vicar of Christ on earth. By the High Middle Ages, "the immanence of the contemporary Christ [*gegenwärtigen Christus*] through the Holy Spirit," once understood as common to the experience of all the faithful, has become exclusively identified with a single Christian — the pope. Over the centuries, then, the primitive power and purity of the presence of Christ has been obscured and obstructed by the developing claims of the Roman papacy.[26]

Harnack's magisterial essay, which introduced the term *Christus praesens* into twentieth-century theology, also illustrates the historicist approach with which liberalism usually addresses the question of the presence of Christ. Historicism sees all human phenomena, on analogy

26. "Christus praesens — Vicarius Christi: Eine kirchengeschichtliche Skizze," *Sitzungsberichte der preussischen Akademie der Wissenschaften (Sitzung der philosophisch-historischen Klasse)* 34 (22 December 1927): 415-17.

with those of nature, as organically occurring within an enclosed system of cause and effect.[27] As Harnack notes in his 1895 lecture *Christianity and History:*

> It is perfectly true that the strength of our modern conception of history lies in the effort which we everywhere make to trace the *development* [*Entwicklung*] of things, and to show how one thing has grown out of another. That this is the true task of the historian is a proposition which can no longer be disputed. There can be no manner of doubt that it is only by this method that a true understanding of history can be attained; and even those who condemn the modern science of history cannot escape the influence of its method.[28]

All historical phenomena are the consequence of others which have preceded them. Therefore, the inviolate law governing historical explanation is that of development.

Accordingly, historicism regards the past as determinative of the present, just as a cause determines its effect. Conversely, if one can reason from cause to effect, then it is equally possible to reason from effect back to cause. Hence, historicism also holds that the present is determinative of the past, insofar as the past is a contemporary reconstruction. As for the future, it is principally understood as the prolongation of the past through and beyond the present.

Given this framework, liberal theology does not regard Christianity as a "supernatural" occurrence which suspends or violates causal relations, but as a historical phenomenon, a *religion,* whose development can be traced from the vocation of Jesus. As for Jesus himself, he is no longer taken for a divine-human being in the Chalcedonian sense — or for the Enlightenment's teacher of eternal truths, the universality and veracity of which are independent of the one who enunciated them. Rather, liberalism regards Jesus as a historical phenomenon, "the founder" of Christianity, a *personality* who "came when the time was fulfilled and spoke what the time required."[29] Since that time, Christianity has evolved. We now find

---

27. On historicism see Bultmann, *History and Eschatology,* pp. 74-90; Weber, *Foundations of Dogmatics,* 2:27-29.

28. Trans. with an Introduction by Thomas Bailey Saunders (London: Adam & Charles Black, 1896), pp. 29-30; pub. in Ger. as *Das Christentum und die Geschichte: Ein Vortrag,* 4th ed. (Leipzig: J. C. Hinrichs'sche Buchhandlung, 1897), p. 7.

29. Harnack, *Christianity and History,* pp. 21-35.

ourselves separated from the historical Jesus by what Harnack terms "an intricate and confusing tradition."[30]

According to Johannes Weiss, this interposing development was well underway even during the formation of the New Testament itself. This is the thesis Weiss presents to the educated German public in 1909 in *Christ: The Beginnings of Dogma*, a brief, but brilliant, inventory of New Testament christological titles. He denies that such familiar titles as "Messiah," "Son of God," and "Lord" could "have sprung from the original thoughts of primitive Christianity, still less from the religious experience and testimony of Jesus." Recent research in the history of religions proved that these concepts were common to the Jewish and Hellenistic environment before Jesus or Christianity ever came on the scene. Christians merely appropriated these already minted titles to express the "tremendous . . . mediate or immediate influence of the personality of Jesus [*Wirkung der Persönlichkeit Jesu*] on the souls of his followers." Therefore, what is constant in Christology is not its categories, but the abiding experience of its animating personality.[31]

The personality of Jesus therefore is held to produce Christian piety (*Frömmigkeit*). For Weiss, this piety is synonymous with Christian faith (*Glaube*).[32] Conversely, Christian piety presents in the pages of the Gospels a portrait of Jesus which Weiss calls a *"Bild der Persönlichkeit,"* an "image of the personality."[33] The christological formulas — both those with which primitive piety constructs its *Bild* of Jesus and those which later piety

30. Ibid., p. 18.

31. Trans. V. D. Davis (London: Philip Green, 1911), pp. 14 and 34. See also p. 158; pub. in Ger. as *Christus: Die Anfänge des Dogmas, Religionsgeschichtliche Volksbücher,* nos. 3/4 (Tübingen: J. C. B. Mohr [Paul Siebeck], 1909), pp. 6 and 17-18. See also p. 87.

32. Weiss elaborates this thesis in *Jesus im Glauben des Urchristentums* (Tübingen: J. C. B. Mohr [Paul Siebeck], 1910). Here is sketched the development of the three types of faith-piety found in the New Testament: (1) the imitation of Jesus, practiced by the earliest church, (2) the relation of prayer to the Risen Lord, characteristic of Paul, and (3) faith in the historical Jesus as the revealer of God, central to John. The common experience, direct or indirect, underlying these forms of faith is that of the personality of Jesus. Indeed, Weiss attributes the post-crucifixion significance of Jesus primarily to his personality rather than to his resurrection. See esp. pp. 9-12 and 38-43. On the interchangeability of *Frömmigkeit* and *Glaube*, see, e.g., p. 2.

33. *Christ of Dogma*, p. 135. Cf. Ger., p. 135. Here is the seed of the form-critical method; namely, that the personality of Jesus and the piety of Christians are correlative: "So in the image of Jesus which they left behind for us, they simultaneously sketched themselves." *Jesus des Urchristentums*, p. 19. See also *Christ of Dogma*, pp. 128-29. Cf. Harnack's term *"sein Lebensbild,"* in *Christentum und Geschichte*, pp. 13 and 15-16.

adopts to express his continuing influence — vary according to their time and place. Hence, these formulas, as such, cannot be accorded normative status for contemporary faith. Indeed, given their milieu, the christological titles of the New Testament must be regarded as mythological.[34]

Nevertheless, this very discovery, so disabling for traditional dogmatics, actually proves salutary for faith:

> What we learn from all those stammering attempts to express the nature of Christ in formulas is simply, how mighty the personality [*Persönlichkeit*] must have been, that inspired men to such faith, quickened their imagination to such an extent, and for centuries furnished food for their thought. The less we are able to understand the Christology and appropriate it to ourselves, the more decisively are we referred back to Jesus in his own personality [*auf die Person Jesu zuruckgewiessen*].[35]

By stripping away the varnished layers of New Testament Christology with the solvent of historical criticism, Weiss restores the original portrait of Jesus on behalf of contemporary faith. Behind the veneer of incomprehensible dogma lies an incomparable personality.

According to Emanuel Hirsch, this modern concept of personality *(Persönlichkeit)*, so prominent in liberal theology, derives from two sources: Immanuel Kant and Romantics such as J. W. von Goethe and J. G. Herder.[36]

---

34. Ibid., pp. 26 and 34.

35. Ibid., p. 160; in Ger., p. 88. Cf. the similar views of Wilhelm Herrmann in *The Communion of the Christian with God Described on the Basis of Luther's Statements,* trans. J. Sandys Stanyon, ed. R. W. Stewart (New York: G. P. Putnam's Sons, 1906; London: Williams & Norgate, 1906; reprint ed., London: SCM, 1972), p. 7; in Ger. *Der Verkehr des Christen mit Gott im Anschluss an Luther Dargestellt,* 7th ed. (Tübingen: J. C. B. Mohr [Paul Siebeck], 1921), pp. 5-6.

Even when *Person* is retained by Harnack, Herrmann, and Weiss, presumably out of deference to traditional usage, an inspection of contexts indicates that they employ it as a synonym for *Persönlichkeit.* See, e.g., Harnack, *Christentum und Geschichte,* pp. 8-9, 12, 16, and 20, where *Person* and *Persönlichkeit* are used interchangeably in common contexts. See also Weiss, *Christus des Dogmas,* pp. 6, 51, and 88; and Herrmann, *Verkehr mit Gott,* pp. 57-63. Thus, translators of liberal theology often render the German *"Person"* by the English "personality." See Harnack, *Christianity and History,* pp. 38, 44, 57, 61, and 66; in Ger., pp. 10, 12, 16, 18, and 20; Weiss, *Christ of Dogma,* pp. 129 and 158; in Ger., pp. 70 and 87; and Herrmann, *Communion with God,* pp. 71, 90, and 93; in Ger., pp. viii, 72, and 74.

36. See Hirsch, *Geschichte der neuern evangelischen Theologie im Zusammenhang mit den allgemein Bewegungen des europäischen Denken,* 5 vols. (Gütersloh: C. Bertelsmann

Kant inherits John Locke's definition of a person as "a thinking intelligent being, that has reason and reflection," self-consciousness, and a continuing identity in space and time.[37] Kant then expands upon Locke's definition when he uses the term *Persönlichkeit* to refer to "the character which submits entirely to moral duty."[38] Personality, then, is the backbone of that austere autonomy, independent of the mechanisms of nature, which marks beings as moral and spiritual, and thus as truly human. In Kant's view, *Persönlichkeit* emphasizes the person as the bearer of moral consciousness, standing upright, over against nature.

By contrast, for the Romantics, *Persönlichkeit* refers to that mysterious creativity revealed in the many-sided, cultured individual.[39] From this standpoint, personality does not so much oppose nature as express in humanity and history the vital forces impelling natural evolution.[40] While Kant fastens on moral agency, the Romantics focus on affective or receptive experience *(Erlebnis)* as the key to personality.[41] These two perspectives — the Kantian and the Romantic — become entwined in liberal Christology.

Albrecht Ritschl observes that personality is a product of both endowment and environment. On the side of endowment, every individual possesses a "formal and original self-distinction" from all others, which Ritschl terms "the Ego." This center of personhood is where Ritschl lodges not only the traditional capacity for thinking, feeling, and willing, but also the "precondition" for personality. The personality emerges as the Ego interacts with its environment. For Ritschl, then, human beings are not born with personality; rather, they are normally endowed with the capacity to acquire it. While environment must be given its due in accounting for the unique shape of an unfolding personality, the *a priori* Ego, upon which the environment works, anteriorly posits every person as an enclave of spirit and freedom within the mechanistic world of space and time. This is confirmed by the appearance

---

Verlag, 1954), 4:299-300 and 341-42; and *Die Religion in Geschichte und Gegenwart: Handwörterbuch für Theologie und Religionswissenschaft,* 3rd ed. (hereafter cited as *RGG*[3]), s.v. *"Persönlichkeit,"* by W. Trillhaas.

37. *An Essay Concerning Human Understanding,* ed. A. S. Pringle-Pattison (Oxford: Clarendon, 1950), p. 188.

38. Hirsch, *Geschichte der Theologie,* 4:299.

39. See ibid., 4:299-300; and Bultmann, *History and Eschatology,* p. 104.

40. See Bultmann, *History and Eschatology,* pp. 80-81, characterizing Herder.

41. See ibid., p. 84.

in history of moral consciousness which transcends the determinisms of nature. Thus, for Ritschl, there can be no such thing as a "mere" (that is, "purely material") human being.[42]

Since persons are made for personality, the acquisition of it — in a mature, independent form — is the goal of human development. Ritschl elaborates on this goal with respect both to activity and to receptivity. A developed personality possesses "the highest possible degree of receptivity to the general relations of things and the common interests of mankind."[43] Likewise, as an agent active within and upon the environment, such a personality also exercises "the highest possible degree of spiritual influence" in and over others.[44] The more developed the personality, the more its receptivity and activity, its openness to others and its influence upon them, converge as love. To live in love is the goal of personality, the true measure of human fullness and wholeness.

The influence of a mature personality continues to exercise its effects, down through the centuries, even after the individual bearing it has died. The stronger the original personality, the deeper and profounder its historical influence. Thus, while the historical environment plays an essential role in the development of personality, the independent personality likewise plays an essential role in historical development.

This historical development is understood by liberal theology not simply as chronological advance, but as civilizing progress. When Harnack inquires as to the causes of this progress, material or economic factors prove inadequate. Indeed, even in the realm of political economy, nonmaterial elements play their part. Nevertheless, ideas alone cannot account for progress. Therefore, the real question is what causes an inert idea to "catch fire" or "take hold." In Harnack's estimation, the answer lies in such factors as insight, courage, conviction, and inspiration, all of which derive from personality. These are the unfathomable forces "along with and above the power of circumstance" which ignite ideas and propel history and humanity onward and upward from a state of nature to the Kingdom of

---

42. *The Christian Doctrine of Justification and Reconciliation,* vol. 3: *The Positive Development of the Doctrine,* ed. and trans. H. R. Mackintosh and A. B. Macaulay (reprint ed., Clifton, N.J.: Reference Book Publishers, 1966), pp. 218-19, 231-37, and 397; pub. in Ger. as *Die christliche Lehre von der Rechtfertigung und Versöhnung,* 3rd ed., vol. 3: *Die positive Entwicklung der Lehre,* 3rd ed. (Bonn: Adolph Marcus, 1895), pp. 207-9, 219-28, and 375-76.

43. Ibid., 3:233.

44. Ibid.

God. Such spiritual powers operating through personality are "the real levers of history."[45]

Within this historicist framework, liberal theology further locates Jesus of Nazareth. His historical, and hence soteriological, significance stems from the incomparability of his personality on the scale of development. Whether Jesus was the first to declare distinctly "the infinite value of the human soul" (Harnack),[46] or the command to love as "the whole moral law" (Herrmann),[47] liberal theology generally claims — as a historical fact — that, among the founders of the world's religions, only Jesus perfectly lived what he taught to others.[48]

For example, Ritschl claims that Jesus "realized in His own experience" that "independence toward the world" which is "the true development(of the spiritual personality [*Entwicklung der geistigen Persönlichkeit*]."[49] This occurred when Jesus "made God's supreme purpose of the union of men in the Kingdom of God the aim of His own personal life."[50] Similarly, Harnack finds the fusion of humility and morality, unique to the Beatitudes, mirrored in Jesus' own life, marked as it is by "the deepest humility and a purity of will."[51] Herrmann, too, takes Jesus for "a man who is conscious that He Himself is not inferior to the ideal for which He sacrifices Himself."[52] Thus, an examination of the teaching and personality of Jesus leads liberal theology to conclude with Harnack that Christianity "had a founder who himself was what he taught."[53]

This unparalleled historical fact, attested by the Gospels, has superla-

45. *Christianity and History,* pp. 30-38. See also Harnack, *What Is Christianity?,* trans. Thomas Bailey Saunders, with an Introduction by Rudolf Bultmann (New York: Harper & Bros., 1957; reprint ed., Philadelphia: Fortress, 1986), pp. 48 and 145; pub. in Ger. as *Das Wesen des Christentums,* new ed., with a Geleitwort by Rudolf Bultmann (Stuttgart: Ehrenfried Klotz Verlag, 1950), pp. 29 and 87.

46. *What Is Christianity?,* pp. 63 and 67-68, where Mark 8:36 is in mind. On pp. 47-49, Harnack stresses that Jesus taught nothing new with respect to his Jewish heritage and environment, in order to emphasize the factor of Jesus' personality as the key to his historical significance. See also *Christianity and History,* p. 35.

47. *Communion with God,* p. 90.

48. See, e.g., Ritschl, *Justification and Reconciliation,* 3:385-89; Harnack, *Christianity and History,* pp. 36-38; and, Herrmann, *Communion with God,* pp. 91-93, and 102-3.

49. *Justification and Reconciliation,* 3:387. Cf. Ger., 3:366.

50. Ibid.

51. *Khristianity and History,* p. 37. See also *What Is Christianity?,* pp. 72-74.

52. *Communion with God,* p. 89.

53. *What Is Christianity?,* p. 11. See also p. 145.

tive soteriological significance. Salvation comes to be seen as the process of acquiring a developed personality that is obedient to the moral law and that exercises an influence for good. Nevertheless, both Harnack and Herrmann hold that, in practice, individuals are powerless, in and of themselves, to will the good that the law of love demands.[54] This human predicament turns to judgment as Jesus himself quickens the conscience by commanding obedience to the moral law. Hence, "the very thoughts which we know are able to set free our inner life only throw us back again into discouragement and despondency."[55] This slough of despond into which we slip is thus the place from which Jesus rescues us. In fulfilling the love he required of others, and so overcoming the world, history shows that Jesus achieved the goal of personality development. Thus, he is the uplifting sign that "the blessed liberty of a moral life" is "not essentially foreign to human nature."[56]

Since the personality of Jesus attained full stature, its unparalleled power for good includes utter openness to others amid their moral struggles and failures.[57] Moreover, Jesus' "invincible confidence that He can uplift and bless perfectly those who do not turn away from Him" — a confidence in which he invites us to share — implies, for Herrmann, "the idea of a Power greater than all things, which will see to it that Jesus, who lost his life in this world, shall be none the less victorious over the world."[58] Thus, our faith in God arises as we come under the winning influence of the inner life of Jesus.

This saving influence of Jesus is continually mediated from one Christian to the next. Weiss explains:

> There is no denying the fact that since the days of Jesus a type of child of God lives among us to the blessing of humankind. This type, on the whole, draws its life from the example of the personality of Jesus [*Persönlichkeit Jesu*]. In this spiritual generation of a life within his followers, he has kept himself living in the world. Those who have mediated this invaluable spiritual good to humankind were the earliest Christians, who, with the words of Jesus, have also guided his Spirit over to us.[59]

---

54. See Harnack, *Christianity and History,* pp. 42-49; and Herrmann, *Communion with God,* p. 99.

55. Herrmann, *Communion with God,* p. 100.

56. Ibid.

57. Ibid., p. 99.

58. Ibid., p. 97. See also p. 92.

59. *Jesus des Urchristentums,* p. 24. Cf. Bultmann's comment on one of Weiss's Easter

Mixing metaphors of fire and water, Harnack offers a similar account:

> One Christian educates another; heart kindles heart; and the strength to
> will what we approve comes from the mysterious Power by which one life
> awakens another. At the end of the series of messengers and agents of God
> stands Jesus Christ. They point back to him, and it is from him that has
> sprung the river of life which they bear in themselves as their own. Various
> indeed is the measure of their conscious relation to him — who could deny
> it! — but they all live on him and through him.
>
> Here we have a fact which gives an incomparable significance to this
> personality [*Person*], as a force still working in history.[60]

For Harnack and Weiss, then, it is the "personality" of Jesus rather than
his "resurrection" from the dead that enables Christians to pass on his
presence in the world.

Acknowledging the role of both Christians and their scriptures as
mediators of divine revelation, Wilhelm Herrmann's *The Communion of
the Christian with God* nevertheless sees this revelation "deepened and
perfected as we become acquainted with Jesus Himself."[61] Here Herrmann
insists with the Reformation that "Jesus Himself [*Jesus selbst*] is an element
of the reality in which we stand," and not simply "the tradition concerning
Jesus [*die Überlieferung von Jesus*]."[62] Thus, within the context of historicism, Herrmann strains to make room for an "I-Thou" encounter between
the believer and Christ.

To do this Herrmann distinguishes between the form of the gospel
narrative, which is its written husk, and the kernel of its content, which
is Jesus' own inner life. When it comes to establishing the truth or reality
of this narrated content, Christians generally rely either on "the trustwor-
thiness of the narrator [*der Zuverlässigkeit des Erzählers*]" (here, the church)
or on "a combination of the narrative [*Erzählung*] with something else
which we know to be real." The first path is taken by Roman Catholicism,
the second, by "historical criticism." Whereas the former demands faith
in the authority of the church to secure the truth of the gospel, historical

---

meditations: "And the confession 'Jesus lives' is still only understood in the 'earthly'
[*diesseitigen*] sense." *GuV* 1:13.

60. *Christianity and History,* p. 44. Cf. Ger., pp. 11-12. See also Herrmann, *Communion with God,* pp. 60, 72-73, 78, and 115.

61. P. 60.

62. Ibid., p. 66, omitting italics. Cf. Ger., p. 52.

criticism evaluates the content of the gospel by an external canon, that is, by how well it fits into the wider horizon of previously established data.[63]

But each of these approaches fails faith. For "a believer cannot base his very existence entirely on what may be given him by other men." Secondhand knowledge *about* God or Christ, whether derived from the priest or the professor, cannot substitute for actual communion with God through Christ. Moreover, Herrmann also insists with G. E. Lessing that faith cannot be based on the "continually changing" results of historical research, and hence on one's educational attainments. Rather, the basis of faith is "the inner life of Jesus," conveyed by the gospel narrative — whether that narrative is "sifted and estimated by historical criticism or not."[64]

Therefore, Herrmann sees the genesis of saving faith not in assent to dogma or in historical reconstruction, but in an encounter between the inner life of Jesus and that of the believer:

> He who has found the inner life of Jesus through the mediation of others, in so far as he has really found it, has become free even of that mediation. . . . If we have experienced His power over us, we need no longer look for the testimony of others to enable us to hold fast to His life as a real thing. We start, indeed, from the records, but we do not grasp the fact they bring us until the enrichment of our own inner life makes us aware that we have touched the Living One. . . . It is thus, therefore, that the inner life of Jesus becomes part of our own sphere of reality, and the man who has experienced that will certainly no longer say that, strictly speaking, he can know only the story [*Überlieferung*] of Jesus as a real thing. Jesus Himself becomes a real power to us when He reveals His inner life to us; . . . Help lies for each of us, not in what we make of the story [*Überlieferung*], but in what the contents of the story [*der Inhalt der Überlieferung*] make of us. And the one thing which the Gospels will give us as an overpowering reality which allows no doubt is . . . the inner life of Jesus itself.[65]

That is to say, the gospel tradition renders into our reality, or inner life, the reality of Jesus, understood as his inner life. This narrative rendering of Jesus, or this self-revelation of Jesus through the Gospels, is bound to

63. Ibid., pp. 67-69. Cf. Ger., pp. 53-54.
64. Ibid., pp. 69 and 76.
65. Ibid., pp. 74-75. Cf. Ger., pp. 58-59.

a historically conditioned record; but this rendering, or revelation, by virtue of its compelling power, is not itself subject to historical criticism.

Nevertheless, Herrmann's use of the title "the Living One" to identify the Jesus revealed in the Gospels does not signify for him the exalted Christ. This becomes clear when Herrmann declares that what is true of our encounter with Jesus also "holds true of every historical personality [*von jeder geschichtlichen Persönlichkeit*]; the inner content of any such personality is laid open only to those who become personally alive to it, and feel themselves aroused by contact with it and see their horizon widened."[66] Thus, the contemporary presence of Jesus, even for Herrmann, remains at the level of an effect traceable to a first-century cause.

Herrmann's offering with one hand what he takes back with the other is reminiscent of Albrecht Ritschl. Ritschl declares, "Our faith in Christ is not faith in Him as One Who was, but faith in Him as One Who continues to work, namely, under the conditions corresponding to His present mode of existence."[67] In traditional dogmatics, this "present mode" of Christ's existence is thought of as his *status exaltationis,* that is, his exalted state as the risen and ascended Lord. By contrast, Ritschl claims that Christ's present activity must "be conceived as the expression of the abiding influence of His historical manifestation."[68] Thus, Jesus Christ does not impinge on the present from the future, "from above." Rather, he continues to influence the present from his position in the first century, "from below."

Likewise, despite Herrmann's serious attempt to speak of God's revelation in Christ as a genuine interpersonal encounter with the believer, the framework of historicism keeps his soteriology from linking up with the Risen Lord:

> We cannot speak of a communion with the exalted Christ. Nor do we find such communion spoken of in the New Testament, apart from the visions therein recorded. . . . It is because the invisible God uses this fact [i.e., "the personal life of Jesus"] to make men certain of Himself, that we can say, He communes with us. In this fact of self-revelation He reaches down into the realm of our earthly experience. But we cannot say that of the exalted Christ. Hence the believer . . . must admit that the risen Christ is still hidden from him. He may, indeed, express a

---

66. Ibid., p. 74. Cf. Ger., p. 58.
67. *Justification and Reconciliation,* 3:400.
68. Ibid., 3:432.

thought of his faith by saying that Christ lives in him; but unless, like Paul, he can appeal to visions, he may not say that he *experiences* the communion of the exalted Christ with himself.[69]

That is to say, the exaltation of Jesus Christ is, at best, an implied doctrine, derived from the experience of our communion with God achieved through the inner life of the man Jesus. Only if we ourselves, like Paul, have a supernatural vision of the Risen Lord — an impossibility given Herrmann's historicist canons — can the exalted Christ become an experience of faith and thereby serve as the presupposition for our communion with God.

Thus, the judgment of H. R. Mackintosh regarding Ritschl extends equally to Herrmann: "The . . . tendency to read everything in terms of the immanental factors of development led him in effect to replace the action of the exalted Lord on the Church by a merely posthumous influence."[70] To the degree that Jesus reigns in our hearts, he does so from his grave.

Before turning to Bultmann's own criticisms of his liberal teachers, we must note one other historicist factor guiding their portrayal of Jesus. While we have spared the reader the more florid descriptions of Jesus' personality found in Harnack, Herrmann, and Weiss, we have noted their primary hues. Jesus is portrayed as embodying the law of love, the humility and purity of the Beatitudes, and the confidence that he can save others.

Now to the degree that liberal theology takes these characterizations of Jesus for historical descriptions, based on the scientific reconstruction of the past, they must be open to revision. As Herrmann recognizes, "We are always prepared to modify our results upon more exact examination of the narrative or upon the discovery of new information."[71] Indeed, Harnack argues that the *Lebensbild* of Jesus recovered from the Gospels would be disproved if historical criticism could demonstrate that the actual personality of Jesus differed significantly from it. This would in fact result if it could be established, for example, that Jesus "was an apocalyptic enthusiast or a visionary, whose image and utterances were advanced to the level of pure aim and lofty thought only by the refining influence of later times."[72]

Such a possibility became at least thinkable with the appearance in 1892 of *Jesus' Proclamation of the Kingdom of God* by Johannes Weiss. In

69. *Communion with God,* pp. 291-93.
70. Hugh Ross Mackintosh, *Types of Modern Theology: Schleiermacher to Barth* (London: Nisbet & Co., 1937), p. 158. See also pp. 163-64.
71. *Communion with God,* p. 69.
72. *Christianity and History,* p. 56.

this monograph, which the author prudently withheld from publication until after the death of his father-in-law, Albrecht Ritschl, Weiss concludes "that the messianic consciousness of Jesus, as expressed in the name Son of man, also participates in the thoroughly transcendental and apocalyptic character of Jesus' idea of the Kingdom of God, and cannot be dissociated from it."[73] While Weiss subsequently "retreated with all speed into the liberal conception of Jesus,"[74] if his exegetical essay were right, then the historical Jesus would be radically different from the heroic, yet genial, personality liberal theologians recovered from the Gospels.

Confronted by these challenging findings of Weiss, Harnack offers an ingenious response. Whatever the four written Gospels may indicate, the historian must equally attend to "a fifth, unwritten"; namely, "the united testimony of the first Christian community." This testimony arising from "the prevailing impression" made by the personality of Jesus is united in its verdict that Jesus was no apocalypticist.[75]

While an appeal to tradition that claims to be "unwritten" is problematic, Harnack's intention is to mitigate the exegesis of Weiss by placing the identity of Jesus into a larger historical context than that of the Gospels. As he later declares in *What is Christianity?*,

> We must not be content to exhibit the mere image of Jesus Christ [*Bild Jesu Christi*] and the main features of his Gospel. We must not be content to stop there, because every great and powerful personality [*Persönlichkeit*] reveals a part of what it is only when seen in those whom it influences. Nay, it may be said that the more powerful the personality [*Persönlichkeit*] which a man possesses, and the more he takes hold of the inner life of others, the less can the sum-total of what he is be known only by what he himself says and does. We must look at the reflection and the effects which he produced in those whose leader and master he became.[76]

---

73. Ed. with an Introduction by Richard Hyde Hiers and David Larrimore Holland (Philadelphia: Fortress, 1971; reprint ed., Chico, Calif.: Scholars Press, 1985), p. 129. Cf. *Christ of Dogma*, pp. 55-60, where Weiss sets aside whether Jesus used "Son of Man" as a self-designation and instead focuses on its role as an ecclesial designation of Jesus derived from Daniel 7.

74. Ernst Käsemann, "On the Subject of Primitive Christian Apocalyptic," in *New Testament Questions of Today*, trans. W. J. Montague (Philadelphia: Fortress, 1969; hereafter cited as *NTQT*), p. 109, n. 2.

75. *Christianity and History*, p. 57.

76. P. 10. Cf. Ger., p. 6. See also Herrmann, *Communion with God*, p. 73.

Here Harnack articulates Hegel's view that a historical phenomenon comprises not simply a punctiliar moment but also its continuing effects.[77] "How, then, can we be silent about the history [*Geschichte*] of the Gospel if we wish to know what he was?"[78] Thus, we know that Jesus was not an apocalyptic enthusiast. The subsequent nonapocalyptic "history of the Gospel" bears this out, whatever revisionist exegetes like Weiss may allege about the gospel record itself.

Harnack pursues this line further when he argues that historians reconstructing the personality of Jesus must accept as a valid datum the experience of the "plain Bible-reader" who encounters the light shining in Jesus as the "true gist and meaning" of the Gospels.[79] For "the spiritual purport of a whole life, of a personality [*Person*], is also an historical fact: it has its reality [*Gewissheit*] in the effect which it produces; and it is here that we find the link that binds us to Jesus Christ."[80] Likewise, Herrmann, while conceding that a historian, as such, may be skeptical of the supernatural elements in the Gospels, nevertheless claims that "on the strength of those elements in Jesus which, beyond all doubt, are with us to-day, every reasonable man will hold the more general features of the common story of His life to be correct."[81] In other words, the contemporary effects of Jesus accurately reveal his original personality and thereby provide a hermeneutical standard for winnowing the true from the fanciful in the Gospels' recounting of his life.

Thus, despite liberal theology's stated openness to having its presentation of Jesus disproved, its controlling historicist presuppositions insure that this possibility will never be seriously entertained. On the one hand, liberalism appeals to the original personality of Jesus over against "dogmatic" forms of piety to which it takes enlightened exception. On the

77. See Stephen Crites, *In the Twilight of Christendom: Hegel vs. Kierkegaard on Faith and History,* AAR Studies in Religion, no. 2 (Chambersburg, Pa.: American Academy of Religion, 1972), p. 41.

78. *What Is Christianity?*, p. 11. Cf. Ger., p. 7.

79. *Christianity and History,* pp. 58-59.

80. Ibid., pp. 61-62. Cf. Ger., p. 18.

81. *Communion with God,* pp. 70-71. Similarly, with respect to Jesus' teaching on the Kingdom of God, Herrmann argues that "on historical grounds it is probable that by the phrase He thought, in the first place, of God's sovereignty. But for those who have begun to understand the inner life of Jesus in its characteristic majesty, it is a certainty that this alone is what Jesus chiefly meant by the words. He placed his whole desire in perfect surrender to God. . . . Therefore, what he understood by the Kingdom of God was the experience of the complete sovereignty of God." P. 95.

other hand, liberal theology appeals to the contemporary Jesus-piety of which it approves, over against an apocalyptic personality who could not possibly be its source. In one case, a cause — the incomparable personality of Jesus — is invoked as the true criterion for piety. In the other instance, an effect — Jesus-piety — is invoked as the true criterion for the antecedent cause, the original personality of a nonapocalyptic Jesus. Conveniently, historicism's circular law of development authorizes an appeal either to cause or effect, whichever is needed, to counter problematic data from the other. No wonder, when faced with the possibility of an apocalyptic Jesus, Harnack could so assuredly reply, "But who has proved that, and who could prove it?"[82] As long as historicism reigned, the Jesus of liberalism was safe from historical criticism.

In conclusion, we have seen from our survey how Harnack, Weiss, and Herrmann, operating within the framework of historicism, explain the presence of Jesus in terms of *Persönlichkeit*. Judged incomparable by Kantian-Romantic standards, Jesus' personality continues to exercise, through the mediation of Christians and their scriptures, a positive influence on the moral and spiritual development of others, extending to that of civilization at large. The theologian enriches piety by retrieving the original personality of the historical Jesus. The historian depicts this original personality — not only on the basis of narrow documentation, but with attention to its influence on subsequent piety. Thus, for Bultmann's liberal teachers, the presence of Jesus is expressed in the continuing influence on piety of his incomparable personality.

The Personality of Jesus:
Bultmann's Analysis and Criticism

Two epochal events overturned the liberal account of the presence of Jesus, and both are reflected in Bultmann's subsequent criticisms. The first was the new approach to Christian origins and texts. Central to this development were the philological studies of Richard Reitzenstein (1861-1931) and his reconstruction of "the Primal Man" myth,[83] the cultic analysis of Hellenistic Christianity in Wilhelm Bousset's (1865-1920) *Kyrios Christos*

---

82. *Christianity and History,* p. 56.
83. See *Das iranische Erlösungsmysterium: Religionsgeschichtliche Untersuchungen* (Bonn a Rh.: A. Marcus & E. Weber, 1921).

(1913),[84] and the emergence of form criticism.[85] The cumulative result of studies such as these challenged the liberal assumption that the Gospels either portray or render the personality of Jesus. The second event that overwhelmed established liberal positions was the World War of 1914-1918. As Bultmann observed in a Marburg sermon of 1938, talk "of the influence of Christ on world history, of the effects of His spirit on human manners and morals, of its uplifting and civilizing influence on nations" all ceased with this ghastly "war between nominally Christian peoples."[86] No longer could Europeans rightly regard their historical development as a plausible sign of progress under the guiding influence of Jesus' inner life. Thus, the Jesus of liberalism perished on two fronts — the one secured by the scholar, the other endured by the soldier.

Bultmann delivered a *postmortem* examination of the liberalism in which he was trained on 29 September 1920, at a theological conference in Eisenach. In his lecture "Ethical and Mystical Religion in Early Christianity," Bultmann sketched the current state of New Testament research with an eye to its negative implications for contemporary Christology and piety.[87] Subsequently published in Martin Rade's periodical *Die christliche Welt,* Bultmann's remarks incurred the displeasure of Paul Wernle, a senior professor at Basel and author of a liberal "life" of Jesus. Wernle wrote Rade that Bultmann's lecture constituted "an affront and mockery to the whole religious line which this journal has advocated for decades."[88] Rade, in

84. Subtitled *A History of the Belief in Christ from the Beginnings of Christianity to Irenaeus,* trans. John E. Steely (Nashville: Abingdon, 1970). For Bultmann's summary of Bousset's position see "The Christology of the New Testament [1933]," in *FaU* 1:269-73; pub. in Ger. as "Die Christologie des Neuen Testaments," in *GuV* 1:252-56.

85. On the origins of form criticism see Erich Fascher, *Die Formgeschichtliche Methode* (Giessen: Alfred Töpelmann, 1924).

86. *This World and the Beyond: Marburg Sermons,* trans. Harold Knight (New York: Charles Scribner's Sons, 1960), p. 68. ET slightly altered. Pub. in Ger. as *Marburger Predigten* (Tübingen: J. C. B. Mohr [Paul Siebeck], 1956), p. 57. For discussion of World War I on Bultmann's life and thought, see Evang, *Bultmann in seiner Frühzeit,* pp. 61-63.

87. In *The Beginnings of Dialectic Theology,* 2 vols., ed. James M. Robinson and trans. Keith R. Crim and Louis De Grazia (Richmond, Va.: John Knox, 1968- ; hereafter cited as *BDT*), 1:221-35; pub. in Ger. as "Ethische und mystische Religion im Urchristentum," in *Anfänge der dialektischen Theologie,* ed. Jürgen Moltmann, pt. 2: *Rudolf Bultmann, Friedrich Gogarten, Eduard Thurneysen, Theologische Bücherei, Neudrucke und Berichte aus dem 20. Jahrhundert, Systematische Theologie,* vol. 17 (München: Chr. Kaiser Verlag, 1963; hereafter cited as *ADT*), pp. 29-47.

88. Wernle to Rade, 6 December 1920, quoted in Bernd Jaspert, "Rudolf Bultmanns

turn, forwarded Wernle's complaining letter to Bultmann. Here is a portion of Bultmann's candid reply to Rade:

> During the first years of my university studies I was nourished by the
> intellectual life which flourished in the theological circle to which
> Wernle belonged. Their way of preaching Jesus seemed to me then the
> right model for proclaiming the gospel today. In my early student years
> I tried to shape my own preaching along these lines. . . . I also felt
> compelled to teach my students this model — until I realized that I had
> been warming myself at an alien fire, and that this kind of piety was
> foreign to me, i.e., that the person of the historical Jesus [*geschichtliche
> Jesus*] meant little or nothing to me. My conviction was strengthened
> by my study of Herrmann's writings in this area, which had always
> seemed to me fuzzy. Moreover, I was troubled again and again by the
> realization that the preaching model advocated by Wernle and his friends
> bore little or no intellectual fruit in our lives. Why, for example, was
> this kind of piety so unintelligible to the lay friends to whom I felt so
> close? My continued study of the sources compelled me to admit that
> we know little of the historical Jesus [*historische Jesus*]. There seemed to
> me but one conclusion: the Jesus-piety of "liberal theology" was the
> fruit of self-deception.[89]

As his letter reveals, Bultmann's disenchantment with liberalism began
when he questioned his own experience of the presence of Jesus. Whether
viewed from the standpoint of the original sources or contemporary piety,
critical research and the cultural crisis conspired to make the incomparable
personality of Jesus as inauthentic a dogma as the Christ myth it had
supposedly replaced. The new exegetical and existential situation of postwar Germany had alienated the Jesus of liberalism from Bultmann's self-understanding.

Thus, throughout the 1920s, Bultmann offers, in a number of contexts, a series of criticisms aimed at the liberal doctrine of the personality
of Jesus. These criticisms of his teachers can be grouped into two kinds:
historical-exegetical criticisms demonstrating that the Gospels do not portray a *Bild* of Jesus' personality and *philosophical-theological* criticisms
arguing that contemporary faith is not the direct effect of a historical

---

Wende von der liberalen zur dialektischen Theologie," in *Rudolf Bultmanns Werk und
Wirkung,* ed. Bernd Jaspert (Darmstadt: Wissenschaftliche Buchgesellschaft, 1984), p. 28.
    89. Bultmann to Rade, 19 December 1920, quoted in ibid., pp. 30-31.

personality. We begin our exposition with Bultmann's historical-exegetical criticisms.

The Personality of Jesus in Light of New Testament Research

In his 1920 Eisenach lecture, Bultmann reports that the view of New Testament theology, prevailing from the time of F. C. Baur, has been overthrown by Bousset's *Kyrios Christos* and form-critical research. The "spiritual content of the message of Jesus," which liberalism, in "antithesis to Judaism," identified as the universal Fatherhood of God, the moral law, and love as the fulfillment of personality, is not "the essence of the Christian religion"; neither does it undergo "a unified, linear development" from Jesus to Paul to John.[90]

Bultmann explains that the New Testament reflects not so much the witness of individual writers, but that of two groups of congregations — "primitive Palestinian and Hellenistic Christian." The Palestinian community regarded Jesus "as the eschatological preacher of repentance and the prophet of the coming rule of God, as a teacher of wisdom and a rabbi," and, "above all, the soon-to-come 'Son of Man.'" The Jesus it reverenced taught that "God is primarily the holy will, demanding a good will from man; and the relation to God is one of obedience and trust." It invented no cultic forms but was essentially "a Jewish sect."[91]

By contrast, as Bousset showed, Hellenistic Christianity centered on the cult of *Kyrios Christos*. Jesus himself is worshipped as the *Kyrios*-deity of the cult, whose sacramental presence is mediated by baptism and the Lord's Supper. The yet-to-come Son of man gives way to the *Kyrios* who comes in the cult. Thus, as Christianity moves geographically from Palestine to Syria, it also moves theologically from anticipation of an eschatological promise to participation in a sacramental presence. The real roots then of the *Christus praesens* are not found in Jewish Palestinian soil (*contra* Harnack) but in the Hellenistic environment of the *Kyrios* cult.[92]

90. "Ethical and Mystical Religion," in *BDT* 1:221-22.
91. Ibid., 1:223-25 and 227-28. By 1926 further research by Reitzenstein, and the Mandaean texts edited by Mark Lidzbarski, led Bultmann to conclude that "it's questionable whether primitive Palestinian Christianity can be regarded as a definite unity." "The New Approach to the Synoptic Problem [1926]," in *EaF,* pp. 53-54.
92. See ibid., 1:224. Cf. Ger. 2:33. See also *The History of the Synoptic Tradition,*

Central to the liturgical drama of this cult was the soteriological narrative of the Christ myth. This myth is a version of the Iranian myth of the Primal Man or Heavenly Redeemer first isolated by Richard Reitzenstein. On the basis of motifs and patterns shared by a number of Hellenistic religious texts, Reitzenstein hypothesized a common archetypal myth, that of the Primal Man, to account for these similarities. As reconstructed by Reitzenstein, this Iranian myth presupposes the contrast between the divine world of light and the darkness of chaos. Into this chaos, the Primal Man descended from the realm of light, was overcome, and dismembered. His fragments remain as human souls, flickers of light in the darkness of chaos. These souls are subsequently visited by an Ambassador from the light world. He reveals their true origin and institutes the sacramental means for their return to the world of light. Although this Ambassador, like the Primal Man, is overcome, he disguises himself, escapes from the powers of chaos, and ascends back to the light whence he came. As bearers of the image of the Primal Man, human souls recognize in the Ambassador not only this selfsame image, but their ultimate destiny as the redeemed.[93]

Bultmann holds that the Gospels derive their essential story-line from this soteriological myth. True, form criticism detects discrete units, such as miracle stories and individual sayings of Jesus, behind the final redaction

---

trans. John Marsh (New York: Harper & Row, 1963; hereafter cited as *HST*), pp. 347-48; pub. in Ger. as *Die Geschichte der synoptischen Tradition*, 3rd rev. ed., *Forschungen zur Religion und Literatur des Alten und Neuen Testaments*, no. 29 (n.s., no. 12) (Göttingen: Vandenhoeck & Ruprecht, 1957; hereafter cited as *GST*, pp. 372-73); *Jesus and the Word*, new ed., trans. Louis Pettibone Smith and Erminie Huntress Lantero (New York: Charles Scribner's Sons, 1958), pp. 137, 152-53 and 214; pub. in Ger. as *Jesus* (Berlin: Deutsche Bibliothek, 1926), pp. 126-27, 141, and 196; *FaU* 1:204; pub. in Ger. as *GuV* 1:172; *FaU* 1:270-71; pub. in Ger. as *GuV* 1:252-54; "Paul [1930]," in *EaF*, p. 126; pub. in Ger. as *Die Religion in Geschichte und Gegenwart: Handwörterbuch für Theologie und Religionswissenschaft*, 2nd ed. (hereafter cited as *RGG²*), s.v. *"Paulus"; TNT* 1:123-24 and 133; and *History and Eschatology*, pp. 51-53.

93. For this summary of Reitzenstein see Johnson, *The Origins of Demythologizing*, pp. 91-96. Johnson also notes Carsten Colpe's influential conclusion "that the so-called pre-Christian Iranian myth of the Heavenly Redeemer is actually a post-Christian creation" and that Reitzenstein's hypothesis "developed out of no firmer a base than an analogical extrapolation from Old Testament research: just as there were prebiblical creation myths, so there must be pre-Christian redeemer myths." P. 114, citing Colpe, *Die Religionsgeschichtliche Schule: Darstellung und Kritik ihres Bild vom gnostischen Erlösermythus* (Göttingen: Vandenhoeck & Ruprecht, 1961). Painter challenges Johnson's contention "that as Reitzenstein was unable to prove his theory it was disproved," and defends the supposition that "the fragments of myth which appear widely spread presuppose the complete myth." *Theology as Hermeneutics*, p. 140.

of the Gospels, but these Palestinian forms are now embedded in a unified editorial framework, "the epiphany of the heavenly Son of God." This narrative framework, imposed by the Hellenistic church and rehearsed in its cult, ultimately derives from the myth of the Primal Man. The Gospels, beginning with Mark, are the literary product of melding Palestinian traditions about Jesus into the soteriological narrative furnished by this myth. Subsequently in John, "the Palestinian material is almost completely supplanted" by "the Christ myth."[94]

Even at the level of the Gospels, it is "not the historical Jesus, the 'religion of Jesus' [*nicht der historische Jesus, die 'Religion Jesu'*], which was operative, but essentially the Christ myth" created by Hellenistic congregations. Christianity, then, as a *religion*, that is, "with its own forms of myth and cult and communal life, begins with primitive Hellenistic Christianity." Given these conclusions, "Jesus is not to be understood in terms of the subsequent Hellenistic development, but only on the basis of the earlier Jewish development." In other words, the historical Jesus belongs to the prophetic and eschatological context of Palestinian Judaism. He is not, at least intentionally, the "founder" of Christianity. Jesus of Nazareth is not the subject matter, but only the background or historical presupposition for New Testament theology.[95]

94. "Ethical and Mystical Religion," in *BDT* 1:223-24. See also *HST,* p. 306. Nevertheless, Bultmann does acknowledge the influence of the Palestinian community upon the Hellenistic. The latter identified its *Kyrios* with Jesus of Nazareth and its congregations with those "at the end of time." The Hellenistic community also accepted the Old Testament, the traditions about Jesus, the tie with Jerusalem, and the synagogal forms of "prayer and preaching, so that alongside the Kyrios cult was the service of the Word of God." 1:227-28.

95. Ibid., 1:224-25 and 227; in Ger. in *AdT* 2:33-34 and 36. Consistent with this view, note Bultmann's subsequent treatment of the eschatological proclamation of Jesus under the heading of "Judaism," rather than "Primitive Christianity," in *Primitive Christianity,* pp. 86-93 and his claim that "*The message of Jesus* is a presupposition for the theology of the New Testament rather than a part of that theology itself," *TNT* 1:3. For Bultmann's defense of assigning the historical Jesus to Judaism, over against the reproaches of Joachim Jeremias and Ernst Käsemann, see "The Primitive Christian Kerygma and the Historical Jesus [1960]," in *The Historical Jesus and the Kerygmatic Christ: Essays on the New Quest of the Historical Jesus,* ed. and trans. Carl E. Braaten and Roy A. Harrisville (New York: Abingdon, 1964; hereafter cited as *HJKC*), p. 19; pub. in Ger. as "Das Verhältnis der urchristlichen Christusbotschaft zum historischen Jesus," in *Exegetica: Aufsätze zur Erforschung des Neuen Testaments,* ed. Erich Dinkler (Tübingen: J. C. B. Mohr [Paul Siebeck], 1967), p. 449; and "Antwort an Ernst Käsemann [1965]," in *GuV* 4:196.

Thus, liberalism's presentation of "the inner life of Jesus" as the absolute anchor for faith becomes highly suspect. In its attempt to transcend the historically conditioned forms of Pauline and Johannine Christianity, all in the name of Jesus, liberal theology overlooks the fact that the Jewish Jesus of the Palestinian community is as limited and conditioned a phenomenon as the Christ myth of the *Kyrios* cult. Moreover, in attempting to replace the Hellenistic tradition with the Palestinian as a criterion for contemporary piety and theology, liberalism transfers this normative function to a phenomenon, which, historically speaking, cannot be called Christianity at all![96]

More important for our study is the implication that the Gospels are not the result of any attempt to portray the personality of Jesus: "There is no historical-biographical interest in the Gospels, and that is why they have nothing to say about Jesus' human personality [*menschlicher Persönlichkeit*], his appearance and character, his origin, education and development."[97] Rather, the Gospels are the literary product of stringing collated sayings and stories on a narrative line afforded by the Christ myth. As Bultmann notes in his introduction to *Jesus*, given the "fragmentary and luxuriantly legendary" character of the Gospels' sources, and, given that "other sources about Jesus do not exist," we are left in virtual ignorance about "the life and personality of Jesus [*Persönlichkeit Jesu*]."[98]

In this same introduction, Bultmann finds further confirmation for this judgment from the lack of scholarly agreement on whether or not Jesus regarded himself as the Messiah; if so, in what sense, and at what point in his development:

> Considering that it was really no trifle to believe oneself Messiah, that, further, whoever so believed must have regulated his whole life in accordance with this belief, we must admit that if this point is obscure we can, strictly speaking, know nothing of the personality [*Persönlichkeit*] of Jesus.[99]

---

96. Ibid., 1:231.
97. *HST,* p. 372. Cf. *GST,* p. 397.
98. P. 12. See also *EaF,* p. 52.
99. *Jesus and the Word,* p. 9. Cf. *Jesus,* p. 12. See also "The Study of the Synoptic Gospels [2nd ed., 1930]," in *Form Criticism: Two Essays on New Testament Research,* by Rudolf Bultmann and Karl Kundsin, trans. Frederick C. Grant (n.p.: Willett, Clark & Co., 1934; reprint ed., New York: Harper & Bros., 1962), p. 23; pub. in Ger. as "Die Erforschung der synoptischen Evangelien" (rev. ed., 1961) in *GuV* 4:8. Macquarrie charges that Bultmann, perhaps "because of the influence of existentialism," has "somewhat

If the community had been concerned to portray the personality of Jesus, the development of his messianic self-consciousness would have provided the obvious plot for the story. But there is no scholarly consensus that it does.

As for the traditional liberal claim, revived in 1926 by Emanuel Hirsch, that Jesus received the name "Son" at his baptism, " 'as clarification of the attitude of inner life already present,' " this, too, is rejected by Bultmann on a number of grounds.[100] (We note here only the exegetical ones, which Bultmann gives as early as 1921 in *The History of the Synoptic Tradition.*) Without denying the historicity of Jesus' baptism by John, Bultmann's form criticism classifies the synoptic account (Mark 1:9-11, pars.) as a faith legend which tells "of Jesus' consecration as messiah." As such, we do not have here a "calling story," as comparison with other biblical texts shows: "Not only is there not so much as a word about the inner experience of Jesus, but there is also no word of commission to the person called, and no answer from him, things which we normally find in proper accounts of a call." Moreover, Bultmann denies *eiden* ("he saw," Mark 1:10) as being predicated of Jesus, and hence reporting his vision. Therefore, in Bultmann's judgment, "Matthew and Luke are quite right to take Mark's story as the description of an objective happening and *kai phone egeneto* ["and a voice came"] in Mark 1:11 displays the same idea." The whole focus of the baptismal account, then, is on divine determination — not personality development.[101]

These exegetical considerations inform Bultmann's subsequent disagreement with Hirsch: "In the view of the Gospels, the community which tells the story of the baptism is thereby rejecting the question of Jesus' human development and personality [*menschlicher Entwicklung und Persönlichkeit*]."[102] As Bultmann puts the matter in 1933 with respect to the

---

dogmatically brushed aside" the messianic consciousness of Jesus. Such characterizations and speculations leave unanswered Bultmann's arguments. What is arbitrary is Macquarrie's own assertion of "the numinous elements in the personality of the historic Jesus" by which, in typical liberal fashion, he finds in Jesus "a big enough figure to found the Christian religion." See *An Existentialist Theology,* pp. 22-23, 80-81, 180, and 185.

100. "On the Question of Christology [1927]," in *FaU* 1:125, where Bultmann quotes Hirsch, *Jesus Christus der Herr* (Göttingen: Theologische Vorlesungen, 1926), p. 85; pub. in Ger. as "Zur Frage der Christologie," in *GuV* 1:94.

101. *HST,* pp. 247-49.

102. *FaU* 1:125. Cf. *GuV* 1:94.

views of his long-deceased teacher, Johannes Weiss: "Weiss's basic assumption is false. The community did *not* preserve an image of the personality of Jesus [*Bild der Persönlichkeit Jesu*] at all."[103] Bultmann does not attempt to drive a wedge between the original, historical personality and its New Testament *Bild.* He simply shows there is no *Bild,* and, therefore, no access to Jesus' personality as a historical datum. The recognition of the Gospels' "fragmentary and luxuriantly legendary" sources, the lack of scholarly consensus on the messianic self-consciousness of Jesus, and the overt dissociation of Jesus' inner development from the synoptic accounts of his baptism, all undermine the historical foundations for the liberal doctrine of Jesus' personality.

The Personality of Jesus and the Nature of Faith

Despite Bultmann's exegetical excision of Jesus' personality from the pages of the Gospels, this operation still leaves intact Harnack's claim that Jesus was an incomparable personality on the basis of his continuing influence in and upon present piety. To analyze this liberal correlation of personality and piety, Bultmann must consider the nature of faith. This he does in his 1927 essay, "On the Question of Christology."[104]

Occasioned, in part, by the publication of Emanuel Hirsch's *Jesus Christus der Herr,* Bultmann's essay criticizes Hirsch's formulation of the presence of Jesus Christ. Despite Hirsch's stated intention of carrying forward the perspective of Søren Kierkegaard on Christ as our "contemporary," an aim Bultmann claims to share,[105] Hirsch relapses into "a Life-of-Jesus theology," which speaks of Jesus' presence in terms of personality.[106] The failure of Hirsch's christological proposal to match his theological intention is reminiscent of that of Bultmann's honored teacher, Wilhelm Herrmann. Indeed, Bultmann finds in Hirsch so many parallels

---

103. *FaU* 1:268. Cf. *GuV* 1:250-51. "Indeed the tradition of the earliest Church did not even unconsciously preserve a picture [*Bild*] of his [Jesus'] personality. Every attempt to reconstruct one remains a play of subjective imagination." *TNT* 1:35. Cf. *TdNT,* pp. 37-38.

104. *FaU* 1:116-44.

105. *FaU* 1:116. For Kierkegaard's discussion, see *Training in Christianity,* ed., trans., and with an Introduction by Walter Lowrie (Princeton: Princeton University Press, 1967), pp. 66-70.

106. *FaU* 1:129.

with Herrmann that, later in the essay, Bultmann begins to recycle his arguments against Hirsch for use against Herrmann.[107] In order to avoid repetition, we shall concentrate on Bultmann's analysis of Herrmann, thereby consolidating his criticisms of Hirsch and Herrmann into a single account.

For Herrmann, faith is a free decision of trust occasioned by, and experienced as, the personal life of Jesus. As such, faith is not an assertion or "work," but a free surrender of our will, as that will is overcome by the compelling personality of Jesus. Faith, then, is not a knowledge of dogmatic propositions about God, but an event, an "experience of trust [*Erlebnis der Vertrauens*]" in Jesus that simultaneously brings us the presence and power of God. While Herrmann retains the liberal emphasis on the *fides qua creditur*, "the faith by which one believes," as the basis for theological assertions, he nevertheless insists with the Reformation that faith is always grounded in and directed to the Lord in whom it trusts.[108]

This pattern of faith, Herrmann argues, is common to every experience of trust. We have this experience "'when a personal life touches us to which we can cleave in trust and reverence.'"[109] Whenever we trust in another, there is simultaneously present in this relationship a higher moral goodness which evokes our trust in the first place. Invariably, those who occasion our consciousness of this presence still fall short of the ideal they represent. Only Jesus' incomparable inner life is completely congruent with the moral goodness we experience through him; this experience implies the ultimate good, or God. Only Jesus is worthy of becoming our conscience, and he alone, by his friendliness toward sinners, can bring us forgiveness for our moral failures.[110]

Against these views of his Marburg mentor, Bultmann argues that "such trust and reverence for moral strength and goodness is clearly not the Christian faith."[111] First, moral goodness does not require the Christian faith. The moral law with its claim of the good is not grounded in Jesus but in human existence. While it is true that Jesus' teaching *may* intensify the claims of conscience, this can be said of any number of

107. Cf. *FaU* 1:126 with 135; 1:126-27 with 136-37; and 1:128 with 137.

108. *FaU* 1:132-34, omitting italics. Cf. *GuV* 1:101-3.

109. *FaU* 1:134, where Bultmann quotes Herrmann, *Die mit der Theologie verknüpfte Not der evangelischen Kirche und ihre Überwindung, Religionsgeschichtliche Volksbücher*, vol. 4, no. 21 (Tübingen: J. C. B. Mohr [Paul Siebeck], 1913), pp. 22-23.

110. *FaU* 1:134-36.

111. *FaU* 1:135.

worthies, from the prophets of the Old Testament to Socrates himself.[112] Second, while our trust is evoked by the power of goodness inherent in an "I-Thou" encounter, so is our mistrust. Precisely in our attempt to preserve the experience of trust, we render this experience uncertain by turning from the power which is its essential condition to the visible and objective factors which accompany its occasioning.[113]

Our oscillating trust and mistrust indicate that insecurity shrouds all interpersonal relationships. Since this is the case, "there is no discoverable reason why, in a relation of trust in Jesus, our own will to be obedient should not be quite as uncertain as in the relation of trust in others."[114] Moreover, precisely in our efforts to preserve our trust in Jesus as an experience, we turn salvation from a gift of God into a work which we perform. This is evident when Herrmann, against his fundamental intention, falls back "either to an idea of goodness as the power of history or to a demand, the authority of which we admit, so that we then stand under the law."[115] Something other than trust, namely, our Kantian-Romantic anthropology, now verifies our experience of Jesus; and if we ask who, in the end, is bestowing forgiveness, we are answered only by the echo of our own voice.[116]

Bultmann goes on to dispute Herrmann's claim that our experience of trust in Jesus is really analogous to that which we experience from our flesh and blood contemporaries. Such an analogy fails to recognize that death ends the trust-creating power of a personality — even that of Jesus: "As a *Thou*, in the sense of a fellow man, he has vanished — as every such *Thou* vanishes when the man dies."[117] As for the effects allegedly traced back to a given personality, they, too, cease when those who have experienced them at first hand are themselves dead. This is why Bultmann can say elsewhere that even if Jesus possessed the sort of personality liberals ascribe to him, its influence ends with the death of the last eyewitness.[118] As with everything human, personality too is circumscribed by death.

Thus, our relation to the historical Jesus, unlike that enjoyed by his

---

112. *FaU* 1:126-27. See also 1:38.

113. *FaU* 1:135.

114. *FaU* 1:137.

115. *FaU* 1:135, omitting italics. See also 1:126. Cf. Herrmann, *Communion with God*, pp. 101-5.

116. *FaU* 1:126. See also 1:38.

117. *FaU* 1:137. Cf. *GuV* 1:106, in which "Thou" [*Du*] is not italicized. See also *FaU* 1:128. Cf. *GuV* 1:97.

118. *FaU* 1:267-68.

original disciples, does not possess the firsthand directness of genuine personal associations. In short, "I have done him no wrong and he has nothing to forgive me."[119] Perhaps recalling his youngest brother killed in France in 1917, Bultmann declares,

> I must say bluntly: it is impossible to see what more was done by the historical Jesus [*der historische Jesus*] who goes to his death in obedient love than was done by all those who, for example, in the World War took the same road, also in obedient love. Their road actually means more to us, not only because we see it more clearly, but chiefly because we were associated with them as with a living *Thou*. To try to create such experiences of encounter with a person of the past seems to me artificial and to lead to sentimentality.[120]

Every "Thou" we have known in our daily associations exercises stronger claims upon us than any made by Jesus of Nazareth.

In a sense, liberals such as Hirsch inadvertently admit this when they, like Herrmann, are forced to fall back on reconstructing "'the inner life of Jesus' as a historical datum present to hand in world history, which can be clearly seen with a little honest effort."[121] Typically this reconstruction makes use of the Gospels as historical sources to support the contention that Jesus truly forgives sinners. But as Bultmann notes elsewhere, all the gospel narratives can ever demonstrate historically is that there were those who claimed to receive forgiveness from Jesus.[122] "And since the forgiveness cannot be verified as a discernible objective event, I am not at all helped by reading touching stories of how Jesus forgave the sinful woman or Zacchaeus."[123]

Typically, too, the reconstruction of Jesus' personality proceeds, as

---

119. *FaU* 1:128.

120. *FaU* 1:127-28. Cf. *GuV* 1:96-97. In his "Autobiographical Reflections [1956, 1965]," Bultmann mentions the death of his youngest brother in 1917 and reveals that yet another perished in a Nazi concentration camp during World War II. See Kegley, *Theology of Bultmann*, p. xxi; pub. in Ger. as "Autobiographische Bemerkungen Rudolf Bultmanns," trans. Meredith Butler and Bernd Jaspert, in Barth, *Gesamtausgabe* 5:1:315-16.

121. *FaU* 1:137, omitting italics. Cf. Herrmann, *Communion with God*, pp. 84-93.

122. "Actually, the forgiveness of sin can never be won through the contemplation of history. Only a *belief* in forgiveness, *acts* of love and forgiveness, *consciousness* of love and forgiveness can be demonstrated in knowable history." *FaU* 1:38.

123. *FaU* 1:128. "The man who is seeking love and forgiveness for himself is not helped by evidence that someone else is confident of having received love and forgiveness." *FaU* 1:38. See also *Jesus and the Word*, p. 212.

with Hirsch, "according to the analogy of our own personal life." But when he, like Herrmann before him, portrays Jesus' inner life as free from sin or guilt, one of "'always prayerful, always obedient surrender,'" and "'a perfect manifestation of the character of God in man,'" we are given pious descriptions for which there is no human analogy. The utter unreality of such characterizations stems from the fact that they are simply abstract descriptions of a moral ideal artificially foisted on Jesus. Hence, when Hirsch speaks of Christ as our "contemporary" and Herrmann of the presence of "Jesus' inner life," they are really speaking of the contemporary presence of their own moral and spiritual values projected on to a figure they reconstruct from the Gospels. Here, again, faith turns into a "work," the very error Herrmann sought to avoid. This is the appalling, if unintended, result of retaining the concept of Jesus' personality as the ground and object of faith's trust.[124]

Despite Bultmann's analysis and criticism of liberal Christology, "the presence of Jesus" does remain as central in his thought as in that of his teachers. Where Bultmann takes leave of liberalism is in his refusal to account for Jesus' presence by appealing to the believer's experience of Jesus' personality. Bultmann is not denying that Jesus is a living "Thou," only that Jesus becomes such *in this way.*[125] To determine in what way Jesus is understood by Bultmann to be a "Thou" for us is the question now before us.

Having reconsidered Bultmann in the light of his liberal heritage, and with a nod to his more recent interpreters, we now turn to his New Testament accounting of "the presence of Jesus," or, to replace Georgi's term with Bultmann's own, "the *Christus praesens.*" This is where the path begins on our way to assessing some of the key theological developments of our post-Bultmann period.

---

124. *FaU* 1:128-29, where Bultmann quotes Hirsch, *Jesus Christus der Herr,* pp. 79-89. Cf. Herrmann, *Communion with God,* pp. 89-91.
    125. *FaU* 1:127.

CHAPTER 2

The Pauline *Christus Praesens*
according to Bultmann

Introduction

IN HIS 1953 Presidential Address before the *Studiorum Novi Testamenti Societas* at Cambridge, England, Bultmann summarizes the eschatological Christology of Paul and John as follows:

> Christ is the eschatological event not as a figure of the past (and this he would be even as centre of history, for the centre lies behind us) but as the *Christus praesens*. And indeed he becomes present in the Word proclaiming Him and in the sacraments, so far as the sacraments are not regarded as infusing supernatural powers, but in so far as by them the death and resurrection of Christ become present events for the recipient, i.e. as *verbum visibile*.[1]

Here Bultmann takes up the term *Christus praesens*, which recalls Harnack's magisterial essay *"Christus praesens — Vicarius Christi,"* to characterize the essential christological claim of the New Testament.

In this chapter, we present Bultmann's case for the Pauline *Christus praesens*, reserving the Johannine for chapter three.[2] We stress at the outset

---

1. "History and Eschatology in the New Testament," *New Testament Studies* (hereafter cited as *NTS*), 1 (1954-55): 15-16; pub. in Ger. as "Geschichte und Eschatologie im Neuen Testament," in *GuV* 3:105. As the polemical parenthesis indicates, Bultmann is taking issue with the thesis of Oscar Cullmann that Christ is the "midpoint" of history. See Cullmann, *Christ and Time: The Primitive Christian Conception of Time and History,* trans. Floyd V. Filson (Philadelphia: Westminster, 1950).

2. Bultmann's interpretation of Paul is based on those letters of the Apostle that are

the reconstructive nature of our project. When in his "more theological" writings Bultmann asserts the presence of Christ in and through the proclamation of the church, the scriptural warrants are usually assumed, or, at best, abridged. It is in his "more exegetical" writings that we find a much fuller exposition of Paul and John on the presence of Christ, one which thus invites systematic analysis. Specifically, the long-delayed publication in 1976 of Bultmann's commentary on 2 Corinthians now makes possible our presentation of the Pauline *Christus praesens* according to Bultmann.[3]

"The Turning Point of the Ages"

Bultmann follows Bousset's *Kyrios Christos* in holding that Paul converted to Christianity in its Hellenistic (Syrian) form.[4] The reader will recall that this community sees Jesus less and less as the coming Son of man, the outlook typical of the Palestinian church, and instead worships him as the *Kyrios* present in the cult.

Nevertheless, as with the preaching of Jesus and the earliest church, so that of Paul "is eschatological through and through."[5] The message of Paul, as with Jesus before him, is saturated with themes common to apocalyptic movements, especially the notion of two aeons dividing the world's career. The present, old aeon, dominated by Satan, is pervaded by pain and sorrow. The anticipated new aeon, the glory of paradise, with its freedom from sin and death, is now at hand. God, or his representative, the Son of man, is about to judge the world. The dead will be raised. All will be rewarded according to their deeds.[6]

What differentiates Paul's proclamation from that of "the historical Jesus," the Jesus whose message can, more or less, be gleaned from the synoptic Gospels, is Paul's recasting of this eschatological expectation:

"unquestionably genuine"; namely, Romans, 1 and 2 Corinthians, Galatians, Philippians, 1 Thessalonians, and Philemon. See *EaF,* p. 111 and *TNT* 1:190.

3. Dinkler reports that the text is based on "Bultmann's handwritten commentary, written down somewhere between 1940 and 1952." *CC,* p. 5.

4. See "The Significance of the Historical Jesus for the Theology of Paul [1929]," in *FaU* 1:221-22; pub. in Ger. as "Die Bedeutung des geschichtlichen Jesus für die Theologie des Paulus," in *GuV* 1:189-90; and *TNT* 1:187-89.

5. *FaU* 1:232.

6. *TNT* 1:5.

Jesus looks to the future, to the *coming* kingdom of God — which is coming or dawning *now*. But Paul looks back; *the turning point of the ages has already come.* "But when the time had fully come, God sent forth his Son, born of woman, born under the law, to redeem those who were under the law, so that we might receive adoption as sons" (Gal. 4:4f.). God *has already* bestowed reconciliation through Christ. "Therefore if anyone is in Christ, he is a new creation; the old has passed away, behold, the new has come. . . . Behold, now is the acceptable time; behold, now is the day of salvation" (2 Cor. 5:17; 6:2). The decisive event which Jesus *expects,* has for Paul already taken place.[7]

While Jesus proclaimed the coming judgment and summoned his listeners to prepare for God's reign, Paul proclaims, by virtue of the crucified Jesus' destiny as the Risen Lord, that salvation from the old age has now occurred. Thus, in Bultmann's celebrated phrase, *"The proclaimer became the proclaimed."*[8]

Bultmann further observes that Paul employs a variety of terms to describe the saving significance of Jesus' destiny. Paul can speak of Jesus' death with concepts taken from Jewish sacrificial practice and juridical theory. The cross is seen as a propitiary sacrifice (*hilastērion,* Rom. 3:25-26) that cancels the guilt of sins or as a vicarious sacrifice by which human beings are ransomed (e.g., Gal. 3:13; 2 Cor. 5:21). Paul can therefore describe salvation as redemption from the punishment of sin dictated by the law (Gal.

---

7. *FaU* 1:233. See also *FaU* 1:195; *Theological Dictionary of the New Testament* (hereafter cited as *TDNT*), s.v. "*zaō* [etc.]," pub. in Ger. as *Theologische Wörterbuch zum Neuen Testament* (hereafter cited as *TWNT*); "Jesus and Paul [1936]," in *EaF,* pp. 196-97; pub. in Ger. as "Jesus und Paulus," in *Exegetica,* pp. 223-24; *TNT* 1:306-7; "Die christliche Hoffnung und das Problem der Entmythologisicrung [1954]," in *GuV* 3:89, ET: "The Christian Hope and the Problem of Demythologizing," trans. Conrad Bonifazi, *The Expository Times* 65 (1954): 277-78; and "The Primitive Christian Kerygma and the Historical Jesus," in *HJKC,* p. 16.

Bultmann discerns in Paul a developing attenuation of the future dimension of primitive Christian eschatology. Gal. 4:4 and 2 Cor. 5:17, 6:2 show a "demythologizing" of views expressed in 1 Thess. 4:16 and 1 Cor. 15:23, 51-53. Thus, Paul is the first to hold that the decisive salvation event has occurred in the cross and resurrection of Jesus Christ. See *Jesus Christ and Mythology* (New York: Charles Scribner's Sons, 1958; hereafter cited as *JCaM*); pub. in Ger. as "Jesus Christus und die Mythologie," in *GuV* 4:154-55; and *History and Eschatology,* pp. 42-43.

8. *TNT* 1:33; *FaU* 1:283; and "The Primitive Christian Kerygma and the Historical Jesus," in *HJKC,* pp. 30 and 38. Cf. Bultmann to Barth, 10 December 1926 in *Letters,* p. 28, in which Bultmann raises the issue of "how it is to be understood (not causally explained) that the proclaimer Jesus becomes the proclaimed Jesus Christ."

3:13), from the law itself (Gal. 4:4-5), and "from the present evil age" (Gal. 1:4), which — subject to the law — is under the power of sin and death. Thus, in Paul's understanding, Christ's death brings freedom from guilt, punishment, and the power of sin and death which manifests itself both in the compulsion to sin (1 Cor. 6:12-20) and in "the standards and evaluations which prevail in this sin-dominated age" (cf. 1 Cor. 7:17-24).[9]

Paul can also speak of salvation in terms of the "grace" or "love" of God. By grace (*charis*), Paul means both God's act and gift: "That is, God's deed of grace consists in the fact that He gave Christ up to die . . . as a propitiatory sacrifice for the sins of men" (Rom. 3:25). But this same deed can also be characterized by Paul as love (*agapē*), "when he says in Rom. 5:8, 'God shows his love for us in that while we were yet sinners Christ died for us.'" When Paul asks the Romans, "Who shall separate us from the love of Christ?" (8:35), Bultmann understands the word "love" as referring back "to the salvation-occurrence named in the preceding verse — the death and resurrection of Christ." Whether described as grace or as love, "the salvation-occurrence, then, includes the death and resurrection of Jesus," as "the eschatological occurrence which puts to an end the old aeon."[10]

This "turning point of the ages" accomplished in and through the cross and resurrection also means and brings for Paul a turning from the judgments typical of the old age to those inaugurated by the new — even with respect to Paul's assessment of Jesus Christ:

> [14] For the love of Christ controls us, because we are convinced that one has died for all; therefore all have died. [15] And he died for all, that those who live might live no longer for themselves but for him who for their sake died and was raised.

9. *TNT* 1:295-98.

10. *TNT* 1:289, 292-93, and 306, omitting italics. That God's saving act in Christ is an eschatological deed is indicated in Paul "by the fact that the blessings of salvation appropriated in faith are eschatological gifts": *dikaiosunē* ("righteousness," Rom. 1:17; 10:10; Phil. 3:9), *sōtēria* ("salvation," in its eschatological sense, Rom. 1:16; 10:10), *zōē* ("life," Rom. 1:17; Gal. 3:11), and *pneuma* ("Spirit," Gal. 3:14; 5:5, etc.). Bultmann adds, "Though the Spirit is given to the believer, *pistis* [faith] is not a gift of the Spirit." *TDNT,* s.v. "*pisteuō* [etc.]." Likewise, Paul's claim that "no one can say 'Jesus is Lord' except by the Holy Spirit" (1 Cor. 12:3) "does not intend to attribute the confession of faith to the Spirit, but to state the means by which spiritual and demonic ecstasy are to be distinguished." *TNT* 1:330, n. Paul's close linking of Christ with the *pneuma* in 2 Cor. 3:17 serves "to bring out the fact that Christ is present and active." *TDNT,* s.v. "*zaō* [etc.]." Thus, the Pauline *Christus praesens* is the *pneuma* of the cross-resurrection kerygma.

[16] From now on, therefore, we regard no one [*hōste hēmeis apo tou nun oudena oidamen*] from a human point of view [*kata sarka*, lit. "according to the flesh"]; even though [*ei kai*] we once regarded Christ from a human point of view [*egnōkamen kata sarka Christon*], we regard him thus no longer (2 Cor. 5:14-16).

In Bultmann's judgment, "therefore" *(hōste)* in the first clause of verse 16 draws its conclusion from verses 14 to 15 which immediately precede it. Thus, "v. 16b does not give the basis for v. 16a," but merely cites its "extreme instance." "Therefore" also indicates that the "from now on" *(apo tou nun)* is not the moment of conversion, but the eschatological turning point. Bultmann writes, "Ever since the event of verse 14 ['one has died for all'] the world is new (v. 17; 6:2), the old has passed away — in the objective sense, of course, and not for me as one converted, however surely it is realized for me through my conversion." Thus, Paul extends the implications of the eschatological salvation event to Christology itself: "Even with respect to Christ it is true that *oudena oidamen kata sarka* [we regard no one according to the flesh]."[11]

Bultmann's analysis of Paul's vocabulary of *sarx* ("flesh") uncovers a variety of meanings. *Sarx* can mean everything from human corporeality (e.g., 2 Cor. 12:7), to the human person (e.g., 2 Cor. 7:5), to humanity or human nature as such (e.g., 1 Cor. 15:50), to carnality (i.e., "weakness and transitoriness . . . in opposition to God and His Spirit," e.g., Gal. 1:16; 1 Cor. 15:50), to "the whole sphere of that which is earthly or 'natural'" (e.g., Rom. 2:28-29). Hence, *sarx* can refer to that which is "outward," or "literal," or "visible," in short, to "the world" *(kosmos)* taken as the source and object of natural life (cf. Gal. 6:14 and 5:24).[12]

To grasp what Paul means by *kata sarka*, Bultmann appeals to the parallel formula *en sarki*, "in the flesh." By this latter phrase, Paul almost always means "in the sphere of the obvious, or the earthly-human, or the natural" (as in Gal. 2:20; Phil. 1:22; and 2 Cor. 10:3). But behind this phrase is the impression, often made explicit, that there is another sphere in which life can move; that is, "in the Spirit" (Rom. 8:9), "in the Lord" (Phlm. 16),

11. *CC*, pp. 153-55. See also *TDNT*, s.v., "*thanatos* [etc.]" and "Exegetische Probleme des zweiten Korintherbriefes [1947]," in *Exegetica*, pp. 309-10.

12. *TNT* 1:233-35, omitting italics. In *TDNT*, Bultmann succinctly identifies Paul's "sphere of the *sarx*" as that "of the visible and demonstrable (Rom. 2:28-29; 2 Cor. 4:18), whether in the form of natural phenomena, of historical circumstances or of palpable achievements." S.v. "*thanatos* [etc.]."

"in faith" (Gal. 2:20). Hence, as Romans 7:5 and 8:7-9 make clear, *en sarki* is the sphere of sinning, that is, the field which opposes God as an enemy. Similarly, *kata sarka* can characterize a person or a human relationship "in regard to facts present within natural life and verifiable by everyone," while simultaneously suggesting another possible point of view. Hence, Paul can speak of "Israel according to the flesh [*Israēl kata sarka*]" (1 Cor. 10:18) in contrast to the "Israel of God [*Israēl tou theou*]" (Gal. 6:16).[13]

As a rule, *kata sarka* modifies both nouns (including proper names) and verbs. "As a modifier of verbs the phrase has an altogether different meaning: It stamps *an existence or an attitude* not as natural-human, but *as sinful*" (e.g., 2 Cor. 1:17-18; 10:2).[14] Thus, the exegetical problem in 2 Cor. 5:16b is whether *kata sarka* is to be understood as the adverbial modifier of the verb "know," or as the adjectival modifier of the noun or proper name "Christ."[15] In light of the eschatological salvation event, does Paul forswear a sinful, *kata sarka* knowing of Christ or a Christ who is himself *kata sarka,* that is, simply natural-human? While Bultmann oscillates between the adverbial and the adjectival reading,[16] he repeatedly resolves the exegetical issue by defining it as a distinction without a difference. To perceive Christ in a sarkic way, hence sinfully, is to perceive Christ as sarkic, or as natural-human: "A 'Christ regarded in the manner of the flesh' is just what a 'Christ after the flesh' is."[17]

Therefore, "the *Christos kata sarka* is Christ as he can be encountered in the world, before his death and resurrection,"[18] that is, apart from his destiny as the eschatological salvation event. In Paul, the phrase so taken could refer to Christ as the Son of David or the worker of miracles, in contrast to Christ crucified in the form of a servant. This interpretation

13. *TNT* 1:235-37.

14. *TNT* 1:237. See also *CC,* p. 154.

15. See *TNT* 1:238; *FaU* 1:217; *Exegetica,* p. 309; and *CC,* p. 154.

16. *TNT* 1:238-39 finds the adverbial sense "more probable"; *CC,* pp. 154-55 inclines toward the adjectival reading. Victor Paul Furnish, overlooking *TNT,* has Bultmann favoring the adjectival reading. See *II Corinthians: A New Translation with Introduction and Commentary,* The Anchor Bible (New York: Doubleday, 1984), pp. 312-13. J. Louis Martyn argues for the adverbial reading in "Epistemology at the Turn of the Ages: 2 Corinthians 5:16," in William R. Farmer, C. F. D. Moule, and Richard R. Niebuhr, eds., *Christian History and Interpretation: Studies Presented to John Knox* (Cambridge: University Press, 1967), pp. 269-87. As Martyn's essay shows, the adverbial reading reinforces the anthropological force of this text.

17. *TNT* 1:239. See also 1:294; *FaU* 1:217, 239; and *CC,* p. 154.

18. *CC,* p. 155.

directs the *kata sarka* in 2 Corinthians 5:16 against "those who pride themselves on a man's position" (2 Cor. 5:12). On the other hand, the phrase could instead refer to Christ in the form of a servant (Phil. 2:7), as opposed to Christ in his present glory (Phil. 3:21; Rom. 8:34). In that case, the polemical point is that Paul "may not be regarded with a view to the *thanatos* [death] at work in him, but with a view to the *zōē tou Iēsou* [life of Jesus] at work through him" (2 Cor. 4:7-12).[19]

Whichever way *Christos kata sarka* is taken, whether as mighty Son of David or as lowly servant,[20] in the context of 2 Corinthians 5:16, both perspectives falsely arise from seeing Christ in a "fleshly" way. That is, both assess him in "human terms,"[21] understand him "as he presents himself to our eyes,"[22] or regard him "as he can be met within the world."[23] Moreover, this sarkic way of knowing is sinful, whether or not the Christology built on its vision is "high" or "low."

Thus, "Paul is concerned neither with the human personality [*menschliche Persönlichkeit*] of Jesus . . . nor with the nature of Christ as a heavenly divine being."[24] Instead, Paul claims "a revelation [*apokalupsis*] of Jesus Christ" (Gal. 1:12), "the substantive content" of which is "the acknowledgment of Jesus as the Messiah":[25]

> Jesus' death-and-resurrection, then, is for Paul the decisive thing about the person of Jesus and his life experience, indeed, in the last analysis it is the sole thing of importance for him — implicitly included are the incarnation and the earthly life of Jesus as bare facts. That is,

19. *CC,* pp. 155-56.

20. The first interpretation, i.e., Son of David or worker of miracles, "could denote personal acquaintance with the earthly Jesus, of which Paul's opponents (or at least their authorities) boasted." Nevertheless, Bultmann rules out this possibility on three grounds: (1) The "we" of 5:16 does not refer to Paul, but to the Christian community (cf. *ei tis* ["if anyone"] in v. 17; Rom. 6:11, 7:6; and Gal. 2:19); (2) *ei kai* ("even if," Bultmann trans.) in v. 16b signifies "a condition contrary to fact" (following Reitzenstein); and (3) "Nowhere . . . does Paul refute claims derived from personal acquaintance with Jesus." *CC,* pp. 155-56. Bultmann leans toward the second interpretation, i.e., Christ as servant, in *CC,* p. 156. It also appears to inform his views in "The Concept of Revelation in the New Testament [1929]," in *EaF,* p. 77; pub. in Ger. as "Der Begriff der Offenbarung im Neuen Testament," in *GuV* 3:20; and in *TNT* 2:50.

21. *FaU* 1:244.

22. *EaF,* p. 77.

23. *CC,* p. 156. See also *FaU* 1:239.

24. *FaU* 1:277. Cf. *GuV* 1:259.

25. *FaU* 1:235-36, omitting italics.

Paul is interested only in the *fact* that Jesus became man and lived on earth. *How* he was born or lived interests him only to the extent of knowing that Jesus was a definite, concrete man, a Jew, "being born in the likeness of man and being found in human form" (Phil. 2:7), "born of woman, born under the law" (Gal. 4:4). But beyond that, Jesus' manner of life, his ministry, his personality [*Persönlichkeit*], his character play no role at all; neither does Jesus' message.[26]

Bultmann therefore regards modern reconstructions of "the historical Jesus," which typically speak of his "natural origin," his "messianic consciousness," his "inner life," his "heroism," and his "faith," to be futile exercises in "Christ after the flesh."[27] In light of Jesus' destiny as the turning point of the ages, to portray his personality is to betray his eschatological significance. Such portrayals are now anachronistic for Christian faith.

To inquire then about how and where Jesus Christ becomes our contemporary is not to trace the perdurable influence of his personality. Rather, as Paul shows, it is to ask how and where his eschatological or messianic reality is manifested in the present. In "that he construes the eschatological event as *present*," Paul leaves behind apocalyptic theology and affirms his affinity with the sacramental *Kyrios* cult of Hellenistic Christianity.[28] Insofar as "he understands the presence of salvation as an *eschatological* phenomenon," Paul still reflects the lingering influence of Jewish apocalypticism.[29] For Paul, the eschatological event, or the saving Lordship of Jesus, becomes present in and through its announcement or

---

26. *TNT* 1:293-94. Cf. *TdNT*, p. 293. Bultmann reaffirms these judgments in 1960 in "The Primitive Christian Kerygma and the Historical Jesus," in *HJKC*, p. 20. But see *FaU* 1:232 and *History and Eschatology*, p. 47, in which Bultmann admits the possibility that Jesus' message may have influenced Paul.

See also Bultmann to Barth, 10 December 1926, in *Letters*, pp. 29-30: "I naturally realize that Kierkegaard is fundamentally right when in the *Philosophical Fragments* [p. 104] he says that the tradition about Jesus is adequately presented if one says that 'we have believed that in such and such a year God showed himself in the lowly form of a servant, lived among us, and taught, and then died.'" Significantly, Bultmann then adds, "In fact, however, the synoptists hand down *more* than Kierkegaard regards as necessary, and since this *more* is in fact handed down, I view it as a concern of theology to be interested in this more and to present it." Insofar as this "more" embraces the eschatological destiny of Jesus and its present import, Bultmann's reading of the New Testament in general, and Paul in particular, is not "Kierkegaardian."

27. See *FaU* 1:124, 126, 132, 239, 241, and 277 and *EaF*, pp. 78-79.

28. *CC*, p. 98, my italics. See also *TNT* 1:144 and 300.

29. *CC*, p. 98, my italics.

proclamation. This proclamation of the Word of God the New Testament calls "the kerygma."[30] Thus, Paul's "eschatologizing" of the presence of Christ and his "presentizing" of the eschaton go hand in hand with his "kerygmatizing" of the sacramental *Kyrios* cult.[31]

The Kerygma

Paul's kerygma announces "Jesus Christ the Crucified and Risen One — to be God's eschatological act of salvation."[32] As such, "the kerygma of Paul proclaims a fact: Jesus Christ, whom God sent when the time was full, who was put to death and rose again 'for our trespasses' or 'for our justification' (Rom. 4:25)."[33] Nevertheless, "the word of proclamation is no mere report about historical incidents" or "teaching . . . which could simply be regarded as true without any transformation of the hearer's own existence. For the word is *kerygma,* personal address [*Anrede*],

30. "The concept of the 'Word of God' . . . refers to that for which it generally stands in the New Testament — *the Christian kerygma.*" *FaU* 1:298.

31. For example, Paul styles the Lord's Supper a "proclaiming" (*kataggellein,* 1 Cor. 11:26), "using the same word that he otherwise uses for preaching" (Rom. 1:8; 1 Cor. 2:1; 9:14; Phil. 1:17-18). *TNT* 1:313. See also 1:298; *FaU* 1:213; and *EaF,* p. 200.

Paul's transposition of salvation from a purely sacramental to a kerygmatic event (1) shifts salvation from the realm of cosmic occurrence to that of human decision, and (2) transfers "incorporation" *en Christō* ("in Christ") from that of a cosmic Christ-sphere to that of an eschatological community, the *ekklēsia* ("church"). On (1), see *TNT* 1:302. See also 1:307; *Primitive Christianity,* pp. 202-3; and *CC,* p. 117 (on 2 Cor. 2:14). On (2), see *CC,* pp. 23 and 63. See also *FaU* 1:202 and 243-44; *TNT* 1:310-11; and *RGG*[3], s.v. "*Mystik* [*IV. Im N.T.*]." For the locative *en Christō,* see *CC,* p. 70 (on 2 Cor. 2:17) and p. 165 (on 2 Cor. 5:17). Cf. Col. 1:15-20 where, stimulated by Paul, the "body" of which Christ is "head" is no longer the cosmos, but "the 'Church' (by means of the addition in v. 18 and again in v. 24)." *TNT* 1:178-79.

32. *TNT* 1:3. "In the kergyma Jesus Christ is proclaimed as the one who died vicariously on the cross for the sins of men and was miraculously raised by God for our salvation." See "The Primitive Christian Kerygma and the Historical Jesus," in *HJKC,* p. 16. See also *FaU* 1:208; "Paul," in *EaF,* pp. 124-25; *TDNT,* s.v. "*zaō,* [etc.]," where the following summaries of the kerygma are noted: Rom. 6:10; 14:9; 2 Cor. 13:4; cf. Rom. 10:9 and 1 Cor. 15:3-5; and *TDNT,* s.v. "*pisteuō,* [etc.]," where 1 Cor. 15:3-5 is summarized, 1 Thess. 4:14 is quoted, and Phil. 2:6-11 is cited. Since "the death and resurrection of Christ are bound together in the unity of one salvation-occurrence" (Rom. 8:34; 2 Cor. 5:15; 13:4), when Paul abbreviates the kerygma as "the word of the cross" (1 Cor. 1:18), this does not alter its status as "the word of life" (Phil. 2:16) and *vice versa. TNT* 1:293. See also 1:292; *FaU* 1:240; *EaF,* p. 71; and *NTaM,* pp. 36-37.

33. *FaU* 1:208, omitting italics. See also 1:241.

demand [*Forderung*], and promise [*Verheissung*]; it is the very act of divine grace."[34]

These characterizations of Paul's kerygma by Bultmann all stem from connotations in Paul's own image of a herald running ahead of the royal entourage to proclaim the monarch's imminent arrival or promulgated mandates. That is to say, *kērygma* ("message" or "proclamation," cf. *kērussein*, "to herald" or "to proclaim"),[35] in the proper sense, is an "authorized, prescribed proclamation, a sovereign edict," the dissemination of which, by definition, "requires authorized messengers, *kērukes, apostoloi* [heralds, apostles] (Rom. 10:13-17)."[36] These heralds proclaim only what the sovereign authorizes. The word of the herald, insofar as it comes from the monarch, is a sovereign word effecting the monarch's will. "So we are ambassadors for Christ," Paul writes, "God making his appeal through us" (2 Cor. 5:20).

Bultmann almost always characterizes kerygma as *Anrede*,[37] a term variously rendered into English by his translators. For example, Louise Pettibone Smith translates *Anrede* as "summons," "direct summons," "address," or "direct address,"[38] while Kendrick Grobel prefers "challenge" or "personal address."[39] Bultmann's exegetical case for kerygma as *Anrede* is based on the New Testament's occasional substitution of both *kērygma*

---

34. *TNT* 1:319. Cf. *TdNT*, p. 319. See also 1:302; in Ger., p. 301, where the proclaimed word is characterized as *"anredenden, fordernden und verheissenden."*

35. See *FaU* 1:219, n. 28 and *TNT* 1:88. The Greek term *to kērygma* refers either to the act of proclamation (e.g., 1 Cor. 2:4) or to the content of what is proclaimed (1 Cor. 15:4). See *TDNT*, s.v. *"kērux* [etc.]," by Gerhard Friedrich.

36. *TdNT*, p. 308. According to Bultmann, "Paul calls all missionaries 'apostles' (1 Cor. 9:5; Rom. 16:7; 2 Cor. 11:5, 13; 12:11f.) and the same usage is still found in Acts 14:4, 14, and Did. 11:4-6." *TNT* 1:60.

37. *GuV* 1:172-73, 175-76, 180, 186, n. 2, 199, 208, 260, 263, and 267; *TdNT*, pp. 306 and 308; and "Das Problem des Verhältnisses von Theologie und Verkündigung im Neuen Testament," in *Aux Sources de la Tradition Chrétienne: Mélanges offerts à M. Maurice Goguel à l'occasion de son soixantedixiéme anniversaire* (Neuchâtel: Delachaux & Niestlé, 1950), p. 35. See also *TdNT*, p. 303, where the present participle *anredender* modifies the noun *Charakter*.

38. *FaU* 1:205, 207, 212, n. 28, 231-32, 241, 277, 281, and 284-85. When Bultmann uses the adjective *direkte* before *Anrede*, Smith usually renders the construction as "direct address," and, less frequently, as "direct summons." See *FaU* 1:204, 208, and 280.

39. *TNT* 1:307 and 319; and 2:128 and 240. The instance where Grobel translates *Anrede* as "challenge" occurs in the context of rendering *persönliche Anrede* as "personal challenge." Grobel renders the construction *anredender Charakter* as "character of direct challenge." See *TNT* 1:304.

and *kērussein* with terms associated with exhortation.[40] "God's Word," Bultmann declares, "is always summons [*Anrede*]."[41] Thus, Paul does not simply announce the kerygma of Christ, he directly addresses it to his listeners.

Bultmann consistently characterizes Paul's kerygma, which is the Word of and from the sovereign God, as both "demand" and "promise," as God's call for obedience and as God's declaration of love.[42] That is to say, the heralded kerygma authoritatively addresses the listener's conscience (*suneidēsis*, 2 Cor. 4:2; 5:11).[43] Bultmann defines conscience as a "state of mind" that judges its own intent with respect to possible or actual conduct, thereby presupposing "a knowledge of good and evil and of the corresponding conduct."[44] The proclaimed kerygma does not constitute conscience, but assumes and confirms its presence (Rom. 2:15). Every hearer has a moral capacity or self-understanding already awaiting God's demand and promise.[45]

Bultmann finds this pattern of addressing announcement, with its call to repent and its promise to save, not only typical of the preaching by Paul but also of the preaching by Jesus and the prophets.[46] What

40. In this regard, Bultmann cites *marturein* ("testify," 1 Cor. 15:15; cf. Gal. 5:3); *marturion* ("testimony," 1 Cor. 1:6; 2:1); *parakalein* ("summon," 2 Cor. 5:20; 6:1); and *paraklēsis* ("appeal," cf. 1 Thess. 2:3 with 1 Cor. 2:4). See *FaU* 1:219, n. 28.

41. *FaU* 1:300, omitting italics. Cf. *GuV* 1:282. See also Bultmann's review of *Die Bedeutung des Wortes bei Paulus,* by Otto Schmitz, in *Theologische Literaturzeitung* (hereafter abbreviated *TLZ*) 53 (1928): 566.

42. *TNT* 1:302 and 319.

43. See Bultmann's review of *Bedeutung des Wortes bei Paulus,* by Schmitz, in *TLZ* 53 (1928): 565-66; *FaU* 1:209, n. 23, 211, 242, 301, 303, and 317; *GuV* 1:260 (correcting a misprint in *FaU* 1:278); *EaF,* p. 139; *TNT* 1:216-20, 250, and 260-61; and *CC,* pp. 102 and 147.

44. *TNT* 1:217. For Macquarrie's attack on this definition as arbitrarily Heideggerian, see *An Existentialist Theology,* p. 151.

45. See *FaU* 1:209, n. 23, 226, 303, 317; *EaF,* pp. 135, 139; and *TNT* 1:218, 250, and 260-61. The Pauline *suneidēsis* is thus an example of that innate human capacity for questioning and the implicit knowledge thereby presupposed which Bultmann terms *Vorverständnis* ("preunderstanding") on the lines of Heidegger's *Vorhabe.* See *GuV* 1:125-26, n. 1, 153, 161, n. 1, 268, n. 1, 295-98, and 311, ET: *FaU* 1:156-57, n. 9, 184, 192, n. 4, 286, n. 2, 315-17, and 330; *GuV* 3:1-8, ET: *EaF,* pp. 58-65; and *History and Eschatology,* pp. 111-15. For Heidegger's discussion of *Vorhabe, Vorsicht,* and *Vorgriff* in his uncovering of the "hermeneutic circle," see *Sein und Zeit,* pp. 150-53. ET: *Being and Time,* pp. 191-95.

46. See *FaU* 1:204, 206, 208, 231-32 and "The Primitive Christian Kerygma and the Historical Jesus," in *HJKC,* pp. 27-28. Bultmann also finds in "the great prophet of

separates the kerygma proclaimed by Jesus from that proclaimed by Paul is Jesus' eschatological destiny; it is this destiny that Paul proclaims. Thus, what distinguishes Paul's kerygma from that of Jesus or the prophets is not its character as direct address, as demand and promise, but its content as "Christian."

According to Bultmann, the content of the Christian kerygma takes form in "dogmas," that is, theological statements or propositions, of which "Jesus, Lord" (2 Cor. 4:5; cf. Rom. 10:9; Phil. 2:11) serves as a prime example.[47] Occasionally, Paul prefaces such statements by "we know" (2 Cor. 5:1), or "you know" (1 Thess. 5:2; 2 Cor. 8:9; Rom. 6:3), thereby indicating that dogmas do convey knowledge (Wissen) about God.[48] These dogmas are conceptually colored by the time and place of their formulation.[49]

Bultmann's talk of the knowledge transmitted by the kerygma's theological statements appears to run counter to his repeated insistence that the kerygma, precisely as Anrede, is directed to moral, rather than theoretical, reason.[50] From this seeming inconsistency come cascading questions. How do dogmatic statements become spoken and heard as kerygma, as Anrede? Do they do so simply through rhetorical convention or merely by claiming to announce the divine will? Moreover, how can a dogmatic statement be distinguished from a kerygmatic one if the kerygma itself is composed of dogmatic statements? Is there, for instance, an "ideal" kerygma, independent of any concrete theological formulation, which can determine when a dogma is truly kerygmatic?[51] Tagging these questions

---

Iran, Zarathustra, a similar association of eschatology and moral demand." *Jesus and the Word*, pp. 129-30.

47. *TNT* 1:318 and 2:239. Cf. *FaU* 1:278 and 280-81 where Bultmann regards the confession "Jesus is Lord" not so much as a statement of the kerygma, but, rather, as a verbal response to the kerygma's summons of God's act in Christ. Such responses, as christological formulations, may subsequently and indirectly serve kerygmatic proclamation. Thus, Bultmann finds in Paul two distinct but interwoven rhetorics of Christology: primary proclamation of the Christ event (direct summons) and secondary explanation of it (indirect summons). The latter also embraces the "new self-understanding of believers" out of which the former issues.

48. See *TNT* 1:318. Cf. *TdNT,* pp. 318-19. See also *TDNT,* s.v. *"agnōstos."* Peter Carnley's comment that "the revelatory Word is heard as call but not as communication" is therefore an overstatement, at least with respect to Bultmann's exegesis of Paul. See *The Structure of Resurrection Belief* (Oxford: Clarendon, 1987), p. 116.

49. See *FaU* 1:213 and 279-80.

50. See, e.g., *EaF,* p. 78; *TDNT,* s.v. *"aphiēmi* [etc.]"; and *JCaM,* p. 36.

51. See *NTaM,* pp. 59-60 and Bultmann's review of *Bedeutung des Wortes bei Paulus,* by Schmitz, in *TLZ* 53 (1928): 566.

for further discussion in chapter four, we simply note here that Bultmann regards the dogmatic content of the kerygma as subordinate to the kerygma's function of direct address.[52] In Bultmann's view, the kerygma demands "obedience to" or "faith in" and not — in the first instance — "discussion of."

Therefore, when Bultmann speaks of "the kerygma," he typically means the Christian message of God's act in Christ. Granted that Paul formulates this message in theological statements, the vital point for Bultmann is that the message is proclaimed as a summons to decision.

The Kerygma and Christ: Patterns of Predication

According to Bultmann, the eschatological event can be predicated by Paul either of Christ or of the word proclaiming him. Of course, this is not to say that the kerygma "suffered under Pontius Pilate, was crucified, dead, and buried"! Rather, what is meant is that, with respect to their soteriological benefits, the event of Christ is synonymous with the event of Christ proclaimed. "As the Christ event is the eschatological event which ends the old aeon and begins the new, so the same is true of the preaching of the apostle: 'Behold now is the acceptable time; behold now is the day of salvation' (2 Cor. 6:2)."[53] Hence, "as Christ can be called the 'power' *(dunamis)* of God (1 Cor. 1:24), so also the preaching itself, the 'gospel' is 'a power of God for salvation to everyone who has faith,' (Rom. 1:16)."[54] Likewise, Paul can name Christ "our righteousness" (1 Cor. 1:30) and the gospel proclaiming him "the righteousness of God" (Rom. 1:17).[55] By bestowing the same eschatological predicates on preaching that he gives to Christ, namely, "power" and "righteousness," Paul testifies to the soteriological synonymy of Christ and the kerygma. Hence, Paul can name either the kerygma or Christ as the object of faith.[56]

---

52. See *EaF,* p. 78 and *TNT* 1:318-19. Cf. *TdNT,* pp. 318-19. Note in the latter how Bultmann almost grudgingly accepts the place of *Wissen* in kerygmatic communication, but hastens to subordinate it to "*existentielle Wandlung* [existential transformation]." See also *FaU* 1:189-90, 193, and 208-12.

53. *FaU* 1:307.

54. *FaU* 1:278. See also 1:242.

55. See *EaF,* p. 80.

56. "Kerygma" is the object of faith *(pistis)* in 1 Cor. 1:21; 2:4-5; 15:11, 14 (as is "gospel" in 1 Cor. 15:2 and Phil. 1:27). The formula "to believe in" *(pisteuein [pistis] eis)*

Since the function of preaching requires a functioning preacher (Rom. 10:14-15), Paul can also predicate of the preacher what he predicates of the preaching with respect to Jesus Christ. As 2 Corinthians 2:14 declares, "But thanks be to God, who in Christ always leads us in triumph, and through us spreads the fragrance of the knowledge of him everywhere."[57] Here, as Bultmann points out, the gospel is the fragrance, while in the very next verse, it is the apostle himself who is called the "aroma of Christ."[58] Thus, "it is the apostle himself who is . . . identical with the *logos tou theou* [Word of God] which he proclaims (v. 17). . . . As the Word, so the apostle himself belongs to the eschatological saving event described in verse 16."[59] Therefore, concludes Bultmann, "Paul, as it were, proclaims himself."[60]

---

can take for its object "Christ Jesus" (Rom. 10:14; Gal 2:16; cf. Phil. 1:29). *Pistis* with the genitive similarly takes the following objects in Paul: "Jesus Christ" (Rom. 3:22; Gal. 2:16; 3:22), "Jesus" (Rom. 3:26), "Christ" (Phil. 3:9), and "the Son of God" (Gal. 2:20). See *TDNT*, s.v. "*pisteuō* [etc.]" and *TNT* 1:317-18.

Significantly, "the believing Jesus [*der glaubende Jesus*] is of no concern at all for Paul; what he calls 'faith' first appears upon the death and resurrection of Christ, not before." *FaU* 1:277. Cf. *GuV* 1:259. See also *TNT* 1:3. For an opposite interpretation of Paul, which reads Gal. 3:22 as a subjective genitive, see Richard B. Hays, *The Faith of Jesus Christ: An Investigation of the Narrative Substructure of Galatians 3:1–4:11,* Society of Biblical Literature Dissertation Series, no. 56 (Chico, Calif.: Scholars Press, 1983), pp. 157-76.

57. Paul's use of *osmē* ("fragrance"), in Bultmann's judgment, "rests on the ancient idea that fragrance is a sign of the divine presence and the divine life." *CC*, p. 64. Note also that *phaneroō* ("spreads") is used "for revelation as this takes place in [Paul's] preaching [as also 2 Cor. 11:16] and indeed his very existence (2 Cor. 4:10-11)." *TDNT*, s.v. "*phainō* [etc.]," with Dieter Lührmann. See also *TDNT*, s.v. "*alētheia*" on 2 Cor. 4:2.

58. See *CC*, pp. 66-67 and 107 and Bultmann's review of *Gnosis: La Connaissance religieuse dans les Epîtres de Saint Paul,* by Jacques Dupont, in *The Journal of Theological Studies* (hereafter cited as *JTS*), n.s. 3, pt. 1 (April 1952), p. 12.

59. *CC*, pp. 66-67. See also p. 107. Commenting on the identity between the apostle and the Word of God, Bultmann notes that "this is not the self-consciousness of the pneumatic but is based upon the fact that God's Word is not a universal truth, an idea, but rather the spoken, accosting Word which as such does not exist without its bearer." *CC*, p. 67. See also *TNT* 1:307 and *CC*, p. 107.

60. *CC*, p. 107. Commenting on 2 Cor. 4:5, "For what we preach is not ourselves, but Jesus Christ as Lord, with ourselves as your servants for Jesus' sake," Bultmann remarks: " 'Not ourselves' — this does not repel the charge that Paul makes himself the object of his preaching, but rather the charge of egoistic motives." *CC*, pp. 106-7. Cf. *TNT* 1:291 on Rom. 15:18. Cf. *CC*, pp. 25-26 on 2 Cor. 1:6-7. Bultmann's interpretation is supported by the fact that just as the kerygma is directed to the listener's conscience, so the apostle — as apostle — "can only be understood by the hearer's *suneidēsis*" (2 Cor. 4:2). *CC*, p. 74; cf. p. 147 on 2 Cor. 5:11.

Hence, "the decision for the gospel and for Paul is one and the same" (2 Cor. 5:12).[61]

To these patterns of predication yet another can be added. Bultmann finds that Paul can also predicate of the preacher what he predicates of the incarnate, crucified, and risen Christ.

In regard to the incarnation, "what is true of the pre-existent Son — he 'did not please himself' but took all reproach upon himself (Rom. 15:3) — is also true of the apostle: 'I please all in all things' (1 Cor. 10:33), and he, too, travels his way through reproach and shame (1 Cor. 4:9-13; 2 Cor. 6:8f.)."[62] Likewise, the servanthood Paul attributes to the One who became incarnate (Phil. 2:8; Gal. 2:20; Rom. 8:35, 39; 15:8), he grants *mutatis mutandis* to those proclaiming Christ, not least himself (Rom. 1:1; Gal. 1:10; Phil. 1:1; 1 Cor. 4:1; 10:19; 2 Cor. 3:6; 4:5; 6:4; and 11:23).[63] Given this pattern of predication, Bultmann comments that "the incarnation of the Preexistent One . . . occurs in the Christian proclamation."[64]

With respect to the cross and resurrection, Bultmann paraphrases 2 Corinthians 4:12 as follows: "As Christ gave himself up to die in order to obtain life for men, so death is at work in the apostle in order that life may be at work in the hearers of his preaching."[65] Moreover, "in the apostle, Christ is present precisely as the Risen One, for in bearing about in his body the dying of Jesus, Paul is manifesting in his body the life of Jesus (2 Cor. 4:10-11)."[66] Bultmann similarly interprets 2 Corinthians 13:4. Paul's statement, "For we are weak in him [Christ], but in dealing with you we shall live with him by the power of God," is taken to mean that "through the apostle, Christ is demonstrating his power to the hearers" or that "the risen Christ himself encounters the hearer in the apostle."[67]

---

61. *CC,* p. 148. See also *FaU* 1:211-12.

62. *TNT* 1:304.

63. See *TNT* 1:304-5.

64. *TdNT,* p. 305. See also p. 304 and *FaU* 1:241.

65. *TNT* 1:304. Cf. *CC,* pp. 25-26 on 2 Cor. 1:6. See also *EaF,* p. 77, where "the preaching apostle himself must be understood as one who reveals life precisely in death" (2 Cor. 5:16–6:10).

66. *TdNT,* p. 306.

67. *TNT* 1:306. See also 1:303, where Gal. 6:17 and 2 Cor. 1:5; 4:10-11 are cited. Cf. 1:350-51, where Bultmann interprets Gal. 6:17; 2 Cor. 4:10-11; 13:4 on the basis of somatic incorporation into the "fellowship" of Christ's sufferings (Phil. 3:10), rather than on the grounds of the preaching ministry. So also 1:299, in regard to 2 Cor. 4:7-12, and 1:328, in regard to 2 Cor. 1:5 and 4:10.

In regard to their soteriological benefits, the death and resurrection of Jesus Christ are replicated in Paul — as an apostle:

> Thus Paul has become Christ himself for his hearers — not because he is deified and is gazed upon by them as a pneumatic, but because he preaches to them. "So we are at work for Christ [*für Christus*] (perhaps we must even translate, 'in Christ's stead' [*an Stelle Christi*]) in such a way that God makes his appeal through us. We beseech you on behalf of Christ [*für Christus*] (or 'in Christ's stead' [*an Christi Statt*]) be reconciled to God!" (2 Cor. 5:20).[68]

As Bultmann reads Paul, Christ — incarnate, crucified, and risen — is our contemporary in addressing us through the heralds who proclaim him: "In them he is speaking (2 Cor. 5:20; 13:3) and through them he is working (Rom. 15:18)."[69]

To those demanding of Paul proof that "Christ is speaking in me" (2 Cor. 13:3), a demand resulting from the perception of Paul as pitifully weak and without power *(dunamis)* (2 Cor. 10:1, 10), hence, without Christ (10:7-8), such proof comes not by way of "demonstrative form," but by the "material content" of preaching itself.[70] Paul is certain that the word will have an effect, and that the power of Christ will prevail even in and through one such as himself, who is abused as "weak." In this regard, the Apostle exhibits the pattern of Christ himself, in whom "*astheneia* [weakness] and *dunamis* [power] are joined" (2 Cor. 13:4).[71] Therefore, Paul can demand of his Corinthian congregation that their "'obedience to Christ' prove itself in obedience to him (2 Cor. 10:5f.)."[72]

---

68. *EaF,* p. 76. Cf. *GuV* 3:19-20. See also *CC,* pp. 106-7. Cf. *BK,* pp. 109-10. Bultmann regards "the typical 'pneumatic' in Hellenism" to be "the 'divine man' *(theois anēr),* who is of higher nature than ordinary mortals, filled with mysterious, divine power, which makes him capable of miraculous insights and deeds." *TNT* 1:157. By contrast, Paul's "emphasis lies upon apostleship as the agency of Christ's being present to his people and of his calling them to obedience." So Furnish, *II Corinthians,* p. 350.

In *CC,* p. 163, Bultmann defends the translation "in Christ's stead" *(an Christi Statt),* for the *huper Christou* of 2 Cor. 5:20, "since the commissioned messenger certainly speaks in place of, as representative of the one commissioning." Cf. *BK,* pp. 164-65. See also *FaU* 1:209. Cf. *GuV* 1:177.

69. *TNT* 1:306. See also 1:345 and *CC,* pp. 191 and 242-43 on 2 Cor. 13:3.

70. *CC,* p. 242.

71. *CC,* pp. 242-43.

72. *TNT* 1:308. Paul's claim to his congregations' obedience (2 Cor. 2:9; 7:15; Phil. 2:2; Phlm. 21) should not be construed as tyranny (2 Cor. 1:24). Paul regards himself as

To sum up: Bultmann's exegesis of Paul uncovers double patterns of predication. The same soteriological benefits attributed to (the death and resurrection of) Christ are also attributed to the proclamation and proclaimers (as proclaimers) of the kerygma. These patterns suggest to Bultmann a unity, if not identity, between the event of Christ and the event of Christ proclaimed. We now turn to Bultmann's further exegetical account of this unity.

The Kerygma and Christ: 2 Corinthians 5 and 6

An examination of Bultmann's more exegetical essays finds several explicitly linking the presence of Christ to the act of kerygmatic proclamation. For example, in "The Christology of the New Testament," Bultmann declares in 1933 that "Christ is present in the word."[73] In another essay of that same year, "The Word of God in the New Testament," Bultmann writes, "Christ becomes contemporary in the preaching";[74] "Christ himself, indeed, God himself, summons men in the preaching of the apostle";[75] "the Christ event is further consummated in the preaching of the Word";[76] and "the proclamation of the Word is a continuation of the Christ event."[77] At the conclusion of his 1936 essay, "Jesus and Paul," Bultmann asserts that what

---

a *doulos* ("slave"), not only of Jesus Christ, but of those to whom he preaches (2 Cor. 4:5; 1 Cor. 9:19-23). Furthermore, Paul demands obedience not on the basis of his person, let alone personality, but on the basis of his apostolic office. See *FaU* 1:244. On 2 Cor. 10:5-6, see *TNT* 1:315 and *CC*, pp. 185-87. On 2 Cor. 1:24, see *CC*, pp. 43-45.

73. "*Christus ist im Wort gegenwärtig.*" *GuV* 1:260. ET: *FaU* 1:278. See also *GuV* 1:289: "*Ist Christus im Wort der Kirche gegenwärtig,*" ET: *FaU* 1:308. Cf. *RGG²*, s.v. "*Paulus,*" where preaching and the sacraments (understood as proclamation) "*das Heilsereignis zur Gegenwart machen.*" ET: *EaF*, p. 140.

74. "*In der Predigt wird Christus vergegenwärtigt,*" *GuV* 1:289. ET: *FaU* 1:307. Cf. *Exegetica*, p. 228: "*Aber Taufe und Abendmahl sind nur eine besondere Vergegenwärtigung des Heilsgeschehens, das im allgemeinen im gepredigten Wort sich vergegenwärtigt.*" ET: *EaF*, p. 200.

75. "*Im predigenden Apostel Christus selbst, ja Gott selbst, anredet.*" *GuV* 1:289. ET: *FaU* 1:307. Cf. *RGG²*, s.v. "*Paulus,*" ET: *EaF*, p. 139; and *Exegetica*, p. 228, ET: *EaF*, p. 200.

76. "*Im gepredigten Wort das Christusgeschehen sich weiter vollzieht,*" *GuV* 1:289. ET: *FaU* 1:308. Cf. *Das Urchristentum*, p. 224: "*In der Verkündigung das eschatologische Geschehen weiter vollzieht.*" ET: *Primitive Christianity,* p. 201.

77. "*Setzt sich so das Christusgeschehen in der Verkündigung des Wortes fort.*" *GuV* 1:289. ET: *FaU* 1:308.

is "encountered" in preaching is "Christ himself, i.e., the address of God."[78] In his 1949 presentation of *Primitive Christianity,* Bultmann notes that as in Gnosticism so in Paul (and John), "the redeemer is present in the word of preaching, the message from above."[79] These citations speak of a Christ who is present both as the proclaimed *and* as the proclaimer of the kerygma.

In the context of every quotation above, Bultmann cites, without elaboration, 2 Corinthians 5:18-19 (or -20) and 6:2. When we turn to Bultmann's exegetical writings on 2 Corinthians, we find him setting forth Paul's connection between kerygmatic proclamation and the presence of Christ in the context of 2 Corinthians 5:11–6:10. Bultmann's structural analysis of this passage shows the overall movement of thought as follows: 5:11-15 is an introduction which picks up the theme, if not the term, of "the apostolic *pepoithēsis* [self-confidence]" over against the reproach of boasting. Next, 5:16–6:2 reveals the basis for this confidence in "the fact that with Christ the old has passed and the new has dawned, and that precisely this salvation event itself continuously takes place in the proclamation." Then, 6:3-10 counters the charge that Paul is a pitiful, powerless apostle by arguing paradoxically, and on analogy with 4:7-12, that "the power of the efficacious *zōē* [life] in the proclamation reveals itself exactly in the lowliness of the proclaimer." Thus, the eschatological life of the new creation is manifested both in the "power" of the apostolic proclamation and in the "weakness" of the apostolic proclaimer.[80]

Within this context, we turn specifically to 2 Corinthians 5:18-19:

> [18] All this is from God, who through Christ reconciled [*katallaxantos . . . dia Christou*] us to himself and gave us [*hēmin*] the ministry of reconciliation [*tēn diakonian tēs katallagēs*]; [19] that is, God was in Christ reconciling the world to himself, not counting their trespasses against them, and entrusting to us [*en hēmin*] the message of reconciliation [*ton logon tēs katallagēs*].

The act of reconciliation, *dia Christou* ("through Christ"), "explained by the *mē logizomenos autois ta paraptōmata autōn* [not counting their tres-

---

78. *"In ihr [der Predigt] begegnet Christus, begegnet Gottes Anrede selbst." Exegetica,* p. 228. ET: *EaF,* p. 200. Cf. *"Jesus Christus ist für Paulus das vergebende Wort Gottes,"* p. 222. ET: p. 195. Cf. *RGG²,* s.v. *"Paulus": "In der Predigt des Apostels begegnet Gottes Wort selbst (2 Kor 5:20) und redet Christus (Rom. 15:18)."* ET: *EaF,* p. 139. See also *GuV* 1:180. ET: *FaU* 1:242.

79. *"Dass im verkündigten Wort, der Botschaft von oben, der Erlöser präsent ist," Das Urchristentum,* p. 224. ET: *Primitive Christianity,* p. 201.

80. *Exegetica,* p. 306. See also *CC,* pp. 145-46 and 167.

passes against them] in verse 19," in which peace replaces "the enmity between God and humankind," Bultmann interprets in tandem with Romans 5 as "the purging of sins" accomplished by God, *dia tou thanatou tou huiou autou* ("through the death of his Son," NRSV) (Rom. 5:10; cf. 5:1, 9).[81] The cross also implies the resurrection, for 5:18-19 draws the consequence of 5:15 where the raising of Christ is explicitly mentioned with his death.[82] Moreover, this "objective state of affairs" wrought in Christ's cross is "God's deed alone."[83] Hence, the *logos tēs katallagēs* ("word of reconciliation") is taken not as "the conciliatory word, but the preaching of reconciliation already accomplished"[84] — in short, as "the kerygma."[85]

Bultmann interprets the *diakonia tēs katallagēs* ("ministry of reconciliation") as synonymous with the *diakonia tou pneumatos* ("ministry of the Spirit," NRSV) or *tēs dikaiosunēs* ("of righteousness") (3:8-9),[86] functioning within the *kainē diathēkē pneumatos* ("new covenant of the Spirit," cf. 3:6).[87] Therefore, "just as the *diakonia* of the *kainē diathēkē* is the apostolic office," in contrast to the *diakonia* of the *palaia diathēkē* ("old covenant") or "the office of Moses,"[88] so the *diakonia tēs katallagēs* of 5:18 is none other than "the apostolic office which proclaims the saving event."[89] Both the kerygmatic word and office have been given *en hēmin* ("to us"), that is, "to the Christian community."[90]

---

81. *CC,* p. 158. Hence, in 2 Cor. 5, "reconciliation denotes the forgiveness of sins (v. 19) or *dikaiosunē* [righteousness] (v. 21)," *CC,* p. 164. See also *TNT* 1:85. Kelsey observes in *Uses of Scripture* (p. 86, n. 41) that the discussion of Paul in *TNT* 1:285-87 does not "relate reconciliation to Christ's death." Kelsey overlooks Bultmann's five references there to Rom. 5:10. See also *FaU* 1:278 and *Exegetica,* p. 309.

82. See *Exegetica,* p. 309 and *CC,* pp. 153 and 158, where Bultmann comments that the phrase "All this is from God" points back to verses 14, 16, and 17, but that the rest of verse 18 and all of verse 19 point back to verse 15. See also *FaU* 1:197 and 241 and *Primitive Christianity,* p. 201, where Bultmann explicitly includes the resurrection with the cross in relation to the act of reconciliation attested by 2 Cor. 5:18-19.

83. *CC,* pp. 158-59. See also p. 164 and *TNT* 1:286-87, where Bultmann notes Rom. 5:6, 10, and 11.

84. *CC,* p. 163. See also p. 159 and *TNT* 1:287.

85. *FaU* 1:298, n. 37, omitting italics.

86. *CC,* p. 160.

87. *CC,* p. 79.

88. *CC,* p. 79.

89. *CC,* p. 160. See also p. 76, where Bultmann infers from 1 Thess. 3:2 and 2 Cor. 3:6, 6:4, 11:15, and 11:23 that "*diakonos* [servant] designates Paul as an apostle." Cf. Col. 1:25, Eph. 3:7, and 1 Tim. 4:6. See also p. 170.

90. "The *hēmin* ["us," of 2 Cor. 5:18] can refer to Paul or to the apostles in general,

Note that 2 Corinthians 5:18-19 predicates two acts of God: (1) reconciling through Christ, restated as "not counting their trespasses," and (2) giving the *diakonia tēs katallagēs* ("ministry of reconciliation"), restated as the *logos tēs katallagēs* ("message," lit. "word," "of reconciliation"). In Bultmann's view, these two acts occur simultaneously — not sequentially. God's reconciling act in Christ and the ministry or word that proclaims it are two simultaneous sides of one eschatological salvation event. As Bultmann paraphrases 2 Corinthians 5:18-20 and 6:2 in *Theology of the New Testament,*

> God simultaneously instituted [*hat zugleich gestiftet*] with reconciliation the *diakonia tēs katallagēs,* the *logos tēs katallagēs* (2 Cor. 5:18-19), so that in the proclamation Christ himself, indeed God himself, is encountered [5:20]; and that the *nun* [now] in which preaching resounds is the *nun* of the eschatological event [6:2].[91]

There is thus, by the will of God, a correspondence between the event of Christ and that of Christ proclaimed.

Nevertheless, is this "simultaneous" interpretation of the text justified by Bultmann's own exegesis? True, Bultmann links the "word of reconciliation" to God's act in Christ by noting that the *logos tēs katallagēs* of 5:19 appears in place of the *diakonia tēs katallagēs* of 5:18. On the basis of this substitution, Bultmann declares that "institution [*Einsetzung*] of the proclamation thus belongs with the *katallagē.*"[92] Yet this line of argument

---

but it more likely refers to the Christian community, for the *en hēmin* in verse 19 clearly means among people, or among the believers, in the community." *CC,* p. 161, cf. p. 151.

91. *TdNT,* p. 302. See also *FaU* 1:241-42, 278, and 307. Cf. *GuV* 1:209, 260, and 289; *TDNT,* s.v. "*pisteuō* [etc.]." Cf. *TWNT; Primitive Christianity,* p. 201; cf. *Das Urchristentum,* p. 224; *TNT* 1:59, 286-87, and 307; cf. *TdNT,* pp. 63, 286-87, and 308; *CC,* pp. 160-61; cf. *BK,* pp. 162-63; and "The Primitive Christian Kergyma and the Historical Jesus," in *HJKC,* p. 40; cf. *Exegetica,* p. 467. Note how in *GuV* 1:260 and 289, *TWNT,* s.v. "*pisteuō* [etc.]," *Das Urchristentum,* p. 224, and *TdNT,* pp. 63, 286, and 308, Bultmann in each case uses, without comment, the adverb *zugleich* to indicate that the divine actions specified in 2 Cor. 5:18-19 are to be taken as occurring simultaneously.

Furnish, citing Bultmann, comments that the ministry of reconciliation "is not regarded merely as responsive to or a consequence of the eschatological event, but as a constituent part of the event itself." *II Corinthians,* p. 336. Charles B. Cousar likewise makes Bultmann's point when he writes, "In the very act in which God breaks through hostility, God gathers up the reconciled into the service of reconciliation." *A Theology of the Cross: The Death of Jesus in the Pauline Letters* (Minneapolis: Fortress, 1990), p. 78.

92. *CC,* pp. 160-61. Cf. *BK,* p. 162. So also Furnish, *II Corinthians,* p. 337.

already assumes that the *diakonia* is instituted simultaneously with reconciliation, an assumption for which Bultmann offers no exegetical account.[93] Thus, despite the fact that his interpretation of Paul on the unity
of Christ and the kerygma hinges on taking the divine acts of 2 Corinthians
5:18-19 as simultaneous rather than sequential, Bultmann's own exegesis
of this passage begs the question. Clearly, then, extra- (or intra-)textual
factors are operating here in Bultmann's interpretation of Paul, a point to
which we shall return in chapter four.

Exegetical problems aside, Bultmann's reading of 2 Corinthians 5:18-
19 does provide his answer as to how it is for Paul that "faith in the
kerygma is inseparable from faith in the person mediated thereby."[94] To
say with Bultmann that God *simultaneously* instituted the deed and word
of reconciliation is to assert that there has never been a Jesus Christ who
is soteriologically present apart from the proclamation of the kerygma:

> The saving fact is therefore the Word (Rom. 10:13-17). Not the word
> as the vehicle of ideas or as a communication of historical information,
> but the Word as preaching [*als Predigt*], validated by the person Jesus
> Christ who is one with it — but in such a way that it, too, is one with
> him and is encountered only in him.[95]

Thus, faith encounters the Crucified and Risen Lord only in and through
the proclamation of his death and resurrection; and faith encounters
authentic proclamation, that is, one that actualizes the eschatological sal-

93. Moreover, Bultmann's claim that 5:18-19 draws the consequence of 5:15 ("who
for their sake died and was raised") does not clarify matters. Is Bultmann saying that
(1) Christ's death and resurrection (5:15), taken together, is equivalent to "reconciled
through Christ" (5:18, which entails "the ministry of reconciliation," 5:19); or (2) is
Bultmann claiming that Christ's death and resurrection (5:15) are parallel equivalents to
5:18, "reconciled through Christ" (= death), and 5:19, "ministry of reconciliation" (= resurrection)? Regardless of the answer, neither resolves the question as to sequentiality or
simultaneity in 5:18-19. Cf. *EaF,* p. 200; *Exegetica,* p. 309; and *CC,* pp. 153 and 158.

94. *TDNT,* s.v. "*pisteuō* [etc.]." In Bultmann's view, "Paul understands faith primarily
as obedience" (Rom. 1:5; cf. 1:8 with 16:19; 2 Cor. 9:13; cf. 10:5-6 with 10:15) and
"simultaneously 'confession'" (Rom. 10:9). Paul describes faith as obedience *(hupakoē)*
because "acknowledgment of the crucified Jesus as Lord" demands the surrender of one's
self-understanding. At the same time, faith is also confession *(homologein =* to confess)
because " 'faith' is 'faith in . . .' That is, it always has reference to its object." "Faith,
therefore, is not 'piety' or trust-in-God in general." *TNT* 1:314-19, omitting italics.

95. *FaU* 1:242. Cf. *GuV* 1:209. Hence, faith in the kerygma simultaneously entails
for Paul what Bultmann terms "a personal relation to Christ" (citing Rom. 6:8; 10:9, 14;
Gal. 2:20; and Phlm. 5). *TDNT,* s.v. "*pisteuō* [etc.]."

vation event, only in and through the presence of the Crucified and Risen Lord. Jesus has risen into the kerygma.[96] Hence, it is what he is, and he is what it is: the power of God unto salvation.

The Kerygma and Christ: Possibility and Actuality

The unity God has bestowed on the event of Christ and that of Christ proclaimed is constituted eschatologically and manifested temporally. Bultmann's position, in effect, distinguishes between the first manifestation of the kerygmatic Christ (2 Cor. 5:18-19) and his subsequent presence in proclamation (2 Cor. 5:20; 6:2). The unity of Christ and the kerygma, actually encountered by faith in Christian proclamation, presupposes the possibility for this unity in an antecedent act of God. Thus, the possibility for salvation, its divine presupposition or condition, is given by God's simultaneous institution of the deed and word of reconciliation. The actuality of salvation, the manifestation of this divine condition, only occurs in and through the occasion of Christian proclamation.[97]

Given the distinction between possibility in principle and possibility in fact which runs throughout Bultmann's exposition of the eschatological salvation event, whenever he speaks of "church," or "faith," or "the kerygma," one must always ask whether he is speaking primarily of a possibility established by God or of one actually encountered in and through Christian proclamation.

With respect to the church, if God simultaneously instituted the

---

96. See *FaU* 1:241 and 245 and "The Primitive Christian Kerygma and the Historical Jesus," in *HJKC*, p. 42. Thus, for Paul, "the preached Word . . . itself belongs to the saving event, continually allotting to the individual the grace of God active in this event." *TDNT*, s.v. "*zaō* [etc.]." See also Bultmann's review of *Bedeutung des Wortes bei Paulus*, by Schmitz: "For Paul, the proclaiming word itself belongs to the proclaimed subject (matter) [*Sache*]." *TLZ* 53 (1928): 565.

97. See *CC*, p. 161. Bultmann also expresses the actualizing of God's eschatological possibility by saying that the *apo tou nun* ("from now on," 2 Cor. 5:16) "must be grasped and realized from time to time in faith (6:1f.)." *Exegetica*, p. 310.

The distinction between the divine "condition" and the human "occasion," the paradoxical coincidence of which results in revelation as a contemporary event, derives from Kierkegaard. The distinction functions to relate God and humanity without "naturalizing" deity or apotheosizing humanity. In this way, an account of revelation is rendered which redraws the line between Creator and creature allegedly blurred during the heyday of Hegelianism. See *Philosophical Fragments*, esp. pp. 104-5.

deed and *diakonia* of reconciliation, as Bultmann holds, then it follows that God simultaneously established with them the church. At the same time that God raised Jesus into eschatological rank, God called the eschatological *ekklēsia* into existence. The apostolic ministry presupposes the church to which it has been given. Christ as God's deed and the church as Christ's witness are thus two inseparable sides of the eschatological event. As a possibility in principle, Christ and the church are coterminous. Neither is antecedent to the other.

By contrast, when Bultmann speaks from the standpoint of the actuality of the church, then Christ and the kerygma are taken as prevenient to it. That is to say, "the church is constituted by this kerygma. It cannot exist at all without the 'ministry' *(diakonia)* of the word."[98] Given the unity between the kerygma and Christ, Bultmann can also say that the church is called into being by Christ himself (see 1 Cor. 7:22).[99] In this regard, Bultmann does not have in view Jesus of Nazareth, the "founder" of Christianity, but Jesus Christ who calls into history from the eschaton the *qāhāl* or True Israel of apocalyptic hope.[100] Thus, Bultmann indicates the church's relation to Christ to be coterminous in principle and consequent in practice.[101]

Similarly, Bultmann speaks of faith both as an actuality that accompanies the proclamation of the Christ kerygma and as a possibility that arises from God's antecedent act uniting Christ and the kerygma.[102] When

---

98. *FaU* 1:212, omitting italics. See also *FaU* 1:274; "The Significance of the Old Testament for the Christian Faith," trans. Bernhard W. Anderson in *The Old Testament and Christian Faith: A Theological Discussion,* ed. Bernhard W. Anderson (New York: Harper & Row, 1963; hereafter cited as *OTaCF*), pp. 30-31; pub. in Ger. as "Die Bedeutung des Alten Testaments für den christlichen Glauben [1933]," in *GuV* 1:332-33; *EaF,* pp. 140, 201; and "The Transformation of the Idea of the Church in the History of Early Christianity," trans. S. MacLean Gilmour, *Canadian Journal of Theology* 1 (1955): 74 and 79; pub. in Ger. as "Die Wandlung des Selbstverständnisses der Kirche in der Geschichte des Urchristentums," in *GuV* 3:132 and 139.

99. See *FaU* 1:195 and 197 and *EaF,* p. 140.

100. See *FaU* 1:233 and *TNT* 1:10, 96-98, and 118. See also *FaU* 1:193-96 and 274; "Prophecy and Fulfillment [1949]," in *EPT,* p. 205; pub. in Ger. as "Weissagung und Erfüllung," in *GuV* 2:183; "Man between the Times according to the New Testament [1952]," in *EaF,* p. 249; pub. in Ger. as "Der Mensch zwischen den Zeiten nach dem Neuen Testament," in *GuV* 3:36; and "The Transformation of the Idea of the Church in the History of Early Christianity," *Canadian Journal of Theology* 1 (1955): 73-74.

101. "As it [the church] was called into existence by the proclaimed word, its existence in turn is the foundation of preaching." *TNT* 1:300. See also *FaU* 1:212-13.

102. "The new life is a historical possibility created by the saving event and it is a reality wherever it is grasped in the resolve to act [i.e., in faith]." *FaU* 1:276, omitting italics.

Paul writes that "faith comes from what is heard, and what is heard comes by the preaching of Christ" (Rom. 10:17), he is speaking of the realization of faith through the event of proclamation. On the other hand, when Paul writes of a time "before faith came . . . until faith should be revealed" (Gal. 3:23), he points, in Bultmann's view, to "the opening up, through God's act, of the possibility of having faith."[103]

Likewise, "kerygma" can refer either to the word in principle (2 Cor. 5:18-19) or to the word in fact (2 Cor. 5:20; 6:2). The simultaneous establishment of the deed and ministry of reconciliation extends to the "word of reconciliation" itself. In this regard, Bultmann notes Paul's substitution of the term *diakonia* ("ministry," 5:18) by that of *logos* ("word," 5:19).[104] This institution of the word in principle establishes the necessary condition for its consequent actuality as the bearer of salvation (2 Cor. 5:20; 6:2).

Summary

As an interpreter of Paul, Bultmann understands Jesus Christ to be God's act which puts an end to the determinative status and standards of the old aeon. By virtue of Jesus' destiny as the Crucified and Risen Lord, he is no longer to be regarded from the standpoint of the old age, but rather as the eschatological salvation event. To inquire then about how and where Jesus Christ becomes our contemporary is not to trace the perdurability of his historical personality, but to focus on how and where his messianic or eschatological reality is revealed in the present. This revelation occurs in the continuing proclamation of the kerygma or Christian message of God's act in Christ.

The unity between the event of Christ and that of Christ proclaimed is indicated by Paul's double patterns of predication. The same soteriological benefits attributed to (the death and resurrection of) Christ are also attributed to the proclamation and proclaimers (as proclaimers) of the kerygma. The possibility for this unity is established by God simultaneously instituting with the reconciliation wrought in Christ the office and word proclaiming it. The actuality of this unity is only encountered in and through the act of proclamation itself.

103. *FaU* 1:210. See also *FaU* 1:203 and *TNT* 1:329.
104. See *EaF,* p. 200; *TNT* 1:286; and *CC,* pp. 160-61.

Jesus Christ is therefore present in the kerygmatic occasion. He is present not as an empirical object, but as the saving power of the gospel known only to faith in and through the humanity and temporality of preaching. He is present not simply as a figure who is proclaimed but as the abiding agent of Christian proclamation.

The inseparable unity between Christ and the kerygma attested by Paul clarifies for Bultmann the way in which both philosophical idealism and theological liberalism misunderstand the relation between Christ and the kerygma. Idealism errs in seeing Christ as a teacher of universal truths or timeless ideas that can be abstracted from an essentially superfluous kerygma. Liberalism errs in going "behind the kerygma, using it as a 'source', in order to reconstruct a 'historical Jesus.'"[105] Thus, despite the oft-repeated accusation of Bultmann's Docetism, this label may better fit many of his opponents. Why? Because both idealism and liberalism shuck the kerygma where alone Christ is enfleshed for faith. Against such attempts, Bultmann declares, "Jesus Christ confronts men in the kerygma and nowhere else, just as he confronted Paul himself and forced him to the decision."[106] The kerygma and Christ — what God has joined together cannot be put asunder!

105. *FaU* 1:241.

106. *FaU* 1:241, omitting italics. By this assertion Bultmann could either mean (1) that Jesus Christ only confronts us in the very same way he once confronted Paul, i.e., through the kerygma; or (2) that Jesus Christ, who once confronted Paul directly, now confronts us only kerygmatically. The logic of Bultmann's argument supports the first interpretation. This judgment is confirmed when Bultmann speaks of Paul's conversion either as the result of his encounter with the kerygma or of his encounter with Jesus Christ. In light of 2 Cor. 5:18-19, an encounter with the one embraces the other. See *TDNT*, s.v. "*pisteuō* [etc.]"; *EaF,* pp. 114-16, 122, 185; and *TNT* 1:60 and 187.

CHAPTER 3

The Johannine *Christus Praesens* according to Bultmann

The Paradox of Revelation

THE "revelation of Jesus Christ" of which Paul wrote to the Galatians (1:12) has its Johannine counterpart in the declaration, "No one has ever seen God; the only Son, who is in the bosom of the Father, he has made him known" (John 1:18). Nevertheless, this eschatological salvation event that Paul perceives primarily through the cross and resurrection appears for John throughout the mission of the *Logos,* the incarnate Son of God.[1] Adapting the whole of the "Gnostic Redeemer myth" for his Christology, John subsumes Good Friday and Easter within a revelatory framework stretching all the way back to "the beginning" (1:1-2).[2]

---

1. Cf. *TNT* 1:292-94 and 2:33-40. See also 2:52-53. By "John" Bultmann means the unknown author of the Fourth Gospel and the unknown authors of the three epistles of the New Testament bearing this name, minus those passages attributable to subsequent ecclesiastical redaction. See *TNT* 2:3 and 10; "Die kirchliche Redaktion des ersten Johannesbriefes," in *Exegetica,* pp. 381-93; *RGG*[3], s.v. *"Johannesevangelium,"* and *The Johannine Epistles: A Commentary on the Johannine Epistles,* trans. R. Philip O'Hara, Lane C. McGaughy, and Robert W. Funk (ed.) (Philadelphia: Fortress, 1973; hereafter cited as *JE,* pp. 1-3); pub. in Ger. as *Die drei Johannesbriefe,* new ed. (Göttingen: Vandenhoeck & Ruprecht, 1967; hereafter cited as *JB*), pp. 9-12 In regard to 1 John, "whether the author is the same as that of the Gospel is disputed and cannot be said to be so with certainty." *RGG*[3], s.v. *"Johannesbriefe."*

2. See *TNT* 2:12-14 and *TDNT,* s.v. *"zaō* [etc.]." For Bultmann's reconstruction of the Gnostic Redeemer myth, itself dependent on the "Primal Man" myth hypothesized earlier by Reitzenstein, see *The Gospel of John: A Commentary,* trans. G. R. Beasley-Murray (gen. ed.), R. W. N. Hoare, and J. K. Riches (Philadelphia: Westminster, 1971; hereafter cited as *JG*), pp. 24-31 and 60-66; pub. in Ger. as *Das Evangelium des Johannes,* 11th rev. ed. (Göttingen: Vandenhoeck & Ruprecht, 1950; hereafter cited as *EJ*), pp. 9-15

In declaring that the *Logos* "was *en archēi,* in the very beginning," John expresses the "absolute otherness" of the *Logos* "from the sphere of the world."[3] By "world" *(kosmos),* John primarily designates humankind, together with the viewpoints which humankind fashions for itself, and which, in turn, fashion humankind.[4] But "in the person and word of Jesus one does not encounter anything that has its origin in the world or in time," but God, who alone "can be thought of as being *en archēi.*"[5]

Yet how can one seriously claim to encounter what is "wholly other"? Is not such an assertion a sheer contradiction? Does not an encounter — even with God — imply by definition an otherness that is less than absolute, as, indeed, the doctrine of creation might itself suggest?

Bultmann takes pains to emphasize on the basis of John's Prologue "that revelation is possible because the world is the creation of the *Logos*" (1:3, 4b).[6] Moreover, he takes the associated claim of 1:4a, "That which has been made was life in him" (margin), as announcing that "the vitality of the whole creation has its origin in the *Logos;* he is the power which creates life."[7] John connects creation and revelation by identifying this

---

and 38-43; *Primitive Christianity,* pp. 163-64; *TNT* 1:165-67; *History and Eschatology,* p. 54; and *RGG*[3], s.v. *"Johannesevangelium."* Since Carsten Colpe's 1961 study *Die Religionsgeschichtliche Schule,* the Gnostic Redeemer myth has played a greatly diminished role in Johannine scholarship. Moreover, in the judgment of Raymond E. Brown, the known texts of the Old Testament and Qumran, as opposed to a hypothesized Gnostic Redeemer source text, "go a long way toward filling in the background of Johannine theological vocabulary and expression." See *The Gospel according to John: Introduction, Translation, and Notes,* 2 vols., The Anchor Bible (Garden City, N.Y.: Doubleday & Co., 1966-70), 1:LVI.

3. *JG,* pp. 31-32.

4. See "The Eschatology of the Gospel of John [1928]," in *FaU* 1:166-70; pub. in Ger. as "Die Eschatologie des Johannes-Evangeliums," in *GuV* 1:135-39; *TDNT,* s.v. *"pisteuō* [etc.]," and *JE,* p. 17.

"Compare the alternation of 'all' with 'men', 'darkness', 'the world' (1:1, 3, 4, 5, 10). And compare the predicates used with 'the world'. The world 'knows' (or 'does not know') (1:10; 14:31; 17:23). The world 'loves' (15:19) or 'hates' (7:7; 15:18f.; 17:14); it 'receives' (or 'does not receive') (14:17); it 'sees' (or 'does not see') (14:19); it 'rejoices' (16:20); it 'believes' (or 'does not believe') (17:21), and 'knows' (or 'does not know') (17:23, 25). Obviously, the 'world' is invariably men. The same holds of the assertions that God loves the world (3:16), that it is to be saved (3:17), that the Son speaks to the world (8:26)." *FaU* 1:166, n. 4.

5. *JG,* p. 32.

6. *JG,* p. 40. Cf. *EJ,* p. 22. *"Logos"* is italicized here and in other direct quotes from *JG* to accord with *EJ.*

7. *JG,* p. 39.

"vitalizing power" or "life" as "the light of all people" (1:4b, NRSV). In the incarnation, this "light of the eternal *Logos,* which shone in creation . . . has now become present [*ist jetzt Gegenwart*]": "The light shines in the darkness" (1:5a).[8]

As creatures, then, human beings already have, in principle, "the light," that is, a preliminary understanding of themselves and God. Nevertheless, that the light illuminating human existence and revealing God now shines in Jesus Christ indicates that it "shone in vain in creation." Where human beings go wrong is in converting their "preunderstanding" of themselves and God — essentially "a negative knowledge of human limitations and . . . estrangement from God" — into a positive claim that this preunderstanding as such "possesses the revelation — the *alēthinon* [truth]." They presume to have in hand the "criteria by which to judge how God must confront" humanity "and how the revelation must become reality." Thus, even though creation furnishes the possibility of revelation, only the event of revelation itself enables one to see existence as the creaturely reality it is.[9]

Nevertheless, the fact that John adopts the Gnostic Redeemer framework for his Christology

> makes it plain that he is recognizing, refashioning and answering the urgent Gnostic question concerning *zōē* [life]. . . . This means that the seeking or questioning is not wrong; it has a positive meaning. . . . The question itself may lead to self-deception, i.e., to the supposed finding of life where it is not (5:39-40). But the question, the *eraunan* [search], is present, as shown in the fact that the *kosmos* [world] has the concept *zōē,* and that revelation adopts the term to lead from false *zōē* to true. . . . What is not true or genuine points in the form of a question to what is.[10]

---

8. *JG,* p. 46. Cf. *EJ,* p. 26. Here Bultmann notes that *phainei* (shines) in 1:5a is John's first use of the present tense with respect to the *Logos.* Based on the "not overcome" of 1:5b, which Bultmann correlates with the respective "knew not" and "received not" of 1:10 and 11, *phainei* does not "indicate a timeless presence [*zeitlosen Gegenwärtigkeit*]" of the pre-temporal *Logos,* but the revelation which has been sent into the world "through the earthly work of the *incarnate Logos,*" and "now lives on in the community."

9. *JG,* pp. 46, 61-62, and 496-97. See also *TDNT,* s.v. *"alētheia," "pisteuō* [etc.]," and "*thanatos* [etc.]." Hence, "for Bultmann, the contradiction is also the point of contact for the revelation with man." Painter, *Theology as Hermeneutics,* p. 36. See also pp. 123 and 127.

10. *TDNT,* s.v. "*zaō* [etc.]."

Revelation is thus the divine answer to the human question concerning life; indeed, the answer presupposes the question.[11]

How does revelation occur without compromising the transcendence of God? Bultmann finds John's answer in "the alternating and apparently contradictory ways in which the *Logos* is defined"; that is, both as *God* (*"theos ēn ho logos,"* 1:1) and as *with* God (*"ho logos ēn pros ton theon,"* 1:1, 2).[12] While "the *Logos* is therefore given the same status as God," the twice-repeated claim that he is "with God" indicates that "no simple identification is intended."[13] From this seeming contradiction Bultmann infers "the paradox that in the Revealer God is really encountered, and yet that God is not directly encountered, but only in the Revealer."[14] Thus, John affirms "the exclusiveness and the absoluteness of the revelation,"[15] apart from which "God is not here and is never here."[16]

---

11. Thus, John's interrogative understanding of revelation is congruent with Bultmann's own, whether stated in Augustinian or modern existentialist terms: "I am convinced that Augustine's words, 'Our heart is restless until it rests in Thee,' are true for all men. In all men, explicitly or implicitly, the question concerning God is a living one. The exclusiveness of the kerygma consists in the fact that it provides the answer to this question by offering the right to say 'God is my God.'" "Reply," in Kegley, *Theology of Bultmann*, p. 275. Cf. "The Problem of a Theological Exegesis of the New Testament": "Existential man is interested not in the personality [*Persönlichkeit*] of Jesus, but in his anxiety about his own existence or in the question of the truth of his concern." 1:247. Cf. *AdT* 2:61. As a category of preunderstanding, *zōē* functions in John much as *suneidēsis* ("conscience") does in Paul.

12. *JG*, p. 34.

13. *JG*, p. 34. "It is as in the O.T.: there, the belief that God works in the historical event, and yet is not limited to this event, not identical with it, but stands beyond it as God, can be expressed by the juxtaposition of God and his name; so here ["and the Word was with God," 1:1] the *Logos* stands beside God, so that God must be understood from the outset as the 'one who speaks,' the God who reveals himself." *JG*, p. 35.

14. *JG*, p. 34. Bultmann's language of paradox with respect to revelation echoes Kierkegaard's own with respect to the God-Man, to "the moment" of the eternal in time, and to Christ as contemporaneous with the believer. See *Philosophical Fragments*, esp. pp. 23-54, 193-94, 222 and *Training in Christianity*, esp. pp. 28 and 66-70. "Paradoxical language" is that "in which two or more aspects of the object persist in their oppositeness and interrelatedness without any possibility of coming to a conceptual, synthetic unification." Weber, *Foundations of Dogmatics*, 1:155. Thus, in revelation the Creator comes to the creature without obliterating the ontological distinction between them assumed by, and characteristic of, their true communion.

15. *JG*, p. 376, omitting italics. Bultmann is commenting here on John 10:8. See also pp. 52-54 (on John 1:9) and pp. 79-80 (on John 1:18).

16. *FaU* 1:173, omitting italics. Bultmann is commenting here on John 1:18. See also 1:282-83.

John frames this paradoxical relation between God and humanity with respect both to "the beginning" and to "the end." In the declaration, "the Word became flesh" (1:14), God is said to be revealed in the history and humanity of a singular human being. The "life" and "light" which were "in the beginning," and which created, conserved, and illumined human existence, are now present in the incarnate *Logos*. Likewise, with regard to "the end," Bultmann interprets John 5:24-25 as saying that in the sojourn of the Son the eschatological event is now present within history.

The Word Became Flesh

Just as the "central theme of the gnostic Redeemer-myth is that a divine being, the Son of the Highest, assumed human form, put on human flesh and blood, in order to bring revelation and redemption,"[17] so likewise "the theme of the whole Gospel of John" is none other than "the Word became flesh" (*"ho logos sarx egeneto,"* 1:14).[18]

According to Bultmann, by *sarx* ("flesh") John refers "to the sphere of the human and the worldly as opposed to the divine" and indicates "its transitoriness, helplessness and vanity (3:6; 6:63)." Therefore, the enfleshment of the *Logos* announces that "the Revealer is nothing but a man." By this claim John suggests no "physiological miracle," only the paradox that "the man Jesus is, as the Revealer, the *Logos,*" and "the *Logos* is . . . God, in so far as he reveals himself."[19]

The emphasis John gives to the real humanity of the Revealer shows, in Bultmann's judgment, "a demarcation of his own position" from that of the Gnosticism to which John is otherwise so indebted for the Revealer figure.[20] Bultmann strongly implies that this Johannine "demarcation" is a form of "demythologization."[21]

---

17. *JG,* p. 61.

18. *TNT* 2:40. See also *JG,* p. 64. Cf. *FaU* 1:308: "The whole Gospel is the elaboration of the theme: Jesus is the Word."

19. *JG,* p. 62, incl. n. 4. Bultmann argues that the humanity of the Revealer is also emphasized in that after 1:14 the title *"Logos"* plays no further role in John: "The *Logos* is now present as the Incarnate, and indeed it is only as the Incarnate that it [i.e., the *Logos figure*] is present at all." *JG,* p. 63. Cf. *FaU* 1:308.

20. *TNT* 2:40. See also *TDNT,* s.v., *"zaō* [etc.]."

21. See *TNT* 2:33, 49-50, and 62. When explicitly characterizing John's project as

In contrast to the Gnostic Redeemer, the Johannine Revealer is no "primal man [*Urmensch*]," who has assumed human nature in general.[22] Rather, he is "a *definite human being in history:* Jesus of Nazareth. His humanity is genuine humanity."[23] Therefore, the redemption wrought in revelation is not "a cosmic process," a matter of *phusis* ("nature"), "which takes no account of the particularity of individual men," but one involving a "specific historical figure," which stands ready, in principle, to become "an event in the history of my own life."[24]

Again, unlike the shining hero or numinous *theios anthrōpos* ("divine human") of the Gnostic Redeemer myth, the Johannine Revealer is neither a mere disguise nor a transparently divine medium. True, "his own" do behold his glory (*"doxa,"* 1:14b); but, in accordance with the paradox of revelation, "the *doxa* is not to be seen *alongside* the *sarx,* nor *through* the *sarx* as through a window; it is to be seen in the *sarx* and nowhere else."[25] Only as "hidden" in the flesh is the glory of God revealed to faith, and only through such "humiliation" will the "glorification" of the Son draw all to himself.[26]

Finally, by way of contrast with the Gnostic Redeemer, who, upon

---

"demythologization," Bultmann has in mind (1) John's transposition of cosmological dualism into a dualism of decision, thereby preserving the world as God's good creation, (2) John's historicizing of apocalyptic eschatology whereby the future life and *parousia* of Jesus Christ are claimed as already present, and (3) John's substitution of the mythological Antichrist figure with "false teachers." See *NTaM*, pp. 11 and 19; *TNT* 2:9-10, 17, 21, and 39; "The Christian Hope and the Problem of Demythologizing," *The Expository Times* 65 (1954): 277-78; *JCaM*, pp. 33-34; and *RGG* 3, s.v. *"Johannesbriefe"* and *"Johannesevangelium."*

22. *JG*, p. 65. Cf. *EJ*, pp. 41-42.

23. *TNT* 2:41. See also 2:69. Cf. Kierkegaard's insistence that "the God-Man is not the unity of God and mankind. . . . The God-Man is the unity of God and an individual man. That the human race is or should be akin to God is ancient paganism; but that an individual man is God is Christianity, and this individual man is the God-Man." *Training in Christianity,* p. 84.

In "The Primitive Christian Kerygma and the Historical Jesus," Bultmann qualifies his judgment that "John gives all due emphasis to the humanity of Jesus" by adding, "but presents none of the characteristics of Jesus' humanity which could be gleaned, for example, from the Synoptic Gospels. The decisive thing is simply the 'that' [of his humanity]." *HJKC*, p. 20.

24. *JG*, pp. 64-65, where Bultmann also notes that, "the destiny of the soul is determined by faith or unbelief, not by its *phusis* [nature] — a concept which never occurs in John." See also *JE*, p. 46, n. 10.

25. *JG*, p. 63. See also *TDNT*, s.v. *"pisteuō* [etc.]."

26. See *JG*, pp. 149-53.

his return to the transcendent realm, sheds the body in which he had been glorified, "the historical figure of Jesus, i.e. his human history [*die historische Gestalt Jesu, seine menschliche Geschichte*], retains its significance of being the revelation of his 'glory' and thereby of God's. It is the eschatological occurrence."[27] Thus, the Johannine Revealer does not "appear as a mystagogue communicating teachings, formulas, and rites as if he himself were only a means to an end who could sink into unimportance to any who had received his 'Gnosis.'"[28]

For John the Revealer is the revelation he himself brings:

> His words are utterances about himself; *for his word is identical with himself* [*denn sein Wort ist er selbst*]. . . . What is said of his word is also said of himself: his words are "life," they are "truth" (6:63; 17:17); but so is he himself— . . . (14:6). Whoever hears his word and believes Him who sent him has Life (5:24), but that is what he himself is — . . . (11:25). His words (12:48; 17:8), his "testimony" (3:11, 32f.), must be "accepted" (*lambanein*) — so must he (1:12; 5:43; *cf.* 13:20). To reject him (*athetein*) is identical with not accepting his words (12:48). That his own "abide" in him and he in them means the same thing as that his words "abide" in them (15:4-7). He is the judge (5:22, 27) — so is his word (12:48).[29]

Bultmann takes these common predications as indicating for John that the person and word of Jesus "are identical."[30] Hence, faith can be directed either to the Revealer or to his word since, soteriologically speaking, they are synonymous.[31] "Thus it becomes clear that in the proclaimed word

27. *TNT* 2:49. Cf. *TdNT,* p. 402.

28. *TNT* 2:41. See also Bultmann to Barth, 10 December 1926, in *Letters,* p. 29; *FaU* 1:173, 309-10; *TDNT,* s.v. "*alētheia*"; and *JG,* pp. 65-66. Bultmann's contrast between John's Jesus and a Gnostic mystagogue parallels Kierkegaard's distinction between Christ and Socrates. See *Philosophical Fragments,* pp. 14-18.

29. *TNT* 2:63-64. Cf. *TdNT,* p. 416. See also *FaU* 1:308-9 and *TDNT,* s.v. "*zaō* [etc.]."

30. *TNT* 2:71. See also 2:63-64 and *FaU* 1:308-12. Cf. Kierkegaard, *Training in Christianity,* p. 13: "He [the Saviour] is true to His word, He is what He says, and in this sense also He is the Word."

31. "Since he [Jesus] and his word are identical . . . therefore his words can also be named as the object [*Gegenstand*] of faith (5:47; cf. 2:22), or, as the case may be, the 'works' (10:38) which are identical with the words. . . . This accounts for the fact that for John 'to believe him' [*'ihm Glauben schenken,'* 5:38, 46; 8:31, 45-46; 10:37-38; 14:11] (*pisteuein* with dative) and 'to believe in him' [*'an ihn glauben,'* 2:11; 3:16, 36; 4:39] (*pisteuein eis*) are identical." *TdNT,* p. 423. See also *FaU* 1:309, n. 53 and n. 54.

the Proclaimer himself is encountered."[32] So it is fitting that the Evangelist bestows on the Revealer, "as the Preexistent One, the mythological title Logos."[33] Whatever its origins, this encoded ascription expresses John's claim that "from beginning to end, Jesus is not meant to be the 'historical Jesus'; he is the 'Word', the Word of the Christian proclamation."[34]

The Eschatological Event in History

The demythologization of the Gnostic Redeemer myth carried out by John extends as well to his treatment of the Jewish apocalyptic eschatology. For John the Revealer is the eschatological "invasion of God into the world."[35] Bultmann argues that the revelation of the Son is asserted as the eschatological event primarily "in those sentences where his coming or going is termed the judgment of the world" (e.g., 3:19 and 9:39).[36] In the person and word of Jesus a crisis occurs in the double sense of *krisis*. There is both a *judgment* on unbelief and a resulting *division* of believers from unbelievers (3:19; 5:22-24; 8:15, 26; 9:39; 12:31, 46-48).[37] In these texts, the final judgment, which apocalyptic thought had associated with God's dramatic destruction and transformation of the world, is transposed into the sojourn of the Son. "The encounter with him and his word makes 'the now' into the eschatological 'now'": "Truly, truly, I say to you, he who hears my word and believes him who sent me, has eternal life; he

---

32. *"So wird deutlich, dass im verkündigten Wort der Verkündiger selbst begegnet"*; Bultmann continues, "the unity of the Proclaimer with the proclaimed stamps itself clearly on that linguistic usage such as 'to reject him' and 'not to receive his word' which are identical (12:48), or as unbelief [i.e., in his words] signifies, 'to be disobedient to the Son' (3:36)." *TdNT*, p. 423. See also *TDNT*, s.v. *"pisteuō* [etc.]."

33. *TdNT*, p. 416. See also *FaU* 1:281 and 308.

34. *FaU* 1:310. See also 1:281. Cf. *NTaM*, pp. 32-33, on John 6:42. Here where the text speaks of Jesus' origins "historically" it does so from the standpoint of "the Jews" who cannot comprehend Jesus' soteriological significance.

For history of religions' background on the *Logos* figure, see *JG*, esp. pp. 19-45 and *RGG*[3], s.v. *"Johannesevangelium."*

35. *JG*, p. 404, where Bultmann is commenting on the eschatological connotation of "he who is coming into the world" in John 11:27.

36. *TNT* 2:37, omitting italics. See also *JG*, pp. 257-59 (on John 5:24-25). The Son's coming as "the eschatological event" is also indicated by the christological titles John accords Jesus, especially that of "Messiah" (1:41; 4:25; 11:27; 20:31; 1 John 5:1). See *TNT* 2:36-37.

37. See *FaU* 1:170; *JG*, p. 111; and *History and Eschatology*, p. 47.

does not come into judgment, but has passed from death to life" (5:24).[38] In other words, John "opens the reader's eyes to see that the *parousia has already occurred!*"[39] "In faith, then, the eschaton is attained already. . . . The eschaton has become the present."[40] Bultmann regards this bringing forward of the climactic *parousia* into time as John's radical "historicizing" of eschatology, a theological development which began with Paul but which John was the first to carry through consistently.[41]

By historicizing the eschaton, John presents the incarnation as both a crisis and an offense for all autonomous preunderstanding. The destabilizing question the incarnation poses is whether the human being will see revelation "as an otherworldly event which passes judgment on him and his word; or whether he will make his own illusory ideas the criterion by which to judge revelation." In other words, the issue is whether salvation is determined by a definitive preunderstanding which one carries into the world — and is "world" in the Johannine sense — or whether salvation is

---

38. See *RGG*[3], s.v. *"Johannesevangelium."* Cf. *TDNT*, s.v. *"zaō* [etc.]": "Now that He [the Revealer] speaks, and on John's view this means also when His Word is proclaimed, the eschatological hour is present (5:25)."

39. *FaU* 1:175. "Similarly his coming as the 'Son of Man' is not put off to a future appearing; he was already the 'Son of Man' in his work on earth." *JG*, p. 634, where Bultmann notes John 1:51; 3:14; 5:27; 6:62; 8:28; 9:35; 12:23, 34. Hence, "John radically describes redemption as a present process," *Das Urchristentum*, p. 222; and "John stresses more strongly than the other scripture writers the contemporaneity of salvation, of 'life' (5:24-25; 11:25-26)." *RGG*[3], s.v. *"Mystik [IV. Im NT]."* But see *History and Eschatology*, p. 49, where Bultmann understands John's "new interpretation of the parousia" as abandoning "the apocalyptic eschatology" of "cosmic catastrophe" in favor of "the future perfection of the present life" in the destiny of the individual (John 14:2-3; 17:24). See similarly "The Christian Hope and the Problem of Demythologizing," *The Expository Times* 65 (1954): 278.

40. *TDNT*, s.v. *"pisteuō* [etc.]." This claim is subject to the proviso that believers exist in the world (17:15), are subject to its assaults (15:18-20), and are bound in faith to the Revealer's word which calls the world into question.

41. See *FaU* 1:176, n. 10, and 282; "The Significance of the O.T. for the Christian Faith," in *OTaCF*, p. 29; *JG*, pp. 154-57 (on John 3:18-19) and pp. 257-59 (on John 5:24-25); *TNT* 2:9-10 and 38; and *History and Eschatology*, p. 47. Thus, the developmental schema of F. C. Baur (i.e., Jesus to Paul to John), which Bultmann rejects (see *RGG*[3], s.v. *Johannesevangelium*), nevertheless persists in his exposition of New Testament eschatology.

Those portions of the Gospel of John (e.g., 5:28-29, 39, 40, 44, and 6:51b-58) which speak of a *future* judgment or salvation, at odds with the *present* emphases of the Fourth Gospel as a whole, Bultmann attributes to a later "ecclesiastical redaction." See *FaU* 1:166; *TDNT*, s.v. *"zaō* [etc.]"; *JG*, pp. 219-20 and 261-62 (on John 5:28-29); *TNT* 2:39; *History and Eschatology*, p. 47, n. 1; and *RGG*[3], s.v. *"Johannesevangelium."*

the eschatological event by which the ultimacy of any "worldly" claim and perspective is annulled.[42]

Thus, Bultmann interprets eternity entering time as "*a historical event* [*historisches Ereignis*] *that is simultaneously the eschatological event*, i.e., the event that signifies the end of the world and its history [*Geschichte*]."[43] It is this "*paradoxical nature* of the *concept of Revelation* . . . which John was the first to see with any distinctness."[44]

The Problem of Revelation

In Bultmann's view the "lifting up" of Jesus means that as a figure of history he is now as removed from believers as he is from unbelievers; "what Jesus said to the Jews, he said also to the disciples: they will seek him and cannot come where he is (13:33; cf. 7:34, 8:21)."[45] Hence, "the Revealer is not present for the community in its worldly affairs: 'I am no longer in the world.' And yet *they* are in the world!" (17:11).[46] By his departure, the Christian community remains "alone in the world. Its insecurity seems to stand in contrast to the assurance that his actual presence [*Anwesenheit*] once gave it."[47]

Bereft of the earthly Jesus, the problem confronting the church is whether, and in what sense, revelation can continue.[48] Throughout his commentary on John, Bultmann poses this problem in a number of ways. He asks, "How does the departing Revealer remain present [*bleibt gegenwär-tig*] for his own?;[49] "how can their relationship with him be retained in the face of this isolation?";[50] and "can the disciples still love him, when he has gone? Can the next generation love him, without having had a personal

---

42. *JG*, p. 62.

43. *GuV* 3:202.

44. *TNT* 2:50. Simlarly, the author of 1 John was "the first in early Christianity to grasp the paradox" that believers are granted freedom from sin (3:6, 9) and at the same time must continually confess their sins in order to be certain of their forgiveness (1:6-10). See *RGG*[3], s.v. "*Johannesbriefe.*"

45. *FaU* 1:180. See also *JG*, p. 524 (on John 13:33).

46. *JG*, p. 502.

47. *JG*, p. 504 (on John 17:12). Cf. *EJ*, p. 385. See also *TDNT*, s.v. "*lupē* [etc.]."

48. *JG*, p. 489, esp. n. 5.

49. *JG*, p. 528. Cf. *EJ*, p. 406.

50. *JG*, p. 524.

relationship to him?"[51] Given Bultmann's exposition of the Johannine paradox of revelation, as both "the Word became flesh" and "the eschatological event in history," we can also state the problem of Jesus' departure this way: How does the enfleshment of the Word and the eschatological event continue to happen after the Revealer has "returned to the Father"? How can John, who speaks of the sending of the Son in the aorist tense, as a completed "fact in time," also speak of it in the perfect tense "as still present"?[52]

The Presence of Revelation

Church and Spirit

What Jesus leaves behind "in the world" (17:11) are "his own," the disciples. They now *do* what he *did:*

> As he is sent into the world, so he sends them (17:18); as he is in the world, and yet not from the world, so too are they (17:14, 16; 15:19); as the world hates him, so too it hates his own (17:14; 15:18ff.). Just as his work was a *marturein* [witness], so too is theirs (15:27); they bring the same works to fruition as he (14:12); the world's fate is determined by its attitude to them (1 Jn. 4:5f.; 5:1), as it is by its attitude to him (8:42; 18:37); just as he has overcome the world (16:33), so will their faith (1 Jn. 5:4).[53]

Accordingly, with 16:27 in view ("for the Father himself loves you"), Bultmann comments that "the disciples have, as it were, stepped alongside Jesus, or even taken his place."[54] Again, commenting on 14:12 ("greater works than these will he do"), Bultmann writes, "Indeed, the Father's work, which began with what Jesus did, is to prove its power more and more in what they [the disciples] do."[55]

The sending forth of the disciples by Jesus to "call the world in

51. *JG,* p. 613.

52. *FaU* 1:177, esp. n. 11. Here Bultmann cites instances of the aorist use in John 1:11; 8:14; 9:39; 10:8, 10; and 12:47; and of the perfect in 3:2, 19; 5:43; 7:28; 8:42; and 12:46.

53. *JG,* p. 516, n. 1.

54. *JG,* p. 588.

55. *JG,* p. 610.

question, and demand a decision," even as he did, also reveals that the church *is* what Jesus *was:* "what was true of the person and word of Jesus is also true of the continuing existence and word of the community in the midst of the world."[56] The church is a community of oneness "even as" *(kathōs)* the Revealer was one with the Father (17:21-23);[57] the church is "not of the world" even as Jesus was "not of the world" (17:14);[58] the church is "holy" (17:17) and "sinless" (1 John 4:6) even as Jesus was "sinless" (8:46-47);[59] and the church is a community of those for whom "death has become insignificant" (11:25-26), since its destiny and life, like that of Jesus himself, "is not enclosed within the limits of temporal-historical existence."[60] As Bultmann notes in relation to 15:11, "the eschatological existence which belongs to him [the Revealer] of right, is given to them [the disciples]" . . . so that "what is already reality in him, is to become reality in them."[61] Given these Johannine predicates shared by Christ and the church, the latter can be seen as "representing the Revealer in the world."[62] The church, to borrow Kierkegaard's term, now provides the continuing "occasion" for that revelation originally occasioned by the earthly Jesus.

According to John 14:16 the departure of the earthly Jesus also elicits the promise to send the disciples One who "will be for them what Jesus had been: a *paraklētos,* a helper."[63] John identifies this Paraclete as the

---

56. *JG,* p. 510. Bultmann also notes that "in 1 John [see 5:4; cf. 2:2, 13-15] the victory over the world has already been achieved by Christ and is continuing in his congregation." This is the "decisive difference" with Qumran where "the eschatological victory is expected soon but is still outstanding." *JE,* p. 78, n. 17.

57. See *JG,* p. 513. In the context of John 17:21, Bultmann takes *kathōs* to signify "not merely a comparison but an explanation." *JG,* p. 382, n. 2, where John 13:15, 34; 15:9-10, 12, etc., and 17:11 are similarly cited. Thus, the unity of the community is not simply analogous to, but grounded in, the unity of the Father and the Son.

58. See *JG,* p. 507.

59. See *JG,* pp. 508-11. Commenting on John 8:46a Bultmann notes that Jesus' "'sinlessness' does not describe his 'personality' [*Persönlichkeit*], which could be judged by human standards. . . . It is the character of his word." *JG,* p. 323. Cf. *EJ,* p. 245. Bultmann then adds, "Thus 'sinlessness' applies not only to the person of the Revealer but also to the community which proclaims him. For what v. 47 says of the former, 1 Jn. 4:6 says of the latter. . . . Thus Luther can dare to say that the preacher qua preacher does not have to pray for the forgiveness of his sins." *JG,* p. 323, n. 6.

60. *JG,* p. 520. Thus, the "strong — one may say arrogant — expression" in 1 John 3:14, "We know that we have passed out of death into life," is "the community . . . thereby saying that the promise of Jn. 5:24 has been fulfilled in it." *JE,* p. 55.

61. *JG,* pp. 541-42. Cf. pp. 408-9.

62. *JG,* p. 517. See also pp. 516, 518, and 528.

63. *JG,* p. 615.

Holy Spirit (14:26), and assigns to him functions which are parallel or identical to those of Jesus himself. As Jesus was sent by God (5:30; 8:16; etc.), or has gone forth from God (8:42; 13:3; etc.), so the Paraclete is sent by the Father (14:16) or proceeds from him (15:26); as Jesus, in his capacity as Revealer, is visible only to believers, and not to the world (1:10, 12; 8:14, 19; 17:8; etc.), so is the Paraclete (14:17); as the Revealer teaches and leads into truth (14:16-17; 8:32, 40-42; etc.), so does the Paraclete (14:26; 16:3); as the Son speaks not on his own account (7:16-17; 12:49-50; etc.), neither does the Paraclete (16:13); and as the Son bears witness to himself (8:14) and convicts the world of sin (3:20; 7:7; etc.), so the Paraclete bears witness to Jesus and convicts the world of sin (15:26; 16:8).[64]

John's attribution to the paracletic Spirit of the properties of revelation associated with the incarnate Son points to the union of Jesus and his word replicating itself in the union of the Spirit with the word of the church. As Bultmann comments on John 16:5-11, "Only in the word was Jesus the Revealer, and only in the word will he continue to be it; for the Paraclete, who is to take his place, is the word." Not the word as a frozen formula, but "the word in its being spoken . . . into the world's situation, and which thereby calls the hearer out of the world." Indeed, the Spirit "is nothing other than the power of proclamation, grounded in Jesus, and at work in the community." As the eschatological power and pole of the paradox of revelation, the Spirit is the continuing condition for revelation.[65]

Thus, both the church and the Spirit "take the place" of the earthly Jesus.[66] The church does so by embodying in its proclamatory mission the incarnational "occasion" for revelation. The Spirit takes Jesus' place by effecting in and through this mediating "occasion" the eschatological "condition" or event. Just as deity and humanity, as well as eschatology and history, are distinguishable but inseparable in the mission of the Son, so too the mission of the church and that of the Spirit can be distinguished but never separated.[67] The church is authorized to preach the revelation

64. See *JG,* pp. 566-67. For history of religions' background on the Paraclete, see *JG,* pp. 566-72.

65. *JG,* pp. 559, n. 1, and 560.

66. "The disciples have, as it were, stepped alongside Jesus, or even taken his place [*oder gar an seine Stelle getretten*]" (see John 16:27), *JG,* p. 588, cf. *EJ,* p. 453; and "The Spirit is, so to speak, to take Jesus' place [*Jesus durch den Geist gleichsam ersetzt werden*]" (see John 16:13), *JG,* p. 574, cf. *EJ,* pp. 442-43.

67. Commenting on the juxtaposition in John 15:26-27 "of the disciples' witness

of Jesus Christ, but only the Spirit can authoritatively consummate this revelation in the present: "Precisely in the community's Spirit-inspired proclamation of the Word he [Jesus] himself is at work as Revealer."[68]

This continuing christological character of revelation is found and forged in that the Son sends the Spirit (15:26), or the Father does so at the Son's request (14:16) or in his name (14:26). The Johannine Revealer describes the Spirit as one who "will teach you all things, and bring to your remembrance all that I have said to you" (14:26) and who "will glorify me, for he will take what is mine and declare it to you" (16:14):

> Here it is said explicitly that the word of the Spirit does not displace or supersede the word of Jesus as if it were something new. Rather it is precisely the word of Jesus that will be alive in the proclamation of the community. The Spirit will "call to mind" his word (14:26). . . . The Spirit is not the "inner Light," which brings the new on its own authority, but he is the continuous new power of the word of Jesus. He preserves the old in the continuous newness of the word being spoken in the present.[69]

Thus, the substituting of the Spirit must be understood in the sense of "duplicating" *(Verdoppelung)*, rather than supplanting, the Son in the work of revelation.[70] The word of the Spirit is the "power" that renders the Revealer.[71] "Jesus himself is therefore present in his Word."[72]

This account of the presence of Jesus Christ finds further confirmation for Bultmann in "the correspondence between the promise of the Spirit (14:16f.; 16:12-15) and the promise of Jesus' return (14:18-21; 16:16-24 . . .)."[73] Jesus' promise, "I will not leave you desolate; I will come to you" (14:18), and his promise to give the disciples "another Counselor,

---

and that of the Spirit," Bultmann notes that, "the witness borne by the disciples is not something secondary, running alongside the witness of the Spirit. How else could e.g. the Paraclete's *elegchein* [convincing], as it is portrayed in 16:8-11, be accomplished than in the community's proclamation?" *JG*, p. 554. See also "The Primitive Christian Kerygma and the Historical Jesus," in *HJKC,* p. 40.

68. *JG*, pp. 617-18.
69. *EJ,* pp. 443-44.
70. *FaU* 1:177-78. Cf. *GuV* 1:146-47.
71. See *JG,* pp. 574-76 (on John 16:13-14) and 626 (on 14:26); and *TNT* 2:69 and 90, where John 16:8-11 is cited.
72. *FaU* 1:178. Cf. *GuV* 1:147: *"Jesus selbst ist also gegenwärtig in seinem Wort."*
73. *TNT* 2:90.

to be with you forever" (14:16), both presuppose "the same background, that of the farewell and the question it raises; both are made on the same condition: *tērein tas entolas* [to keep the commandments, 14:15, 21]; and both have the same meaning."[74] John thereby fuses "the primitive expectation of the Parousia" with the "early Christian idea of Pentecost" so that "precisely in the coming of the Spirit, Jesus comes himself."[75]

Furthermore, John's insistence that "the 'world' will perceive nothing of his coming again" (14:21-22)[76] underscores his polemic against conceiving the *parousia* as a world-historical happening. The *parousia* happens whenever and wherever the word is proclaimed in the power of the Spirit. In this way, Jesus "comes again; he is always coming again."[77] But this coming is hidden to the world and its explanations. It is an inner event, not an externally verifiable happening.[78] The presence of the Son effected by the Spirit in the proclamation of the church is visible only to faith.

This interpretation of John by Bultmann stands apart from those offered by liberalism, mysticism, and sacramentalism. Before proceeding further, we pause to note the exegetical case Bultmann makes against these alternative versions of the Johannine *Christus praesens*.

Liberalism

According to John, the sending of Jesus is, to be sure, a historical event involving a singular, concrete human being — Jesus of Nazareth. As such, revelation is open to the possibility of being misunderstood. That is, "it has — like every historical event [*wie jedes geschichtliche Ereignis*] — the possibility of being understood [merely] as a past event which existed in the past and which enters the present through memory." Indeed, this is how liberalism accounts for the use of the aorist and perfect tenses in John. Bultmann's dictum, "Because Jesus has come, he is here," is one that liberalism too embraces. But whereas Bultmann understands this statement

74. *JG,* p. 617. The locution, *tērein tas entolas,* as well as *tērein ton logon* (8:51-52; 15:20; 17:6; cf. 14:23-24), can serve "as alternatives for *pisteuein* [to believe]," "denote obedience to a command," and thereby show that for John, as for Paul, "faith has the character of obedience." *TDNT,* s.v. "*pisteuō* [etc.]."

75. *JG,* pp. 617-18.

76. *TdNT,* p. 437.

77. *FaU* 1:177.

78. *TNT* 2:57-58. See also *JG* (on John 14:17), p. 617.

paradoxically in relation to the eschaton, liberalism takes it in a causal, historicist way: Because Jesus has come (aorist tense), his "effects" are still with us (perfect tense), like those, say, of the French Revolution or Goethe. Moreover, liberalism programmatically aims to further the influence of Jesus through biographical portrayal.[79]

Bultmann charges that this liberal interpretation disregards the eschatological framework of the Fourth Gospel:

> Because Jesus has come, he *is here* [*ist er da*]. But this perfect of his being here [*dies perfektische Praesens seines Da-seins*] is made into the aorist of a past event, into an objective fact of the past, by unbelief. And it is characteristic of John that Jesus as a fact of history [*als Faktum der Geschichte*] is not an objective fact of the past which would be present only in its effects on history [*nur in seinen historischen Wirkungen*] or in the memory which recalls it. He is not to be seen as an object. Therefore his coming is not understood when it is critically attested and a "position" taken in regard to it. Then it would be seen as an object, understood as "world" instead of as an eschatological event. A reconstructed "life of Jesus" is "world." As the fact, "Jesus," which is universally demonstrable, Jesus is made into world. But the living Jesus — that is, Jesus as eschatological fact — is not visible at all to the world (14:22).[80]

Liberalism misunderstands the presence of Jesus Christ in a "worldly" way. He is a publicly accessible object over which historical judgment exercises control. Repressing the eschatological side of the paradox of revelation, liberalism restricts the soteriological significance of Jesus Christ to what historical inquiry and reconstruction can produce.

In contrast to this liberal model, Bultmann declares:

> The authentic form of the re-presentation of the historical fact of Jesus is, therefore, not historical recollection and reconstruction, but proclamation [*Die echte Form der Vergegenwärtigung des geschichtlichen Faktums Jesus ist also nicht die historische Erinnerung und Rekonstruktion, sondern die Verkündigung*]. Jesus, as it were, is duplicated in it: he comes again, and he is always coming again.[81]

---

79. *FaU* 1:176-77, omitting italics. Cf. *GuV* 1:145-46.

80. *FaU* 1:177. Cf. *GuV* 1:146. See also *JG*, p. 493. Note here, in 1928, Bultmann's appropriation of Heideggerian terminology in exegetical exposition.

81. *GuV* 1:146, omitting italics.

In this regard, Bultmann later notes that the role of "recollection" in Christian revelation in 14:26 ("But the Counselor [*paraklētos*] . . . will bring to your remembrance all that I have said to you") is not essentially a matter of "historical reconstruction, but . . . the act whereby the eschatological event that broke in in him [Jesus] is realised in the present."[82] This is borne out for Bultmann by John 16:13b: "He [the Spirit of truth] will not speak on his own authority, but whatever he hears he will speak, and he will declare to you the things that are to come." Here the subject is not "the *content* of the future . . . but *the future as such*."[83] Jesus does not leave a body of knowledge that covers every contingency and can be exhumed by the historian from Christianity's literary remains. Rather, the Spirit propels the church in its mission of interpreting the word, so that the word is heard as contemporary with every situation the future brings.

Likewise, Bultmann notes the parallelism in John 15:26-27 between the witness to Jesus borne by the Spirit and that borne by the disciples, "because you are [*este*] with me from the beginning." Bultmann discerns here the key to "the calling to mind" of 14:26. He comments,

> It is very remarkable, however, that the term *este* [are] is used and not *ēte* [were]. Thus their being with him *ap archēs* [from the beginning] has not come to an end with his farewell, but continues further; and this is the only basis on which their witness is possible. Their witness is not, therefore, a historical account of that which was, but — however much it is based on that which was — it is "repetition," "a calling to mind," in the light of their present relationship with him. In that case it is perfectly clear that their witness and that of the Spirit are identical. The Gospel is itself evidence of the kind of witness this is, and of how that which was is taken up again.[84]

That is to say, the witness to Jesus Christ borne by the Spirit and the church is not the attempt to breathe life into a dead past, but rather the interpretation of "that which was" on the basis of the One who *is*, namely, the *Christus praesens*.

82. *JG,* p. 626.
83. *JG,* p. 573.
84. *JG,* p. 554.

Mysticism

In his discussion of John 10:14-15a ("I am the good shepherd"), Bultmann notes that the language of reciprocal "knowing" (*ginōskein*) "is taken from the terminology of mysticism." By mysticism Bultmann means "the reciprocal relationship between God and mystic" in which "all differences between them disappear." Nevertheless, while "the believer's *ginōskein* means that his being is *grounded* in the Revealer's *ginōskein*, the Revealer's being, although it is 'being for' them in an absolute sense, is in no way *grounded* in their *ginōskein*." This is the import of v. 15, which Bultmann renders, " 'because (on the grounds that) the Father knows me, and I know the Father'; i.e. the relationship of believers to him is grounded in his relationship to God." Thus, there can be no question here of a "circular" relationship, but only one which originates "from above."[85]

With respect to John 15:1-8 ("I am the true vine"), with its language of mutual "abiding," Bultmann holds that the command, "Abide in me, and I in you" (15:4), must be interpreted in the light of Jesus' farewell. The imperative, *Meinate* ("Abide!"), demands "loyalty" from the disciples who remain in the world. Nevertheless, Bultmann denies that this loyalty is a "personal" one, "in which what is given and what is demanded are always equally shared by both sides." Rather, this loyalty "is not primarily a continued being *for*, but a being *from* . . . corresponding to the relationship of the *klēma* [branch] to the *ampelos* [vine]."[86]

Again, if Jesus calls the disciples "friends" (*philoi*, 15:15), "this is not because they had sought his friendship, nor does Jesus call himself their friend, but only them his friends. 'You have not chosen me, but I have chosen you' " (15:16).[87] "Their relationship to him cannot be a direct response to his amicable love, which would mean that he could be called their friend. They can respond to his friendship only indirectly; how, is stated in the words that follow: 'And I have appointed you, that you go forth and bear fruit, and that your fruit abide.' "[88] This fruitbearing embraces both love for one another (15:2) and a witness to the world in the face of its hatred and persecution (15:8–16:4a).

Here Bultmann cautions against Protestant pietism's mawkish eager-

---

85. *JG*, pp. 380-82.
86. *JG*, pp. 534-36.
87. *JG*, p. 544, omitting italics.
88. *JG*, p. 545, omitting italics.

ness to fraternize with Jesus. This form of piety, a mutation of mysticism, also afflicts the liberalism of Harnack, Weiss, and Herrmann. While in mysticism the distinction between God and the mystic is erased, in pietism the friendship analogy is pushed so hard that the earthly Jesus is taken for the believer's constant companion. His humanity is regarded "not as an offence and a paradox, but as an act of condescension which makes the Revealer visible, removing all fear from the man who encounters him, and enabling . . . a merely human and personal relationship with the Revealer."[89] Moreover, pietism overlooks the departure of Jesus, a departure which means "a vast *distance* persists . . . which precludes all familiarity, all mysticism."[90] Thus, for Bultmann, neither in his coming nor his going does Jesus "yield himself up to man's tender emotions: for he is none other than the Revealer, in whom God addresses man."[91]

Bultmann further rejects the mystical account of the *Christus praesens* because it demands "the complete elimination of the future in a mystical present,"[92] a *"nunc aeternum"* or "eternal now."[93] This objection of Bultmann's may seem surprising given his own view that John understands the final judgment and *parousia* of the Son as present now to faith. Bultmann's point is not that John abolishes the future of judgment and forgiveness or the future of Jesus Christ with believers. Indeed, insofar as the Fourth Gospel presents the Revealer as contemporary with those who will hear and bear his paracletic word, the future character of revelation is assumed and assured. What John eliminates from the future of revelation is the mythological or apocalyptic "idea that the time of salvation ushered in by God will be a permanent state on earth," that is, an event or a reality, which will be demonstrably visible to all on the stage of world history.[94] Jesus Christ, as God's eschatological act, circumscribes every present yet to come. Mysticism, therefore, cannot detain him within its atemporal consciousness. In looking to Jesus Christ, faith — here and now — looks forward to the future.

89. *JG*, p. 66.

90. *FaU* 1:179.

91. *JG*, p. 382.

92. *JG*, p. 258, n. 3.

93. See *JG*, p. 257, n. 3. For a recent Benedictine treatment of the mystical *Christus praesens* that appropriates the language of the Fourth Gospel, see John Main, *The Present Christ: Further Steps in Meditation* (London: Darton, Longman and Todd, 1985), esp. pp. 49-59.

94. *TDNT*, s.v. "*pisteuō* [etc.]." See also "The Significance of the O.T. for the Christian Faith," in *OTaCF*, p. 29 and *JG*, p. 560 (on John 16:7). Cf. *RGG*[3], s.v. "*Johannesbriefe*."

Sacramentalism

"The sacramentalism of ecclesiastical piety"[95] traditionally appeals to John 6:51b-58 ("He who eats my flesh and drinks my blood abides in me and I in him," v. 56). Unlike those exegetes who deny any sacramental referent in this passage, Bultmann freely accepts it.[96] Indeed, the text reflects a sacramentalism based on an animistic concept of power. The "living power" of Jesus, it is held, now fills the sacraments. By receiving them, believers are united to Jesus. "Those who participate in the sacramental meal bear within them the power which guarantees their [future] resurrection," while "those who do not eat the Lord's Supper are thus denied all claim to life."[97] The Lord's Supper thus becomes "the *pharmakon athanasias*" or "medicine of immortality" (cf. Ignatius, *Ephesians* 20:2).[98]

While Bultmann acknowledges, in the footsteps of Bousset, that such a sacramental theology was part and parcel of Hellenistic Christianity, he argues that it is one which John actually rejects. John could not have authored 6:51b-58b, for it is alien "to the Evangelist's thought in general, and specifically to his eschatology," and "it also stands in contradiction to what has been said just before":[99]

> For here [6:27-51a] the bread of life which the Father gives by sending the Son from heaven (vv. 32f.) is the Son himself, the Revealer. He gives (v. 27) and is (vv. 35, 48, 51) the bread of life, in the same way that he gives the water of life (4:10) and is the light of the world (8:12), and as the Revealer gives life to the world (v. 33, cp. 10:28; 17:2) — to those, that is, who "come" to him (v. 35; cp. 3:20f.; 5:40), who believe in him (v. 35; and cp. 3:20f. with 3:18). In all this there is no need for a sacramental act, by means of which the believer must make the life his own.[100]

Thus, 6:51b-58 betrays the hand of ecclesiastical redaction.

95. *JG*, p. 138, n. 3.
96. See *JG*, p. 219, n. 1 and *RGG*³, s.v. *"Johannesevangelium."*
97. *JG*, pp. 235-36.
98. *JG*, p. 235. See also p. 219 and "Ignatius and Paul," in *EaF*, p. 271; pub. in Ger. as "Ignatius und Paulus," in *Exegetica*, p. 404. For history of religions' background on the "medicine of immortality," see *TDNT*, s.v. "*thanatos* [etc.]."
99. *JG*, p. 219.
100. *JG*, p. 219.

Furthermore, John "makes no mention at all of the Lord's Supper; in his account of the last meal Jesus' prayer takes its place." Bultmann interprets this to mean that "the sacraments are superfluous" for John, since "the disciples are 'clean' through the word (15:3), just as they are 'holy' through the word . . . (17:17)." Bultmann takes John's pointed silence on the Lord's Supper as indicating that abuses of the rite had made it suspect. His solution is to retain them "in the sense that in them the word is made present in a special way." Only by such "kerygmatizing," analogous to that carried on by Paul, can sacraments be redeemed from the magic of the mysteries for responsible use by the church.[101]

Jesus Christ — The Agent of Revelation

In contrast to liberalism, mysticism, and sacramentalism, Bultmann understands John to say that the presence of Jesus Christ is effected by the Spirit in and through church proclamation. Nevertheless, Bultmann also understands John to say that Jesus Christ himself remains the abiding agent of revelation. Bultmann's emphasis on the contemporary agency of Jesus Christ appeals both to the unity of Jesus and his word, and to the "glorification" of Jesus (13:31) in answer to his petition (17:1-5).

We have already noted that John repeatedly predicates of Jesus the same soteriological benefits that he predicates of Jesus' word. Bultmann infers from this pattern that "such an identification establishes the fact that the 'Word' does not represent a complex of ideas," but *is* the event of God's judgment and forgiveness known as Jesus Christ. "Jesus speaks this Christian proclamation, he *is* this proclamation." That is to say, whenever the proclaimed word of the church effects "judgment and forgiveness," faith attributes this performative power to the eschatological agency of Jesus Christ.[102]

For Bultmann, this Johannine understanding of the Word of God is in sharp contrast to that found in the Old Testament. There the Word of God, as law or prophecy, stands over against, or in judgment upon, Israel's national or ethnic history *(Volksgeschichte)*. At the same time, the present "unity with the past is established by the fact that the Word which

---

101. *JG,* p. 472. Bultmann speculates that the love command restrains John from a direct attack on the sacraments. See *JG,* p. 486.
102. *FaU* 1:309-10.

now confronts the nation recalls the past and thereby makes that history contemporary and continues it."[103] Thus, the preaching of the prophets places its hearer in the saving stream of national or ethnic history.[104] As a Jew I am reminded that God delivered me from Egypt, because I am a member of the nation in whose history the Exodus occurred. With John it is otherwise. The Word of God is not set over against the history of revelation, that is, Jesus Christ, but *is* this history in its very act of being proclaimed or consummated.[105] To "recall" Jesus Christ, therefore, is not to recollect or to reconstruct the *ipsissima verba* of "the historical Jesus," but to participate, albeit paradoxically, in "the act whereby the eschatological event that broke in in him is realised in the present."[106] Thus, the Word of God, who is Jesus Christ, does not integrate the hearer into a narrative of salvation, as if it were a segment of national or world history. Rather, this Word lifts the hearer outside of the determinative status of all such histories and into eschatological existence.[107]

This contemporary agency of Jesus Christ in and through the proclamation of the word is further indicated by the "glorification" of the Johannine Revealer: "Now is the Son of Man glorified, and in him God is glorified" (13:31). So John signals, in the discourses which follow, that Jesus is already speaking "as the *doxastheis* [Glorified], and it is also as the *doxastheis,* that he moves through the event of the passion."[108] Likewise, even before the Easter story, John's Jesus declares, "Because I live [*zō*], you will live also" (14:19b). Bultmann takes the present tense of *zō* to indicate that Jesus "is already speaking as the resurrected one, as the *doxastheis* (13:31)."[109]

From parallels in the history of religions, Bultmann notes that the concept of *doxa* [glory] connotes "divine power in action." Hence, "Jesus' *doxasthēnai* [glorification] also means that he is equipped with power, that he becomes fully effectual." Within the context of 17:1-5, John links the contemporary work of Jesus Christ to the glorification. The declaration

103. *FaU* 1:311.
104. See "The Significance of the O.T. for the Christian Faith," in *OTaCF,* p. 30.
105. See *FaU* 1:311.
106. *JG,* p. 626.
107. See *FaU* 1:311.
108. *JG,* p. 490.
109. *JG,* p. 619. "As the One who speaks ["and on John's view this means also when His Word is proclaimed"] He is the *anastasis* [resurrection] and the *zōē* [life]." *TDNT,* s.v. "*zaō* [etc.]."

of 17:2 that the Father has given the Son "power over all flesh, to give eternal life to all whom thou hast given him," Bultmann interprets as saying that "he who is *doxastheis* is at work in his community." Furthermore, "he is at work there as the Revealer; for, according to v. 3, the life which he bestows is nothing other than the knowledge of God and of himself as the Revealer. . . . Thus, by his *doxa* he is portrayed as the active bearer of the revelation." That is to say, the glory of Jesus Christ does not bring an end to his revelatory work in the world. Rather, it is precisely his glory which enables the Revealer to proclaim his word beyond the confines of the first century.[110]

Summary

As an interpreter of John, Bultmann understands Jesus Christ as the incarnate *Logos* or Son of God; hence, on the model of the Gnostic Redeemer myth, as the Revealer of God. The paradox that God is to be encountered only in (the word and work of) Jesus is expressed by John's declaration that "the Word became flesh" (1:14) and by his radical "historicizing" of the eschatological event (5:24-25). To inquire then about how and where Jesus Christ becomes our contemporary is to ask how and where the enfleshment of the word and the eschatological event continue to happen — even after the Revealer departs from the world.

John locates the presence of Jesus Christ in the word of the church proclaimed in the power of the Paraclete. The same soteriological predicates attributed to the Son, or to his word and work, are transferred to the church and the Spirit, principally in relation to their common mission of bearing witness to the Son. Thus, the church and the Spirit take the place of the earthly Jesus within the world. The church, by its preaching, provides the temporal "occasion" for revelation; the Spirit, in and through the proclaimed word, provides the efficacious eschatological "condition." In this way, the paradox which is Jesus Christ, namely, the eschatological event in history or the Word of God in human form, continues in and

---

110. *JG,* p. 491. See also p. 522. Thus, "in the word of the community, Jesus himself is speaking." *TdNT,* p. 443. For a summary of Bultmann's comparative studies on *doxa,* see *JG,* p. 67, n. 2. Bultmann's interpretation of Jesus' glorification disputes Kierkegaard's claim that "from the seat of His glory He has not spoken one word." See *Training in Christianity,* p. 26. See also pp. 27 and 161-62.

through the coincident witness of the church and the Spirit. The paracletic proclamation of the word renders for faith the presence of Jesus Christ.

The Gospel of John therefore posits no *Christus praesens* in the sense held by liberalism, mysticism, or sacramentalism. All of these traditionally traveled routes into the presence of Christ bypass the Evangelist's eschatological outlook. Each erroneously exalts some human work, whether scientific or religious, to conjure up what only God's Word and Spirit can grant — the presence of Jesus Christ.

As the Glorified of God, Jesus must be understood not only as the object but also as the abiding agent of revelation. That is to say, the Evangelist presents the proclamation of the community as the word of the Glorified himself. Therefore, the Gospel of John is not an account of "the historical Jesus," but is rather, in the words of Ernst Käsemann, "the history of the *Christus praesens.*"[111]

The Pauline and Johannine *Christus Praesens* according to Bultmann

Bultmann's exposition of the Johannine *Christus praesens* shows "the deep relatedness in substance [*sachliche Verwandschaft*] that exists between John and Paul."[112] "Granting all differences in their manner of thought, nevertheless a deep, essential commonality [*sachliche Gemeinschaft*] persists, above all, in that both understand the eschatological event as lifting up Jesus' coming into existence and its continual consummation in the present."[113] Thus, behind their specific conceptual frameworks and terminological differences, Bultmann uncovers in both Paul and John a subject matter *(Sache)* common to each. This Pauline-Johannine subject matter can be expressed for human salvation in both christological and eschatological "event language," as Bultmann's own shorthand formula, *"Christus praesens,"* may now suggest.

---

111. "The Problem of the Historical Jesus," in *Essays on New Testament Themes,* trans. W. J. Montague (London: SCM, 1964; reprint ed., Philadelphia: Fortress, 1982), p. 22. See also p. 28 and Käsemann, "The Structure and Purpose of the Prologue to John's Gospel," in *NTQT,* p. 165. Cf. *JG,* pp. 554-55, 576, n. 2 and *TNT* 2:91.

112. *TNT* 2:9, omitting italics. Cf. *TdNT,* p. 361. See also *FaU* 1:281-83. For Bultmann's discussion of the formal differences between John and Paul, see esp. *TNT* 2:6-10.

113. *RGG*³, s.v. *"Johannesevangelium."*

In Paul, Bultmann discerns a developing attenuation of Jewish apoc-alyptic eschatology. The longed-for "turning point of the ages" has now arrived in the cross and resurrection of Jesus Christ. The "new creation," the "day of salvation," and the "reconciliation" of humanity wrought by God are not far off but are now at hand in and through the office and word proclaiming them. Likewise, for John the final judgment and *parousia* of the Messiah, which took place in the sojourn of the Son of God, now take place in and through the paracletic word of the church. Thus, for both Paul and John, "the eschatological occurrence is understood as already taking place in the present."[114]

What links this eschatological salvation to the present activity of preaching? The answer common to both Paul and John is the presence of Jesus Christ. In Paul the same soteriological benefits attributed to (the death and resurrection of) Christ are also predicated of the proclamation and proclaimers (as proclaimers) of the kerygma. The possibility for this unity is established by God simultaneously instituting with the reconcil-iation wrought in Christ the office and word proclaiming it. In this sense, Jesus has indeed risen into the heralds and kerygma of the cross. In John the same soteriological benefits attributed to the Son, or to his word and work, are also predicated of the church and the Spirit, principally in relation to their common mission of bearing witness to the Son. The church, by its preaching, provides the temporal "occasion" for revelation; the Spirit, in and through the proclaimed word, provides the efficacious eschatological "condition." The paradox which is Jesus Christ, namely, the eschatological event in history or the Word of God in human form, thereby continues in and through the coincident witness of the church and Spirit. In this sense, the glorification of the Son, as God's eschatological Revealer hidden in "the flesh," continues in the humanity and temporality of its contemporary proclamation. Whether they employ the language of glori-fication or that of resurrection with respect to the Crucified, for both John and Paul the event of Jesus Christ continues in the preaching that witnesses to it.[115]

114. *TNT* 2:9-10. See also *FaU* 1:282; *NTaM*, p. 19; "The Christian Hope and the Problem of Demythologizing," *The Expository Times* 65 (1954): 277-78; *JCaM*, pp. 32-34; *History and Eschatology*, p. 151; "The Primitive Christian Kerygma and the His-torical Jesus," in *HJKC*, pp. 16, 40-41; and "Ist die Apokalyptik die Mutter der christlichen Theologie?: Eine Auseinandersetzung mit Ernst Käsemann [1964]," in *Exegetica*, p. 477.

115. Hence, for both, "Christology is proclamation, is summons [*Anrede*]." *GuV* 1:264. See also 1:261 and 267. Since Paul and John share a common subject matter,

Thus, for both Paul and John, "Christ is the eschatological event not as a figure of the past . . . but as the *Christus praesens*."[116] Jesus Christ not only came, he comes; he not only spoke, he speaks; he not only judged and forgave, he judges and forgives. Combining the distinctive formulations of Paul and John, Bultmann can summarize the eschatological *Christus praesens* common to each:

> In Jesus Christ God has reconciled the world with himself [2 Cor. 5:18]. Christ is God's Word [John 1:14]. When this Word is preached, the hour of decision is here [2 Cor. 5:20 and 6:2; John 5:24-25]. Whoever hears him, hears the Father; whoever sees him, sees the Father; whoever honours him, honours the Father [John 5:23-27 and 14:9].[117]

In and through the word of the church, the Christ who is proclaimed is the Christ who is present as the proclaimer.

Confronted by this conclusion, we recall from chapter one those characterizations of Bultmann's views given by Dietrich Ritschl, Charles David Barrett, J. Louis Martyn, and David H. Kelsey. This chorus of critics charged Bultmann with passing over the presence of Jesus Christ as the contemporary agent of salvation. Our examination of Bultmann's exegesis of Paul and John proves these critics wrong. Whether their judgment holds truer for Bultmann's "more theological" writings remains to be seen. To these we now turn to round out our presentation.

Bultmann can expound Paul's Christology with John's language of incarnation and discuss John's Christology in terms of Paul's "turning point of the ages" (cf. Gal. 4:4-5). For examples of the former, see *FaU* 1:241 and *TdNT,* p. 305; for the latter, see *FaU* 1:175 and *JG,* pp. 377, 431, and 634.

116. "History and Eschatology in the N.T.," *NTS* 1 (1954-55): 15-16.
117. *FaU* 1:285.

The *Christus Praesens*
according to Bultmann

Introduction

IN CHAPTER one, we presented the liberal paradigm of the presence of Jesus and Bultmann's analysis of its anomalies. History of religions research, comparative philology, and form criticism had demonstrated for New Testament scholarship what World War I had made plain to European civilization at large: the presence of Jesus was no longer plausible as the continuing influence on modern piety and sensibility of an extraordinary, historic personality. Bultmann did not dispute that Jesus was a living "Thou" for us in the present; but he did dispute that Jesus could be such in the way proposed by the liberal doctrine of personality.

In chapters two and three, we examined Bultmann's "more exegetical" writings and found that the presence of Jesus, for both Paul and John, can be formulated as "the *Christus praesens*." In the hands of Bultmann, this formula of Harnack's now signifies the status and significance of Jesus Christ as the kerygmatic eschatological salvation event, who, as such, forms the subject matter of the New Testament kerygma and, hence, of the Christian faith.

Before we examine how Bultmann, the theologian, accounts for Jesus as our contemporary "Thou" without recourse to personality, we recall our forewarning from Bultmann's critics to expect little from his "more theological" writings with regard to the *Christus praesens*. Yet a survey of his lectures, essays, sermons, and letters finds over a dozen, written between 1936 and 1965, explicitly asserting the presence of Jesus Christ in and through Christian proclamation. Moreover, far from being marginal works, these writings include Bultmann's programmatic essay of 1941,

"New Testament and Mythology," as well as his subsequent responses to Julius Schniewind, Helmut Thielicke, Karl Barth, Karl Jaspers, and Ernst Käsemann.

Among Bultmann's more striking statements are those that claim the kerygma as the exclusive locus for the presence of Christ. For example, in "New Testament and Mythology," Bultmann writes, "Christ, the Crucified and Risen One, encounters us in the word of proclamation — nowhere else"; and "in the preached word, and only in it, is the Risen One encountered."[1] Bultmann repeats this claim in 1948 in response to Schniewind's "Theses" and again in 1952 in reply to Barth's "Attempt to Understand Him." To Schniewind, Bultmann declares, "The *Kyrios Christos* encounters us only in the kerygma of the church."[2] To Barth, Bultmann explains, "Yes, I aim at the thesis that Christ (insofar as he affects us) is the kerygma, because he is the Christ only as the Christ *pro me,* and as such he encounters me only in the kerygma."[3]

In another series of statements, Bultmann identifies the contem-

---

1. "Neues Testament und Mythologie: Das Problem der Entmythologisierung der neutestamentlichen Verkündigung [1941]" (hereafter cited as "NTuM" in Hans Werner Bartsch, ed., *Kerygma und Mythos: Ein theologisches Gespräch* (Hamburg: Reich & Heidrich, 1948; hereafter cited as *KuM* 1), p. 51, omitting italics. ET: "New Testament and Mythology: The Problem of Demythologizing the New Testament Proclamation," in *NTaM*, p. 40. Bultmann does not restrict the proclamation of the church to the sermon of an ordained minister. Such proclamation occurs through the varied forms of lay witness as well. See *Marburg Sermons*, p. 70; "On the Problem of Demythologizing [1952]," in Werner Bartsch, ed. *NTaM*, p. 119; pub. in Ger. as "Zum Problem der Entmythologisierung" (hereafter cited as "PdE"), in *Kerygma und Mythos: Diskussionen und Stimmen zum Problem der Entmythologisierung* (Hamburg: Herbert Reich, 1952; hereafter cited as *KuM* 2), p. 204; and "Preaching: Genuine and Secularized," trans. Harold O. J. Brown, in *Religion and Culture: Essays in Honor of Paul Tillich*, ed. Walter Leibrecht (New York: Harper & Bros., 1959), p. 242; pub. in Ger. as "Echte und säkularisierte Verkündigung im 20. Jahrhundert [1955]," in *GuV* 3:129-30.
2. "Zu J. Schniewinds Thesen: Das Problem der Entmythologisierung betreffend [1948]," in *KuM* 1:134. For Schniewind's criticisms, see "Antwort an Rudolf Bultmann: Thesen zum Problem der Entmythologisierung [1943]," in *KuM* 1:85-134. ET: "A Reply to Bultmann: Theses on the Emancipation of the Kerygma from Mythology," in Rudolf Bultmann et al., *Kerygma and Myth: A Theological Debate,* ed. Hans Werner Bartsch, trans. Reginald H. Fuller (London: SPCK, 1953; reprint ed., New York: Harper & Row, Harper Torchbooks, 1961; hereafter cited as *KaM* 1), pp. 45-101.
3. Bultmann to Barth, 11-15 November 1952, in Barth, *Gesamtausgabe,* 5:1:178. For Barth's criticisms, see "Rudolf Bultmann — An Attempt to Understand Him," in *KaM* 2: esp. 95-97.

poraneity of Jesus Christ with Christian preaching. In an Advent sermon from 1938, Bultmann declares, "A wonder is every act . . . and every event which occurs where Jesus reigns. And where does he reign? Where the word of the gospel is preached and heard."[4] Commenting in 1958 on "Das Befremdliche des christlichen Glaubens [The Strangeness of Christian Faith]," Bultmann writes, "Christianity proclaims an event, or rather *in the proclamation,* the event that is called Jesus Christ takes place continually, the revelation of God in a human word."[5] That same year, with the publication of *Jesus Christ and Mythology,* Bultmann uses similar language when he notes that "the eschatological event which is Jesus Christ happens here and now as the Word is being preached (2 Cor. 6:2; John 5:24) regardless of whether this Word is accepted or rejected."[6]

In yet a third set of statements, Bultmann asserts the agency of Jesus Christ with respect to contemporary church proclamation. For example, Bultmann concludes a Marburg sermon of 1936 on Acts 17:22-32 by claiming that "the unknown God has made himself known to us in his Word . . . which Jesus Christ, as the Crucified and Risen, proclaims to us."[7] In his 1955 reflections on the character of authentic proclamation, Bultmann asserts that "to believe in Christ means . . . to believe the word in which he addresses us [*er uns anredet*], through which he wills to become our Lord."[8] Again, in his Gifford Lectures of that same year, Bultmann explains that "Jesus Christ is the eschatological event not as an established fact of past time but as repeatedly present, as addressing you and me here and now in preaching."[9] In 1957, turning again to issues of authentic proclamation, Bultmann declares that in Christian preaching "the proclaimed is simultaneously present as the proclaimer."[10] Likewise, in 1960 when Bultmann accepts the formulation, coined by Eduard Ellwein, that "Jesus has risen in the kerygma," he does so provided "it expresses the fact that Jesus is really present in the kerygma [*dass Jesus im Kerygma wirklich gegenwärtig ist*], that it is *his* word which involves the hearer in the kerygma."[11]

4. *Marburger Predigten,* p. 94.

5. *GuV* 3:207.

6. P. 81. From the standpoint of faith, outright rejection of Jesus Christ is itself a sign, or countersign, of his presence.

7. *Marburger Predigten,* p. 12, omitting italics.

8. *GuV* 3:126.

9. *History and Eschatology,* pp. 151-52.

10. *"Der Verkündigte zugleich als der Verkünder präsent ist." GuV* 3:168-69.

11. "The Primitive Christian Kerygma and the Historical Jesus," in *HJKC,* p. 42. See

By claiming the kerygma as the exclusive locus for the presence of Jesus Christ, by identifying the contemporaneity of Jesus Christ with that of Christian preaching, and by asserting the agency of Jesus Christ with respect to Christian proclamation, Bultmann, the theologian, advances themes we have already uncovered throughout his exposition of Paul and John. Thus, our preliminary soundings offer initial evidence that Bultmann no more overlooks the *Christus praesens* in his theological writings than in his exegetical ones.

Nevertheless, Bultmann's striking affirmations are neither self-explanatory nor free of ambiguity. They require interpretation. In light of Bultmann's exposition of the Pauline and Johannine *Christus praesens,* we now turn to his "more theological" writings to uncover his own teaching on the presence of Jesus Christ.

Who is Jesus Christ?

If we approach Bultmann's programmatic essay "New Testament and Mythology,"[12] with the question "Who is Jesus Christ?" the following answers emerge:

First, "Jesus Christ" is a "mythical person" [*mythische Person*] or character in the central soteriological narrative of the New Testament.[13] The "individual motifs" of this narrative, embracing the titles "Messiah" and "Son of God," and including the incarnation, atonement, resurrection, ascension, and imminent return, "may be easily traced to the contemporary mythology of Jewish apocalypticism and of the Gnostic myth of redemption."[14]

---

also p. 30. Cf. *Exegetica,* p. 469. See also p. 458 and *GuV* 4:197. Cf. Ellwein, "Fragen zu Bultmanns Interpretation des neutestamentlichen Kerygmas," in Ernst Kinder, ed., *Ein Wort lutherischer Theologie zur Entmythologisierung* (München: Ev. Pressverband für Bayern, 1952), p. 24.

12. To the degree that Bultmann has a "systematic theological position," Schubert M. Ogden finds it "classically formulated" here. See Preface, *NTaM,* p. vii. For a brilliant commentary on Bultmann's essay, see Ogden, *Christ without Myth: A Study Based on the Theology of Rudolf Bultmann* (New York: Harper & Row, 1961; reprint ed., Dallas: SMU Press, 1991), esp. pp. 22-126. Cf. Macquarrie, *An Existentialist Theology,* pp. 159-92.

13. *NTaM,* p. 14. Cf. "NTuM," in *KuM* 1:2. See also p. 13, in Ger., 1:26; *JCaM,* pp. 16-17; and "The Primitive Christian Kerygma and the Historical Jesus," in *HJKC,* p. 16, cf. *Exegetica,* p. 446.

14. *NTaM,* p. 2. See also p. 14 and *JCaM,* pp. 16-17.

Second, "Jesus Christ" is "at the same time a certain historical person [*historischer Mensch*], Jesus of Nazareth," whose "human destiny . . . ends with crucifixion." This crucifixion, reported in the New Testament, Bultmann takes for a "historical event [*historisches Ereignis*]," that is, an event of the past that can be retrieved and reconstructed by the historian.[15]

Third, "Jesus Christ" is "he in whom God acts in the present [*der, in dem Gott gegenwärtig handelt*]" whenever "the person and destiny [*der Person und des Schicksals*] of Jesus of Nazareth" are proclaimed "in their significance as history of salvation."[16]

Therefore, in "New Testament and Mythology" Bultmann understands "Jesus Christ" to signify (1) a mythical character, (2) a historical figure, and (3) the contemporary kerygmatic and eschatological locus of God's saving activity, that is, the *Christus praesens*. These three significations, which we can abbreviate as JC-1, JC-2, and JC-3, form an interrelated configuration that comprises Bultmann's Christology. Hence, while our inquiry continues to focus upon the *Christus praesens* or JC-3, this signification of "Jesus Christ" can only be understood in relation to the other two; that is, as mythical character or JC-1 and as historical figure or JC-2.[17]

"Jesus Christ" as Mythical Character and Historical Figure

We noted in chapter one that as early as 1920 Bultmann labels the narrative (*Erzählung*) of the Gospels and its central character as "mythical," insofar as both reflect parallels and antecedents known to the history of religions.[18] Then, in 1941, with characteristic consistency, Bultmann repeats this judgment in "New Testament and Mythology." Yet in this essay the emphasis shifts from that of 1920. Now Bultmann stresses that the New Testament speaks mythologically when it makes reality claims that are implausible or incredible, not to say false, when compared to the modern "world picture" *(Weltbild)*.

15. *NTaM*, p. 32. Cf. "NTuM," in *KuM* 1:44.

16. *NTaM*, p. 41. ET slightly altered. Cf. "NTuM," in *KuM* 1:52.

17. Cf. my formulations with those of Macquarrie, *An Existentialist Theology*, pp. 166, 168-69, and 171, and Gareth Jones, *Bultmann: Towards a Critical Theology* (Cambridge: Polity Press, 1991), p. 34.

18. See "Ethical and Mystical Religion," in *BDT* 1:223-24. Cf. "Ethische und mystische Religion," in *AdT* 2:32-33.

Unlike the world picture of the New Testament, that of the modern age regards the scientific method as sovereign. This method, as characterized by Bultmann, assumes that empirical reality is constituted by a network of purely immanent causal relations. Thereby precluded is any suspension of the laws of nature or perforation of the unity of the self by intrusive, supernatural powers. Where the scientific method prevails, therefore, the resurrection of a dead man or the infusion of divine life through the ingestion of food can only be regarded as mythological. Given the modern world picture, such typical accounts in the New Testament cannot be taken as recording or referring to real facts and events, inasmuch as facts and events are held to be recovered or reconstructed through scientific means.[19]

Nevertheless, not everything in the Gospels is mythological. Indeed, what distinguishes the Christ myth of the New Testament from similar parallels is that its central character, JC-1, is also a historical figure, JC-2:

> The Jesus Christ who is God's Son, a preexistent divine being, is at the same time a certain historical person [*historischer Mensch*], Jesus of Nazareth; and his destiny as a person [*Person*] is not only a mythical occurrence but at the same time a human destiny that ends with crucifixion. The historical [*Historisches*] and the mythical [*Mythisches*] here are peculiarly intertwined.[20]

By virtue of this "intertwining" of JC-1 and JC-2, Bultmann claims that "the Christ occurrence is not a myth like the cult myths of the Greek or Hellenistic gods."[21]

While "New Testament and Mythology" does not set forth the facts about JC-2 as such, and while Bultmann finds the personality of Jesus

---

19. See *NTaM*, pp. 2-8. Cf. "NTuM," in *KuM* 1:16-21. Throughout this essay, Bultmann uses the term *Weltbild* to characterize the given outlooks of particular historical epochs. For Bultmann's further discussion of the scientific method and its world picture, see *NTaM*, pp. 95-105 and 147-48 and *JCaM*, pp. 15-16, 38, and 65-66.

20. *NTaM*, p. 32. Cf. "NTuM," in *KuM* 1:44.

21. *NTaM*, p. 32. Similarly in "The Primitive Christian Kerygma and the Historical Jesus," Bultmann writes, "The kerygma maintains that God has made the historical Jesus [*der historischer Jesus*] the Christ, the *Kyrios* (Acts 2:36). . . . It is therefore obvious that the kerygma presupposes the historical Jesus, however much it may have mythologized him. Without him there would be no kerygma." *HJKC*, p. 18. Cf. *Exegetica*, p. 448. Conversely, the Synoptics, by preserving and transmitting the tradition of the historical Jesus, insure that the *Kyrios* would not become simply a mythical figure. See *GuV* 4:196.

beyond the historian's grasp, nevertheless, Bultmann holds as credible several facts about the historical Jesus.

Writing in 1926 Bultmann claims that "the doubt as to whether Jesus really existed is unfounded and not worth refutation." Jesus was a male Jew of Nazareth who "lived in Palestine and spoke Aramaic," and who, in all likelihood, "actually lived as a Jewish rabbi." If so, "Jesus being a scribe, had received the necessary scribal training and had passed the requisite scribal tests." Significantly, Jesus' "adherents (not the twelve only) are called pupils (disciples) . . . a technical term" designating "the pupils of a rabbi, not the members of a religious fellowship." Numbered among these followers were former "disciples of the Baptist" and "even a Zealot." Nevertheless, in many respects Jesus did "not correspond to the typical figure of a rabbi." This is seen not only in the fact "that among his adherents were women," or in his apparent "affection for children," but also in his interactions "with sinners, prostitutes, and publicans, which is surely historical." Despite his occasional conduct in opposition to the Law, "Jesus did not attack the Law, but assumed its authority and interpreted it."[22]

Moreover, "there can be no doubt that Jesus did the kind of deeds which were miracles to his mind and to the minds of his contemporaries, . . . undoubtedly he healed the sick and cast out demons."[23]

Jesus was also a preacher of an eschatological message, "who really spoke as a Messianic prophet." His preaching was "addressed first of all to the poor and sinful," and "he allowed himself to be blamed as the friend of tax collectors and sinners." Hence, "his personal qualities . . . apparently aroused in his contemporaries antagonism rather than faith." "Outsiders could not recognize the essentially unpolitical character of the leadership of Jesus." "He seems to have entered Jerusalem with a crowd of enthusiastic adherents; all were full of joy and of confidence that now the Kingdom of God was beginning. . . . Jesus . . . with his followers . . . took possession (as it seems) of the temple, in order to cleanse the holy precincts from all evil in

---

22. *Jesus and the Word,* pp. 12-13, 25, 57-58, and 60-63, omitting italics. In 1960, in "The Primitive Christian Kerygma and the Historical Jesus," Bultmann reiterates many of his 1926 assertions about JC-2. The following differences are noteworthy: In 1960, Bultmann denies Jesus appeared "as a teacher or rabbi" and drops explicit references to Jesus' positive regard for the Law and to his disciples as consisting in part of former "disciples of the Baptist" and "even a Zealot"; he adds that "Jesus was not an ascetic like John the Baptist, but gladly ate and drank a glass of wine." *HJKC,* pp. 22-23 and 26.

23. *Jesus and the Word,* p. 173. See also "The Primitive Christian Kerygma and the Historical Jesus," in *HJKC,* p. 22.

preparation for the coming Kingdom." Arousing "considerable popular excitement," his movement was "suppressed quickly." "Jesus was crucified by the Roman procurator Pontius Pilate as a Messianic prophet."[24]

Given these historical assertions, Jesus Christ, even as a character in a mythical narrative, is not entirely fictitious. Rather, he is analogous to, say, the Abraham Lincoln of Gore Vidal's historical novel. While Vidal's "Lincoln" develops within the plot of a novel, there are many places in the story where this character aligns with the historical facts surrounding the sixteenth president of the United States. Likewise, for Bultmann the New Testament's mythology of the cross "originates," or has a factual basis, in the crucifixion of Jesus of Nazareth.[25] Where the analogy between the gospel narratives and modern works of historical fiction breaks down is at the point of salvation. Vidal, for example, does not claim for Lincoln a transcendent soteriological significance, even if this chief executive did "save" the Union. Yet it is precisely such significance that the New Testament attributes to Jesus Christ. How then can a mythical-historical figure possess saving significance in and for a modern scientific age?

Bultmann, of course, is not the first to struggle with this question. It also preoccupies his liberal teachers as heirs of the Enlightenment. For example, we have already noted how Johannes Weiss relates the mythical and historical strands of New Testament Christology. The mythological titles express the tremendous "mediate or immediate influence of the personality of Jesus on the souls of his followers."[26] Hence, the real referent of the myths adhering to Jesus is not a supernatural person, a preexistent Messiah, but a historical personality whose continuing influence shapes subsequent piety. In this way, liberalism redirects Christian faith around the mythical Messiah

---

24. *Jesus and the Word,* pp. 25-26, 29, 124, 203, and 215. In "The Primitive Christian Kerygma and the Historical Jesus," Bultmann ascribes to Jesus "a prophetic consciousness, indeed, a 'consciousness of authority.'" Yet this bolder evaluation of Jesus' personality, inferred from the Synoptics, is mitigated by Bultmann's starker skepticism regarding Jesus' fate. Bultmann's earlier view that Jesus probably seized the temple in preparation for the Kingdom, a line subsequently developed by Günther Bornkamm and Hans Conzelmann, now becomes downgraded to an uncertain "assumption." As for Jesus' death, Bultmann denies that it can be "understood as an inherent and necessary consequence of his activity; rather it took place because his activity was misconstrued as a political activity. In that case it would have been — historically speaking — a meaningless fate. We cannot tell whether or how Jesus found meaning in it. We may not veil from ourselves the possibility that he suffered a collapse." *HJKC,* pp. 23-24.

25. See *NTaM,* p. 35.

26. *Christ of Dogma,* p. 14.

to the historical figure of Jesus. If the New Testament sees the soteriological referent of JC-2 as JC-1, as liberal exegesis assumes, then the resultant problem myth poses for moderns can be resolved by reversing the relation: the soteriological referent of JC-1 is really JC-2. Only the historical Jesus, and not the mythical Messiah, is determinative for faith.

What Bultmann finds anomalous in this liberal reversal, constituting its christological paradigm, is the claim that soteriological significance can be "read off" or reconstructed from JC-2 as such. Even if the Gospels furnished sufficient data to recover the personality of Jesus, which form criticism disputes, historical reconstructions in the service of apologetics, precisely by basing faith on historical science, convert faith into its opposite, namely, a "work" of self-justification. Soteriologically speaking, therefore, JC-2 cannot be the real referent of JC-1. Thus, the liberal reversal fails to explain how the mythical-historical Jesus Christ, and a mythical-historical kerygma, can exercise saving significance in an age of science.

"Jesus Christ" as the Christus Praesens

Bultmann follows his teachers in accepting the characteristic liberal distinction between JC-1 and JC-2. Yet given the inability of the historian as historian to speak directly of God as God, or salvation as salvation, Bultmann refuses to discard myth once the historical strands in the tradition about Jesus are disentangled from it. Rather, Bultmann speaks of the "New Testament *and* Mythology" because he finds the saving import of Jesus Christ, or the significance of his eschatological destiny, permanently lodged in the mythology of the New Testament.[27]

Nevertheless, the modern shift to a scientific world picture means that the mythical language of the New Testament can no longer bear simple reiteration in church proclamation. It requires interpretation. In order to interpret myth one must understand what myth is and how it functions. Bultmann, drawing from the history of religions, sets forth in "New Testament and Mythology" a comprehensive definition of myth that becomes key to his understanding of the presence of Christ:

27. "It is not for the objectifying view of the historian that Jesus of Nazareth is the Logos of God. On the contrary, the very fact that in the New Testament the person and work of Christ are described in a mythological conceptuality shows that they cannot be understood in the context of world history if they are to be understood as a divine act of salvation." *NTaM*, p. 120. See also *JCaM*, p. 80.

The real point of myth is not to give an objective world picture; what is expressed in it, rather, is how we human beings understand ourselves in our world. Thus, myth does not want to be interpreted in cosmological terms but in anthropological terms — or, better, in existentialist terms. . . . What is expressed in myth is the faith that the familiar and disposable world in which we live does not have its ground and aim in itself but that its ground and limit lie beyond all that is familiar and disposable and that this is all constantly threatened and controlled by the uncanny powers that are its ground and limit. In unity with this[,] myth also gives expression to the knowledge that we are not lords of ourselves, that we are not only dependent within the familiar world but that we are especially dependent on the powers that hold sway beyond all that is familiar, and that it is precisely in dependence on them that we can become free from the familiar powers. Therefore, the motive for criticizing myth, that is, its objectifying representations, is present in myth itself, insofar as its real intention to talk about a transcendent power to which both we and the world are subject is hampered and obscured by the objectifying character of its assertions.[28]

On the basis of this comprehensive definition or general theory of myth, the following observations can be ventured:

First, myth expresses the self-understanding of those who employ it. Here we see a presupposition of form criticism, namely, that ancient texts about transcendent realities reflect the self-understanding of the authorial communities out of which they emerge. This assumption, present in Bultmann's theory of myth, also dovetails with Wilhelm Herrmann's theological dictum, "We cannot say of God how he is in himself but only what he does to us."[29] Thus, in Bultmann's judgment, "when Paul speaks of the

---

28. *NTaM*, pp. 9-10. See also pp. 42-43, n. 5, and 98-99; and *JCaM*, p. 19. In *NTaM*, p. 15, Bultmann acknowledges his indebtedness to Hans Jonas, *Gnosis und spätantiker Geist, Die mythologische Gnosis*, 2 vols. (Göttingen: Vandenhoeck & Ruprecht, 1934-64), vol. 1: *Die mythologische Gnosis, mit einer Einleitung zur Geschichte und Methodologie der Forschung, Forschungen zur Religion und Literatur des Alten und Neuen Testaments*, n.s. 33. For opposite assessments of the influence of Jonas' existentialist analysis of Gnosticism on Bultmann's program of demythologization, cf. Johnson, *Origins of Demythologizing*, pp. 114-26, who sees Bultmann's conceptual dependence, and Painter, *Theology as Hermeneutics*, pp. 140-42 and 146-47, who finds Jonas articulating what he learned from Bultmann.

29. For Bultmann's citations and allusions to this dictum by Herrmann, see *NTaM*, p. 99 (cf. p. 115); *FaU* 1:63; "The Question of 'Dialectic' Theology: A Discussion with Erik Peterson," in *BDT* 1:269; pub. in Ger. as "Die Frage der 'dialektischen' Theologie: Ein Auseinandersetzung mit Peterson," in *AdT* 2:87; and *JCaM*, pp. 43 and 73.

resurrection of the dead, it is clear that he means to speak of *us*, of our reality, of our existence, of a reality in which *we* stand [cf. 1 Cor. 15:1]."[30]

Second, myth expresses what Heidegger's existential analytic of *Dasein* also reveals, namely, the situation of human beings as those whose finitude poses the question or possibility of "authentic existence." Myth, in its particular concrete formulations of this possibility, understands human beings as poised between freedom and bondage, that is, freedom from or bondage to other finite or penultimate powers that falsely require our ultimate allegiance.[31]

Third, myth is not simply a Feuerbach-like projection of human virtues, powers, and values on the sacred canopy of transcendence. While Bultmann rejects the notion that myth has an objective referent divorced from the self, he does not accept the view that myth speaks only of the self. Myth is not simply language for subjective states. Myth also speaks of the ultimate power that mysteriously surrounds life on every side, thereby forcing the question and possibility of authentic existence. Thus, while myth reflects the human hankering for transcendence, Bultmann's theory of myth does not regard this hunger reductionistically as its own referent. Myth, often unsatisfactorily to be sure, points to the transcendent "ground and limit" of this human yearning.[32]

Fourth, the theological error of myth is not that it speaks of transcendence or of divine revelation, but that it does so in an "objectivized" way. Bultmann holds that God cannot be an object of human devotion or inquiry in the manner otherwise appropriate for an observable phenomenon:

> It is the essence of God not to be encompassed, because God encompasses everything else. God does not stand still, so to speak, for seeing, because even in human seeing it is God who sees, provided God is omnipotent. God is not at the disposal of a seeing that is outside of God, for there is no outside of God. Thus, seeing God cannot be objective.[33]

In turning God into a phenomenal or empirical object of thought, myth reifies God and brazenly trespasses upon transcendence by depicting God as visible, accessible, or controllable in the manner of an idol.

---

30. *FaU* 1:81. See also *Exegetica*, p. 481: "Paul thanks God who gives *us* the victory" (1 Cor. 15:57)."

31. See Macquarrie, *An Existentialist Theology*, pp. 67-78 and 204-9.

32. See *NTaM*, pp. 31, 110 and *JCaM*, pp. 70-71.

33. *NTaM*, p. 49.

Yet the "objectification" of God by myth is not overcome by liberalism's replacement of the mythical Messiah or JC-1 with the scientifically reconstructed "historical Jesus" or JC-2. Liberal theology, in speaking assuredly of the revelation of God in the visible and demonstrably incomparable personality of the historical Jesus, only substitutes scientific objectifications for mythical ones — but objectifications nevertheless.[34]

Given these considerations, when Bultmann applies an existentialist interpretation of myth to the New Testament, the referent of JC-1 becomes reoriented away from JC-2 to the "Beyond," that is, to the nonobjectifiable transcendent God *in relation* to the human possibility of authentic existence. The mythically couched confession of salvation through Jesus Christ refers, in the end — neither to the preexistent or imminent Messiah nor to the historical Jesus, but rather — to him "in whom God acts in the present" — *for us*.[35] Thus, soteriologically speaking, the real referent of JC-1 is JC-3, the *Christus praesens*.

This conclusion is confirmed by Bultmann's existentialist interpretation of Paul's kerygma of the cross-resurrection and of John's theme of the incarnation of the *Logos*. We now return to these motifs, previously discussed under Bultmann's exegesis, to grasp more fully his own "imaginative construal" of the presence of Christ.

Cross-resurrection

Bultmann presents the crucifixion of Jesus as a historical event to which Paul's apocalyptic mythology attaches a transcendent significance. When Paul writes of "Jesus Christ and him crucified" before whom "the rulers of this age . . . are doomed to pass away" (1 Cor. 2:6-8; cf. Col. 2:13-15), Bultmann sees "the historical event of the cross [*das historische Ereignis des Kreuzes*] . . . raised to cosmic dimensions."[36] Here is a specific instance of

34. See *FaU* 1:33-40.

35. *NTaM*, p. 41. ET slightly altered. Cf. "NTuM," in *KuM* 1:52. In "Zu Schniewinds Thesen," in *KuM* 1:136, Bultmann amends the phrase *"der, in dem Gott gegenwärtig handelt"* by inserting *"sc. an uns"* [i.e., for us] after the adverb *gegenwärtig*. In this way, Bultmann emphasizes the soteriological correlation of theology and anthropology in the event of Jesus Christ.

36. *NTaM*, p. 34. Cf. "NTuM," in *KuM* 1:45. See also "Johannes 6:60-69: Echtes Bekenntnis [1935]," in Bultmann, *Das verkündigte Wort: Predigten, Andachten, Ansprachen, 1906-1941,* ed. Martin Evang and (with an Introduction by) Erich Grässer (Tübingen:

that "intertwining" of the historical and the mythical that Bultmann finds so typical of the New Testament kerygma.

In Bultmann's view this "raising" of the crucifixion of Jesus to the cosmic plane is really Paul's way of conveying the permanent significance of the cross for human existence. When Paul speaks of the judgment "of the rulers of this age" wrought in the cross of Christ, "this means that what takes place in the cross is the judgment against us ourselves, as those who have fallen under the powers of the 'world'." Thus, "to believe in the cross of Christ" does not mean to accept Paul's mythological formulation as such. Rather, in accord with its deeper intention, "to believe in the cross of Christ means to accept the cross as one's own and to allow oneself to be crucified with Christ" (Gal. 2:19-20; 5:24; and 6:14). This means "overcoming fear of suffering and flight from it and carrying out one's freedom from the world by accepting suffering."[37]

As Bultmann proclaims from his Marburg pulpit in the spring of 1943,

> Only the one who is ready to enter with Jesus into the hour of God-forsakenness on the cross, will also share in the life of the Risen One. To share in the cross of Jesus, however, means to surrender our wishes and plans to the will of God, so that we place under the cross all that concerns us, both our hopes and our work. This means that we enter the ultimate solitude before God, and, as Paul says, that we decree the sentence of death on ourselves, so that we put our trust not in ourselves but in God who raises the dead (2 Cor. 1:9).[38]

As this sermonic excerpt shows, Bultmann's own "word of the cross" existentializes Paul's apocalyptic formulations in order that they be heard anew as "the word of life."

J. C. B. Mohr [Paul Siebeck], 1984), p. 282; and *Marburger Predigten*, p. 198: "For Paul, the cross of Christ is not only a historical event [*ein historisches Ereignis*] of the past, but an event which, begun in Christ, pierces [*durchdringt*] all of human history [*Geschichte*]."

37. *NTaM*, pp. 34-36. Cf. "NTuM," in *KuM* 1:45-47. Here "the world" is "this world [*ho kosmos houtos*]" "of transience and of death," "the sphere that we suppose we can dispose of in order to achieve security." This attitude ironically makes us dependent on "what is visible and disposable," and, hence, subjects our present existence to the power of death. See pp. 15-17.

38. *Marburger Predigten*, p. 175. See also "Faith in God the Creator [1934]," in *EaF*, pp. 180-81; pub. in Ger. as "1. Korinther 8:4–6: Der Glaube an Gott den Schöpfer," in *Das verkündigte Wort*, pp. 271-72.

This existentialist interpretation fastens upon Paul's representation of the cross "as the eschatological event." By "eschatological event," Bultmann means neither "an event of the past to which one looks back," that is, a historical event [*historisches Ereignis*], nor a future apocalyptic occurrence, but an "event in time and beyond time insofar as it is constantly present [*stets Gegenwart ist*] wherever it is understood in its significance, that is, for faith." Hence, the saving work of the cross of Jesus Christ does not reach us through the public percolation of its effects down through the centuries or by anticipating its universal manifestation in the future. Rather, this saving work breaks in upon us "in time" from "beyond time" as faith accepts here and now God's judgment on the world in solidarity with Christ's sufferings.[39]

In regard to the resurrection of Christ, Bultmann denies its status as "an objective historical fact" guaranteed by eyewitnesses.[40] Moreover, the resurrection of Christ is not a discrete, historical event following upon the cross, and which, in turn, will be followed by the *parousia's* inauguration of the "closing scene of history [*Schlussgeschichte*]."[41] According to Bultmann, these views of Paul in 1 Corinthians 15 must be given up for three reasons. First, from the standpoint of a scientific *Weltbild,* the resurrection as the account of "a dead person's returning to life in this world . . . is incredible."[42] Second, "the resurrection cannot be established as an objective fact by ever so many witnesses, so that it could be unhesitatingly believed in."[43] Thus, and third, the resurrection of Christ is purely the "eschatological fact" and "event" known only to faith; that is, the power of life, or freedom from the world, rendered for existence by the word of the cross.[44]

---

39. *NTaM*, pp. 34-35. Cf. "NTuM," in *KuM* 1:46. See also *Marburger Predigten,* p. 198: "This dying of Christ [cf. 2 Cor. 4:10] occurs, above all, where a human being understands that his or her suffering should serve in bringing to consciousness the provisional character and ultimate nothingness of this earthly world."

40. *NTaM*, pp. 37-38 and *FaU* 1:83.

41. *FaU* 1:80-81. Cf. *GuV* 1:51-52. See also *NTaM*, p. 9. The term *Schlussgeschichte* is taken by Bultmann from Karl Barth, *Die Auferstehung der Toten: Eine akademische Vorlesung über 1. Kor. 15* (München: Chr. Kaiser, 1924).

42. *NTaM*, p. 37. Cf. "NTuM," in *KuM* 1:49. Note a slight, but significant, misprint in the ET. Schubert M. Ogden to James F. Kay, 14 November 1989.

43. *NTaM*, pp. 37-38. All the historian can demonstrate is that some people believed Jesus rose from the dead. While this *belief* is a historical fact, the historian cannot demonstrate the belief to be true. See pp. 39-40. See also "The Case for Demythologizing: A Reply [1954]," in *KaM* 2:190-91; and *GuV* 3:204.

44. *NTaM*, p. 38. Paul contradicts the resurrection as the eschatological fact when

The proclaimed kerygma, therefore, is not only the *occasion* for the decision as to faith, but it conveys the *condition* for faith because it is itself "the eschatological event," or Jesus Christ, "constantly present" in and through its very proclamation.[45] Thus, "according to the New Testament, Jesus Christ is the eschatological event, the action of God by which God has set an end to the old world. In the preaching of the Christian Church the eschatological event will ever again become present and does become present ever and again in faith."[46] In other words, "Christ, the Crucified and Risen One, encounters us in the word of proclamation — nowhere else. And faith in this word is in truth the faith of Easter."[47] As Bultmann reiterates in 1960, "the Easter faith . . . consists in the belief that Jesus Christ is present in the kerygma [*dass im Kerygma Jesus Christus präsent ist*]"; and "to believe in the Christ present in the kerygma [*an den in Kerygma präsenten Christus glauben*] is the meaning of the Easter faith."[48] Bultmann thus transposes the mythical-historical account of Jesus' destiny (JC-1 + JC-2) into an eschatological-existentialist account of the Christ who is present in the word of the church (JC-3).[49]

In Bultmann's view, then, we neither await nor expect the *parousia* of Jesus Christ as a God-directed future event which will bring down the curtain on human history. The career of Jesus Christ is essentially finished.

---

he tries to adduce a historical proof on its behalf in 1 Cor. 15:3-8. Bultmann terms Paul's argument "fatal" and consequently declares, "I cannot accept 1 Cor. 15:3-8 as kerygma." See *NTaM*, p. 37 and "Reply to Schniewind," in *KaM* 1:112.

45. Cf. Bultmann's previously cited definition of "the eschatological event" as one "in time and beyond time insofar as it is constantly present wherever it is understood in its significance, that is, for faith," *NTaM*, pp. 34-35, with his speaking of *"Das eschatologische Geschehen, das Christus ist,"* in "PdE," in *KuM* 2:206, and *"Das eschatologische Ereignis, das Jesus Christus ist,"* in *GuV* 4:186. Thus, "the fullness of time," by which Paul marks God's sending of his Son into the world (Gal. 4:4), is applied by Bultmann to the proclaiming of the kerygma (2 Cor. 6:2). See "Reply to Schniewind," in *KaM* 1:116. See also *GuV* 3:205.

46. *History and Eschatology,* p. 151, omitting italics.

47. "NTuM," in *KuM* 1:50, omitting italics. Moreover, in the context of this assertion, Bultmann appears to read Paul's reference to "the preaching of Christ" [*hrēma tou Christou*] in Rom. 10:17 as a subjective genitive, thereby stressing the agency of the Risen Lord in and through the proclaimed word. See p. 51.

48. "The Primitive Christian Kerygma and the Historical Jesus," in *HJKC*, p. 42. Cf. *Exegetica*, p. 469.

49. "Where and how is Christ encountered? . . . In the word of the church addressed to me, in which he becomes present [*in dem er präsent wird*]." *GuV* 4:198.

The future will bring forth nothing new from Jesus Christ for human salvation beyond his continuing presence and activity in the occasion of proclamation. This raises the question, posed by some critics, whether Bultmann's "presentist" version of "the eschatological event" deflates Christian hope by eliminating the expectation of the yet-outstanding, manifest triumph of God over all that continues to resist the will and way of Jesus Christ.

In response, Bultmann claims that this very transposition of the kerygma's ultimate referent is authorized by Paul himself in 2 Corinthians:

> With the judging and liberating death of Christ, God has also established [*ist auch eingesetzt worden*] the "ministry of reconciliation" or the "word of reconciliation" (2 Cor. 5:18-19). It is this word that is "added" to the cross and makes it understandable as the salvation occurrence by demanding faith, putting to each of us the question whether we are willing to understand ourselves as crucified with Christ and as thereby also risen with him [cf. Gal. 2:19-20; 5:24; and 6:14]. In the sounding forth of the word, cross and resurrection become present [*werden Gegenwart*] and the eschatological now takes place. The eschatological promise of Isa. 49:8 is fulfilled: "Behold, now is the acceptable time! Behold, now is the day of salvation!" (2 Cor. 6:2).[50]

Thus, 2 Corinthians points to Paul's own breakout from the mythical-historical constraints of 1 Corinthians 15, a breakout authorizing Bultmann's own.[51] In this way, Bultmann argues that, even for Paul, the real referent of the Christ myth is not the imminent, apocalyptic Messiah, but the *Christus praesens,* or "he in whom God acts for us in the present."[52]

Bultmann's transposition of the resurrection from a mythical-historical event of the past to an eschatological-existential event in the present

50. *NTaM,* p. 40. Cf. "NTuM," in *KuM* 1:51. Exclamation marks added to accord with Ger. The term "added" [*hinzukommt*] appears in quotation marks to indicate an allusion to Luther, who often says "God's word is added and enables us to understand the particular moment in its light." *NTaM,* p. 119. Cf. "PdE," in *KuM* 2:204.

51. Cf. *FaU* 1:242, n. 17: "In my judgment, it is clear that Paul in 1 Cor. 15 (esp. vv. 20-8 and 44-9) is endeavouring to express the idea that the resurrection of Jesus is not an isolated objective fact of the past. He is trying, with the help of the cosmological myth of the Gnostics, to express the contemporaneousness of the fact of salvation. Exegesis therefore may not stop at the reproduction of the mythical presentation but must seek to penetrate to the real purpose of the writer. *In this case it must let itself be guided by the explanations in 2 Cor. 2:14–6:10.*" My italics.

52. "Zu Schniewinds Thesen," in "NTuM," in *KuM* 1:136. Cf. *NTaM,* p. 41.

also effects a corollary transposition in the way one conceptualizes the unity between the cross and the resurrection. Soteriologically speaking, their unity is not a sequential one between two proximate historical events of the past, but the simultaneous unity of a historical event (the cross) with its contemporary existential significance (the resurrection). That is to say, the proclamation of God's act in Christ's cross is itself God's act, insofar as it places before us, here and now, the offer of salvation.[53]

In this regard, we noted in chapter two that Bultmann's exegesis of 2 Corinthians 5:18-19(-20; 6:2) accounts for this unity between God's deed and word of reconciliation in terms of their "simultaneous institution."[54] Yet we also questioned whether Bultmann's exegesis could support the weight of this claim. In "New Testament and Mythology," Bultmann does not use the adverb *zugleich* to indicate that the divine actions specified in 2 Corinthians 5:18-19 occur "simultaneously."[55] Nevertheless, by respectively identifying God's deed and word with the cross and resurrection, Bultmann does suggest in this essay why the unity between God's deed and word is one of simultaneity. For Bultmann, sequentiality pertains only to temporal events. By contrast, the resurrection is the eschatological event, and, hence, as God's word revealing the significance of the cross, the eternal and transcendent condition for salvation. As Bultmann states in his reply to Schniewind, "What happened on the cross and at Easter are two very different things only under the aspect [*sub specie*] of human temporality, but not as an eschatological event."[56] As such, this event is present when and where God so wills. God so wills the event of Christ's resurrection when and where the church proclaims God's judging and liberating deed in Christ's cross. In this sense, the resurrection does not follow upon the cross, but accompanies it, effects it, and *is* it, insofar as the cross carries significance for salvation.

A close reading of "New Testament and Mythology" also reveals that the simultaneous unity Bultmann ascribes to the cross and resurrection in Paul is actually reached by way of John:

<hr/>

53. Bultmann to Barth, 11-15 November 1952, in *Letters,* p. 93.

54. See *GuV* 1:260 and 289, *TWNT,* s.v. "*pisteuō* [etc.]," *Das Urchristentum,* p. 224, and *TdNT,* pp. 61, 297, and 303, where Bultmann in each case uses the adverb *zugleich* to indicate that the divine actions specified in 2 Cor. 5:18-19 are to be taken as occurring simultaneously.

55. Cf. "NTuM," in *KuM* 1:51. In what I am terming the "more theological" writings of Bultmann, the locution "*zugleich eingesetzt hat*" does appear in *GuV* 3:124.

56. "Zu Schniewinds Thesen," in *KuM* 1:144.

Thus, it is not as though the cross could be seen in itself as Jesus' death and defeat, upon which, then, the resurrection ensued, nullifying his death. He who suffers death is already the Son of God, and his death itself is already the overcoming of death's power. This finds its strongest expression in John when he presents Jesus' passion as the "hour" of his "glorification," and thus understands his "being lifted up" in a double sense, as his being lifted up on the cross and as his exaltation to glory.[57]

In the context of this comment on John, Bultmann also cites Romans 4:25 ("who was put to death for our trespasses and raised for our justification"). By juxtaposing this citation from Paul with his comment on John, Bultmann suggests strongly that the relation between the cross and resurrection specified in Romans 4:25 is one of simultaneity rather than sequentiality. In the absence of sufficient exegetical reasons why the divine acts specified in 2 Corinthians 5:18-19 should not be seen as sequential, we may properly conclude that Bultmann reads this key Pauline text, as he does Romans 4:25, "intratextually" through the "simultaneous" lenses of John.[58] Thus, Bultmann appropriates Paul — on Johannine grounds — to translate the mythical concept of Christ's resurrection into faith's acknowledgment that God has established, through Christ's death and for all time, the saving word of reconciliation.

Bultmann's construal of the cross-resurrection event, in terms of God's simultaneous institution of the deed and word of reconciliation, dismayed Karl Barth:

> Apparently the kerygma must suppress or even deny the fact that the cross and resurrection of Jesus Christ, the total Christ event, is the event of our redemption, that it possessed an intrinsic significance of its own, and that only because it has that primary significance has it a derived significance here and now. Yet this event is the ground of our faith and of the kerygma, and faith and kerygma are only secondary to it and derivative from it. . . . All this would, it seems, have to go by the board if we demythologized the New Testament à la Bultmann.[59]

---

57. *NTaM*, pp. 36-37. See also *TNT* 2:56 and *GuV* 3:205.

58. Hence, Schniewind's criticism of "NTaM" that "John only appears as a satellite of Paul" is true only in the formal sense. "Antwort an Bultmann," in *KuM* 1:104. Materially, John is decisive for Bultmann's hermeneutics and theology as Barth ventures to suggest in "Bultmann — An Attempt to Understand Him," in *KaM* 2:120.

59. "Bultmann — An Attempt to Understand Him," in *KaM* 2:110. While Barth

From Barth's standpoint, Bultmann erases the chronological and, hence, ontic priority of Christ to the kerygma. Thereby erased as well is the objective *extra nos* that is "the ground of our faith and the kerygma" itself.

In the wake of Barth's criticism, Bultmann concedes "that in the NT the cross of Christ is described as an *intrinsically* significant event which *then* may and can become significant for faith too." Nevertheless, from Bultmann's vantage point, the issue cannot be resolved by "arguments that simply play off the statements of the NT against me. The question is always that of their interpretation." Hence, to the degree that the formulations of the New Testament (and of Barth) retain the sequential, "'then and therefore'" relation between the events of salvation, they remain at the level of mythical-historical thinking. Moreover, for Bultmann, no event possesses "intrinsic" significance but only acquires significance in relation to human existence. The issue, then, is how Jesus Christ, in his cross and resurrection, relates to human existence as the salvation event. Does he do so through a sequence of events reaching us from the past or by encountering us "from the end of time" as the word is proclaimed "in time"?[60]

Certainly, as a past historical event, the crucifixion of Jesus is chronologically prior to the kerygma. This is not in dispute. Nevertheless, for Bultmann, there is no way "to establish *first* that Christ's crucifixion is the saving event and *then* to believe (for that would mean seeing Jesus as Christ *before* believing him to be so)." Rather, "the crucifixion can be seen as the saving event (and Jesus as Christ) only *in* faith." Again, the emergence of belief in the resurrection of Jesus is a historical event that follows upon his crucifixion. Nevertheless, to acknowledge the emergence of this belief is not the same as believing that Jesus is risen. Thus, the significance of the cross and the resurrection for salvation does not derive from their location on a time-line between the birth of Jesus and subsequent Christian proclamation. Rather, the cross-resurrection, as the indivisible eschatological salvation event, is "always present (in proclamation)."[61]

To say with Bultmann that God simultaneously instituted the deed and word of reconciliation is to declare that there has never been a Jesus

---

can speak in the singular of the cross and resurrection of Jesus Christ as "the total Christ event," the context of his comment clearly shows that he regards the cross and resurrection of Jesus Christ soteriologically as two discrete events "in space and time" each of which chronologically precedes the kerygma *ad seriatim.* See pp. 101 and 109-10.

60. Bultmann to Barth, 11-15 November 1952, in *Letters,* pp. 93-94 and 97.
61. Ibid., p. 94.

Christ, who is soteriologically determinative, apart from the word or message of the cross. Here is the paradox of faith; namely, that in and through the temporal event of preaching, the eschatological event of salvation in Christ is occurring. Hence Bultmann's reply to Barth: "I would rather not say, then, that there is a 'Therefore' but instead a 'Therein.' "[62] By so transposing the relation of God's deed and word of reconciliation from a sequential to a simultaneous occurrence, Bultmann's appeal to 2 Corinthians 5 and 6 aims to honor the eschatological reality both of Christ and of faith, and, hence, of the *Christus praesens*.

Incarnation

Bultmann extends his existentialist interpretation of the cross-resurrection kerygma in Paul to the very theme of the Fourth Gospel: "the Word became flesh" (1:14).[63] As indicated in chapter three, Bultmann regards the incarnation of the *Logos* in Jesus to be a variant of the Gnostic Redeemer myth.[64] As such, this claim is as incredible to the modern scientific *Weltbild* as is Paul's mythology of the cross and resurrection.[65] As Bultmann writes in response to Karl Barth's rebuking paraphrases of John 1:14 and 1 John 1:1, "The statement that the first disciples beheld the 'glory' of the incarnate Word in a resurrection from the dead in time and space, that they saw this with their eyes, heard it with their ears, and touched it with their hands, I regard as sheer mythology."[66] Moreover, this "sheer mythology" becomes entwined with mere history whenever the incarnation is "conceived of as a miracle that happened about 1950 years ago," in other words, as "an objective event in a remote past."[67] By formulating the incarnation in these mythical-historical terms, the traditional doctrine falsely objectifies the *Logos,* both as a metaphysical entity and as a historical fact.[68] Hence, the doctrine er-

---

62. Ibid., p. 97.

63. See *NTaM*, p. 42.

64. See *TNT* 2:12-14 and *JCaM*, p. 17.

65. See *NTaM*, pp. 2-3.

66. Bultmann to Barth, 11-15 November 1952, in *Letters*, p. 97. Bultmann later wrote of 1 John 1:1, "It can now only with difficulty be said whether or to what extent the author understands the incarnation of Jesus Christ mythologically, or whether he interprets the mythological assertion on the basis of the idea of revelation, as does the Gospel of John." *JE*, p. 39.

67. "The Case for Demythologizing," in *KaM* 2:191-92. See also *GuV* 3:205.

68. From Bultmann's analysis of "The Christological Confession of the World Council of Churches," we can safely infer that he would judge not only "God and Savior"

roneously suggests that the object of faith can be known outside of faith either as an eternal truth or as a public piece of the past, rather than as the eschatological salvation event known only in faith.

Nevertheless, just as Paul in 2 Corinthians 5:18–6:2 demythologizes the mythical-historical Christology he advances in 1 Corinthians 15:3-8, so the Gospel of John may be said to demythologize its own Gnostic theme of the incarnate *Logos*. As we discovered in chapter three, John's demarcation from Gnosticism proceeds by stressing both the singularity of Jesus of Nazareth, "a definite human being in history,"[69] and the inseparable identity of this person with the word or message he bears. In the Fourth Gospel, Jesus is the revelation he reveals, the *Logos* or Word of God he speaks: "His words are utterances about himself; for his word is identical with himself [*denn sein Wort ist er selbst*]."[70] The Word of God does not expire with the departure of the earthly Jesus, but continues in the witness of the church through the power of the paracletic Spirit.[71] Thus, the referent of the Gnostic title *Logos* is transposed, from a mythological entity alongside God enfleshed in the historical Jesus, to "the Word of the Christian proclamation."[72] Soteriologically, then, the demythologized *Logos* no longer refers to the mythical-historical Jesus Christ (JC-1 + JC-2), but to the eschatological *Christus praesens* of existential encounter (JC-3).

---

to be "false" when applied to Jesus, but also *"Logos,"* insofar as any of these titles are taken to refer to "an entity which can be objectivized, whether it is understood in an Arian or Nicene, an Orthodox or Liberal sense." Likewise, he would judge any or all of these titles "true," insofar as they refer to "the event of God's acting." *EPT,* p. 287. Hence, as Painter points out, "Christology is a way of speaking about God acting"; and "the [christological] titles are confessions of faith in Jesus as God's act." *Theology as Hermeneutics,* pp. 189-90.

69. *TNT* 2:41, omitting italics. See also 2:69 and *JG,* pp. 64-65.

70. *TNT* 2:63, omitting italics. Cf. *TdNT,* p. 410. See also "NTaM," in *NTaM,* p. 13.

71. See *JG,* pp. 554, 559, n. 1, and 560. Outside of *JG* and *TNT,* Bultmann's allusions to the Spirit are perfunctory. One exception to this pattern is the 1926 essay "The Question of 'Dialectic' Theology," in *BDT* 1:257-74. Here Bultmann assigns to the Holy Spirit the role in actualizing revelation he elsewhere attributes to the *Christus praesens.* In "The Primitive Christian Kerygma and the Historical Jesus," Bultmann distinguishes the Holy Spirit and the presence of Christ in such a way as to recall his interpretation in *JG:* The church takes the place of the earthly Jesus by incarnating in its preaching the occasion for revelation. The Spirit takes Jesus' place in effecting through this occasion the eschatological condition for salvation. In this way, the paradox which is Jesus Christ, the eschatological event in history or the Word of God in human form, continues in the coincident witness of the church and the Spirit. See *HJKC,* pp. 41-42.

72. *FaU* 1:310. See also Bultmann, "In eigener Sache [1957]," in *GuV* 3:189.

Bultmann's transposition of the referent of the *Logos*, as faithful to John's own intention, led Barth to charge, "Docetism!"[73] But this is to miss Bultmann's point. Bultmann does not deny the incarnation of the Word of God. As he later declared to Käsemann, "Without corporeality [*Verleiblichung*] there is not an eschatological occurrence in history."[74] God's Word of judgment and grace once enfleshed in the earthly Jesus is now enfleshed in and through the preaching of the church (John 5:24-25): "The eschatological occurrence is seen in Jesus' coming as the Word, the Word of God that becomes present here and now in the proclaimed word [*im verkündigten Worte jeweils Gegenwart wird*]."[75] Thus, the incarnation does not refer, for Bultmann, to the historical Jesus, as "a datable event of the past,"[76] but to "Jesus as the Christ, as eschatological phenomenon,"[77] whose Word is continually enfleshed as "an ever new event in the event of proclamation."[78] The paradox of faith is that "a human being like myself thus speaks God's Word to me; the *Logos* of God incarnates Himself in him or her."[79] Thus, in and through preaching, Jesus Christ is manifested as the acting agent of salvation.[80]

73. "I am most embarrassed: much as I am loath to charge Bultmann with heresy, I cannot deny that his demythologized New Testament looks suspiciously like docetism." "Bultmann — An Attempt to Understand Him," in *KaM* 2:111. Since Barth, "Docetism" has become a standard shibboleth in polemics against Bultmann. See, e.g., G. Ernest Wright, *God Who Acts: Biblical Theology as Recital*, Studies in Biblical Theology, no. 8 (London: SCM, 1952), pp. 126-27; Ritschl, *Memory and Hope*, pp. 45-57; and J. Christiaan Beker, *Paul the Apostle: The Triumph of God in Life and Thought*, 1st pb. ed. (Philadelphia: Fortress, 1984), p. 155. James H. Cone, in *God of the Oppressed* (New York: Seabury Press, 1975), p. 117, manages to apply the label to Bultmann *and* Barth.

74. *GuV* 4:198.

75. *NTaM*, p. 120. ET slightly altered. Cf. "PdE," in *KuM* 2:205.

76. *NTaM*, p. 130, n. 58.

77. "Zu Schniewinds Thesen," in *KuM* 1:148. See also *NTaM*, p. 40.

78. *NTaM*, p. 130, n. 58. "My interest does not address itself to a 'Life of Jesus,' but to the living message in which the *sarx genomenos* [becoming flesh] is encountered." *GuV* 3:187. See also Bultmann, "General Truths and Christian Proclamation," in *History and Hermeneutic*, p. 154.

79. "PdE," in *KuM* 2:206, n. 1. "The 'demythologized' sense of the Christian doctrine of incarnation, of the word that 'was made flesh' is precisely this, that God manifests himself not merely as the idea of God . . . but as 'my' God, who speaks to me here and now, through a human mouth." "The Case for Demythologizing," in *KaM* 2:193. See also "Preaching: Genuine and Secularized," in *Religion and Culture*, p. 237.

80. See Bultmann's Introduction to *What Is Christianity?*, by Adolf von Harnack, p. xvi; "Preaching: Genuine and Secularized," in *Religion and Culture*, pp. 240 and 242; "General Truths and Christian Proclamation," in *History and Hermeneutic*, p. 155; and "The Primitive Christian Kerygma and the Historical Jesus," in *HJKC*, pp. 30 and 42.

By transposing the doctrine of the incarnation from a claim about the mythical-historical Jesus Christ to that of the eschatological *Christus praesens* of existential encounter, Bultmann is saying that, "now" or soteriologically, the only manifestation of the Word of God is the proclamation of the gospel. The saving significance of Jesus Christ is not grounded in the incarnation, understood as a mythical-historical event, anymore than it is grounded in the cross and resurrection, when similarly understood. Rather, according to Bultmann's existentialist interpretation, the saving significance of Jesus Christ becomes incarnate only in and through the word proclaimed and heard in faith.

For Barth this transposition of the incarnation into an event of the present means that "the real life of Jesus Christ is confined to the kerygma and to faith."[81] Yet, we may ask on Bultmann's behalf, where else is "the real life of Jesus Christ" to be found? As Bultmann replies to Barth, "Christ (insofar as he affects us) is the kerygma, because he is the Christ only as the Christ *pro me,* and as such he encounters me only in the kerygma."[82] Thus, Jesus Christ is enfleshed for faith only when proclaimed. To seek the incarnation elsewhere is the real Docetism to which Bultmann stands opposed.

Jesus Christ as God's Speech Act

In speaking of Jesus Christ as "he in whom God acts in the present," the conclusion of "New Testament and Mythology" inextricably ties Bultmann's understanding of the *Christus praesens* to that of an "act of God," a term that occurs more than a dozen times in this treatise.[83] Moreover, the link between God's act and Christ's presence is reinforced when Bultmann locates this act "in Christ," identifies it with Jesus' "person," and, by appealing to 2 Corinthians 5:19 and 21, speaks of it not only in the past, but in the present tense. By way of apposition, Bultmann also indicates God's act to be synonymous with "the Christ occurrence [*Das Christusgeschehen*]," "the love of God revealed in Christ," and "the self-

---

81. "Bultmann — An Attempt to Understand Him," in *KaM* 2:101.
82. Bultmann to Barth, 11-15 November 1952, in Barth, *Gesamtausgabe* 5:1:178.
83. See, e.g., *"Handeln Gottes,"* pp. 26 and 27; *"Gottes Handeln,"* p. 52; *"Gottes Tun,"* pp. 43 and 52; *"Tun Gottes,"* p. 43; and, *"Tat Gottes,"* pp. 28, 38, 39, 43, and 51. All in "NTuM," in *KuM* 1.

manifestation of the Risen One [*Selbstbekundung des Auferstandenen*]."
Speaking soteriologically, Bultmann characterizes this act as "decisive,"
"redeeming," "liberating," "saving [*Heilstat Gottes*]," and "eschatological."[84]

Responding to critics of "New Testament and Mythology," Bultmann in his 1952 essay "On the Problem of Demythologizing" devotes
the last third of his discussion to "Talk about the Act of God." Here he
again locates this act "in Christ," and, again, speaks of it both in the
past and, more frequently, in the present tense, and notes its futurity as
well. By way of apposition, Bultmann indicates God's act to be synonymous with "a wonder," "the eschatological occurrence . . . that is Christ
[*Das eschatologische Geschehen, das Christus ist*],"and, the "person and
work of Christ [*Gestalt und Werk Christi*]." Bultmann can also substitute
the noun "grace" for that of "God" as the subject of the verb "to act."
Bultmann again characterizes this act as "saving [*göttliche Heilstat*]," but
now, accenting its nonobjectifiable character, further describes it as "un-
worldly," "transcendent," and, more frequently, as "hidden." Importantly,
"God's acting" is also indicated, by way of apposition, to be synonymous
with "God's speaking." Indeed, Bultmann further specifies this speaking
by God, that is simultaneously God's act, as the "event of being addressed,
questioned, judged and blessed by God here and now." Summarizing
Bultmann's discussion, we can say that Jesus Christ is God's "speech
act."[85]

Bultmann accepts as axiomatic that only God can save humanity
and that God acts to do so in the event of deed and word called Jesus
Christ. Nevertheless, as we have seen, Bultmann argues that God's action
in the world should no longer be construed or signified by "objectivized"
and univocal predications, whether of myth or of historical science. Hence,
when Bultmann speaks of the *Christus praesens* as the saving power of
Christian proclamation he is not referring to Jesus Christ as a mythical-

---

84. "NTuM," in *KuM* 1:26-28, 38-39, 42-43, and 51-52. See also *JCaM*, p. 73,
where God's action = God's revelation.

85. *NTaM*, pp. 110-23. Cf. "PdE," in *KuM* 2:196-208. See also *JCaM*, pp. 60-85.
Cf. *GuV* 4:172-89. Here is foreshadowed the subsequent theological transition from
Bultmann's "Christ event" (*Christusereignis, Christusgeschehen*) to Ernst Fuch's "language
event" (*Sprachereignis*) and Gerhard Ebeling's "word event" (*Wortgeschehen*). For an overview of this development, see Paul J. Achtemeier, *An Introduction to the New Hermeneutic*
(Philadelphia: Westminster, 1974). David James Randolph takes up its implications for
homiletics in *The Renewal of Preaching* (Philadelphia: Fortress, 1969).

historical character of the kerygma, a cultural artifact from the past; rather, he is referring to Jesus Christ as the living subject of the kerygma, the eschatological event of direct address.

Thus, when Bultmann speaks with Paul of a divine establishment of the deed and word of reconciliation (2 Cor. 5:18-19), he is not saying that the kerygma, in the sense of propositional formulations bequeathed by the past, has been raised into eschatological standing with Christ. If such were the case, that which pertains only to the temporal occasion of Christian revelation would be falsely regarded as its eternal condition, the perennial error of conceptual fundamentalism. The presence of Christ in the world would then be tantamount to mouthing dogmatic code words. Proclamation would be reduced to incantation. Personal summons would degenerate into mystagogical magic. Evangelical preaching would simply instance the *ex opere operato* of the Roman Mass. God would thereby become "objectified," a predicate of the preacher. To claim Jesus Christ as God's speech act is to say that God, in principle, has elected creaturely language, specifically, *Anrede* or direct address, to be the carrier or mode of Christ's saving presence in the world. It is not to say that any particular formulation of the significance of Jesus Christ is, as such, unsubstitutable, irreformable, or retrievable only by rote.

Nevertheless, because all formulations of the kerygma are temporal and not eternal, even the most responsible interpretations, including those of Bultmann himself, cannot guarantee a correspondence between human speech about God and speech from God.[86] Even formally "Christian" *Anrede* cannot secure its own material actuality as gospel. So what transforms the kerygma from mythical narrative, historical information, or doctrine *about* Jesus Christ — that is, mere artifact or dead letter — into the kerygma as the lively summons *from* Jesus Christ in which are encountered the demand and the promise of authentic existence? Bultmann answers:

86. "Certainly in the framework of theology, homiletics is necessary as a doctrine of preaching. However, no homiletics can transmit to an individual preacher a method which guarantees to him that his sermon will be genuine proclamation, any more than there can be a church order through which it is guaranteed that the Church in any particular historical form achieves its authentic meaning: to be the scene of the eschatological occurrence." Bultmann, "Reply," in Kegley, *Theology of Bultmann,* p. 277. See also "What Does It Mean to Speak of God? [1925]," in *FaU* 1:55; pub. in Ger. as "Welchen Sinn hat es, von Gott zu reden?," in *GuV* 1:28; *FaU* 1:298-99; and esp. "The Question of Dialectic Theology" in *BDT* 1:257-74.

Only Christ can give the kerygmatic character to everything which is "taught" as Christian. It is only Christ who transfigures the doctrine into kerygma. Therefore, Christ is correctly preached not where something is said *about* him, but only where he himself becomes the proclaimer.[87]

Jesus Christ, therefore, is not simply the object of discourse, but, rather, the essential agent of proclamation. Only his presence as the proclaimer enables a creaturely word to become kerygmatic. Christ himself, as the One in whom God acts, is the eschatological condition, the saving content, of the kerygmatic occasion.

Once again we see the transposition Bultmann makes in traditional Christian teaching. The resurrection or revelation of Jesus Christ is no longer regarded as a mythical-historical event of the past on the basis of which Christian witness becomes efficacious by its accurate portrayal of this event. Rather, for Bultmann, the efficacy of Christian witness *is* the resurrection or revelation of Jesus Christ. Yet in this transposition wrought by demythologization, Bultmann appeals to a miraculous, supernatural act by Christ who makes the ordinary language of witness extraordinarily efficacious. This raises the question whether Bultmann's understanding of preaching as the event of Christ's resurrection or revelation is not a form of "word magic." If Bultmann is opposed to supernatural interventionism, should this not extend to his account of the language of revelation itself?

In fact, Bultmann does attempt to explain the encounter between the believer and Christ in ways that anticipate discussions in Anglo-American analytic philosophy on such topics as "performative utterance" and "commissive self-involvement."[88] For his part, Bultmann begins with Herrmann's

---

87. Introduction to *What Is Christianity?*, by Adolf von Harnack, p. xvi. Cf. Yngve Brilioth's claim that the proclaimed "Lord of Scripture . . . is the one who gives to every text its interpretation and its address for every time and place; he is the one who gives to every text its eternal content." *A Brief History of Preaching*, trans. Karl E. Mattson (Philadelphia: Fortress, 1965), p. 10.

88. In this regard cf. *EaF,* pp. 58-60 and 86-87 with the following studies in analytic philosophy: J. L. Austin, "Performative Utterances [1956]," in *Philosophical Papers* (Oxford: Clarendon, 1961), pp. 220-39 and *How to Do Things with Words,* ed. J. O. Urmson (Cambridge, Mass.: Harvard University Press, 1962); Donald D. Evans, *The Logic of Self-Involvement: A Philosophical Study of Everyday Language with Special Reference to the Christian Use of Language about God as Creator* (London: SCM Press, 1963); and John R. Searle, *Speech Acts: An Essay in the Philosophy of Language* (Cambridge: Cambridge University Press, 1969).

insight that we can only speak of God's act in Christ in relation to ourselves. This is true not only because of the nonobjectifiable character of God as the Encompasser of every object, but also because of the nonobjectifiable character of our own existence.[89] Hence, "there is knowledge of God only as existential knowing."[90] This means that the objectivized language of science and mythology must give way, at least where authentic knowledge of God and the self are concerned, to existential language.[91]

Such language proceeds analogically on the model of the personal communion between one human being and another.[92] Specifically, Bultmann construes the presence of Christ as analogous to the encounter of an Addresser with an Addressee when and where the former says to the latter, "I love you."[93] The statement "I love you" is an existential statement in that it does not simply convey information but a self-involving declaration. In saying "I love you" the speaker does not discourse *about* love but *enacts* love concretely. This word of love *is* the love of which it speaks.

In chapter two, we noted Bultmann's description of the proclaimed kerygma as "personal address [*Anrede*], demand [*Forderung*], and promise [*Verheissung*]; it is the very act of divine grace."[94] The theme of the kerygma as promise is not developed by Bultmann, but his discussions of existential language do suggest its connections with promise-making. When the kerygma is heard as Christ saying, "I love you," then the kerygma functions as a personal promise, since "I love you" unreservedly commits the speaker to the hearer with regard to any possible future. As a promise, "I love you" also functions as a demand, insofar as it places the Addressee in a new situation, namely, of being the Beloved, which requires a response, whether positive or negative, that is determinative for self-understanding.[95] In Bultmann's view, such a response can only

89. *NTaM*, pp. 112-13.

90. *NTaM*, p. 50.

91. See *NTaM*, p. 101. Existential statements cannot be grasped "by rational thinking, neither by logical inference from the attitude of others nor by psychological analysis, nor even by existentialist analysis. Rather, I grasp them only in the existential openness of my person for encounter." *NTaM*, p. 105.

92. See *NTaM*, pp. 110-11 and *JCaM*, p. 68.

93. See *EaF,* p. 71; *NTaM*, pp. 114 and 116-17; *JCaM*, pp. 75-76; and *GuV* 4:198. For Bultmann's homiletical use of this analogy, see *Marburg Sermons,* pp. 34, 80-81, and 132.

94. *TNT* 1:319. Cf. *TdNT*, p. 319. See similarly *TNT* 1:302. Cf. *TdNT*, p. 301.

95. See *EaF,* pp. 58-60 and 86-87; *NTaM*, pp. 114 and 116-17; and *JCaM*, pp. 74-76. Cf. *Jesus and the Word,* pp. 202-3.

be made within the context of the Lover's self-declaration. The intention of the Addresser "cannot be observed by objective methods but only by personal experience and response."[96]

To acknowledge the kerygma as a promise is to say, in analytic terms, that it commits the speaker to doing something either by assuming an obligation or declaring an intention, what J. L. Austin calls a "commissive."[97] Words heard with commissive force "involve" an agent or subject. A promise, therefore, always entails its promisor. When the kerygma is heard as a promise of Christ, then it is heard as a promise from Christ himself (Rom 10:17; 2 Cor. 5:20; 13:3). Thus, the *Christus praesens* is logically entailed by the promissory character of his word.[98]

This is not to deny that Jesus Christ, as God's speech act, is always accompanied, mediated, and occasioned in and through ordinary language that is itself subject to the objective analyses of the social sciences. But this is precisely the scandal and "incognito" of the gospel: there is no Word of God without the word of the human herald. Whereas the psychologist or anthropologist, as such, only hears the sounds of solemn assemblies amid the patterns of culture, faith, nevertheless, hears the voice of "the good shepherd" (John 10). Ever hidden "in, with, and under" the visibility of the kerygmatic occasion, Jesus Christ is acknowledged by faith "only against appearances."[99]

This paradoxical understanding of the *Christus praesens* makes Bultmann's theology one of the cross rather than one of glory and places it in opposition to ecclesial or clerical triumphalism. At the same time, the presence of Jesus Christ, precisely in view of its paradoxical character, does not visibly appear to modify or affect in any way the conditions of the observable world. Such theological modesty accords well with the dominant scientific world picture of the Enlightenment. Yet critics of Bultmann claim that the paradoxical word presence of Christ excludes from the scope

---

96. *JCaM*, p. 72. See also *NTaM*, p. 114. Cf. *Jesus*, pp. 194-95: "For the event of forgiveness itself, as between individuals so also between an individual and God, eludes observation. There is not any forgiveness in an empty room, unrelated, so to speak; but it is only real in its relation to the specific individual. Therefore, only the one who is forgiven truly receives the event of forgiveness."

97. See *How to Do Things with Words*, esp. pp. 150-51 and 162.

98. Cf. John Calvin, "We enjoy Christ only as we embrace Christ clad in his own promises." *Calvin: Institutes of the Christian Religion*, trans. Ford Lewis Battles and ed. John T. McNeill, 2 vols., The Library of Christian Classics (Philadelphia: Westminster, 1960), 1:426 (II, ix, 3).

99. *NTaM*, p. 111. See also *JCaM*, p. 62. Cf. *Jesus and the Word*, pp. 178-79.

of salvation any evident sign of, or concern for, social or political trans-formation. Apparently, God acts in Christ only covertly. Faith thereby becomes a matter of private judgment rather than public concern.

To sum up our discussion, Jesus Christ, as God's speech act, addresses us individually, here and now, with God's Word of promise. From beyond all penultimate horizons of historical and cultural contexts comes the final Word that we are powerless to speak to ourselves: "Beloved, you are forgiven." This encounter of loving Addresser to beloved Addressee, occa-sioned by the proclamation of the kerygma, demands of its hearers an acceptance or rejection that is decisive for self-understanding. As the addressing "Thou," Jesus Christ speaks as the *Christus praesens,* that is, as "he in whom God acts for us in the present."[100]

According to Bultmann this speaking by God occurs whenever "the person and destiny of Jesus of Nazareth" are proclaimed "in their signifi-cance as history of salvation [*heilsgeschichtlichen Bedeutsamkeit*]."[101] Thus, before concluding this chapter we must consider the relation of God's speech act, the *Christus praesens* or JC-3, to Jesus of Nazareth or JC-2.

The Identity of the *Christus Praesens*

In "New Testament and Mythology," Bultmann identifies the *Christus praesens* when he declares that "he in whom God acts in the present [JC-3], through whom God has reconciled the world [JC-1], is a real historical person [*ein wirklicher historischer Mensch ist*]," that is, JC-2.[102] Likewise, when evaluating "The Christological Confession of the World Council of Churches" a decade later, Bultmann speaks of "the historical person of Jesus of Nazareth [*die historische Person Jesu von Nazareth*] as the eschato-logical event . . . which becomes present [*präsent wird*] in the proclaimed word at any given time"; and of "the paradox" of "the eschatological event as the occurrence of the Christian proclamation in which now the historical Jesus becomes present [*in der jetzt der historische Jesus präsent wird*]."[103] These respective statements of 1941 and 1951 indicate the identity of

100. See "Zu Schniewinds Thesen," *KuM* 1:136. Cf. *NTaM,* p. 41 and *Jesus and the Word,* pp. 202-3 and 206-8.

101. *NTaM,* p. 41. Cf. "NTuM," in *KuM* 1:52.

102. *NTaM,* p. 41. ET slightly altered. Cf. "NTuM," in *KuM* 1:52.

103. *GuV* 2:259-60. Cf. 4:197.

JC-3 as that of JC-2. If so, Bultmann appears to affirm that the *Christus praesens* is none other than the contemporary presence of Jesus of Nazareth.

The problem with these statements is that they stand in apparent contradiction to statements Bultmann makes elsewhere. For example, consider his emphatic declarations of 1948 to Schniewind:

> I am turning my back on all historical encounters [*allen geschichtlichen Begegnungen*] (along with the *Christos kata sarka* as well), and towards the unique encounter with the proclaimed Christ, who encounters me in the kerygma which concerns me in my historical [*geschichtlichen*] situation. . . . I still deny that historical research [*historische Forschung*] can ever encounter traces of the epiphany of God in Christ. . . . It can only bring us to a historical encounter with the historical Jesus [*zur geschichtlichen Begegnung mit dem historischen Jesus*]; but the *Kyrios Christos* encounters us only in the kerygma of the church.[104]

Similarly, amid the "new quest" for the historical Jesus led by his own students, Bultmann reminds them in 1960 that "the Christ of the kerygma is not a historical figure [*historische Gestalt*] which could enjoy continuity with the historical Jesus [*mit dem historischen Jesus*]"; and, again, that "the Christ of the kerygma has, as it were, displaced the historical Jesus [*hat den historischen Jesus sozusagen verdrängt*] and authoritatively addresses the hearer — every hearer."[105] Far from asserting the identity, or even continuity, of the historical Jesus or JC-2 with the *Christus praesens* or JC-3, Bultmann's statements of 1948 and 1960 emphasize their sharp discontinuity from one another.

These two sets of apparently contradictory statements regarding the identity of the *Christus praesens* pose the question as to whether they are reconcilable within the overall framework of Bultmann's position. In my judgment, the clue is found in Bultmann's operating distinction between the "occasion of" and the "condition for" revelation, a distinction he derives from Kierkegaard.

Bultmann's emphatic denial of any historical continuity between JC-3 and JC-2 does not require a denial of the contemporary presence of Jesus of Nazareth. Even if we accept a sharp discontinuity between JC-3 and JC-2, still JC-2 (and, for that matter, JC-1) could be termed "keryg-

---

104. "Zu Schniewinds Thesen," in *KuM* 1:148.
105. "The Primitive Christian Kerygma and the Historical Jesus," in *HJCK*, pp. 18 and 30. Cf. *Exegetica*, pp. 448 and 458.

matic," insofar as they are presupposed by, or make an appearance in, the formulations of the New Testament kerygma. In this sense, Jesus' "presence" to us, whether as mythical character (JC-1), historical figure (JC-2), or a combination thereof, is precisely like that of any other literary character or historical personage. This Jesus is present to us as the kerygma's literary object and cultural deposit. Hence, people today can indeed have a "historical encounter" with Jesus of Nazareth, just as they can with Abraham Lincoln or Madame Bovary. They may even encounter Jesus of Nazareth in the kerygma as the kerygma's "primal source."[106] From Bultmann's perspective such an encounter with Jesus of Nazareth, that is, JC-2, may indeed occasion, but can never causally effect, the presence of what he variously calls "the Risen One," "the Christ," "the Lord Jesus Christ," "the *Kyrios Christos,*" "the Christ *pro me,*" or "the *Christus praesens,*" in short, JC-3.

When Bultmann refers to "the Christ of the kerygma," as in his polemical remarks from 1960, he is clearly speaking of JC-3. The *Christus praesens,* therefore, is not an object of the kerygma, an artifact, or even the *occasion* for revelation (as are JC-1 and JC-2), but JC-3 is the acting agent, the performing subject, the very *condition* of the eschatological event. He it is who "authoritatively addresses the hearer — every hearer," who "proclaims the word of God," and who "addresses you and me here and now in the preaching." Other than the relation of occasion to condition — a relation established by the electing will of God and to which the human will contributes nothing (and which, therefore, outside of faith, may only appear arbitrary) — there is no connection between JC-2 and JC-3.

As we have seen, Bultmann takes this position for two basic reasons. First, the form-critical analysis of the New Testament leads to "the negative conclusion that the outline of the Gospels does not enable us to know either the outer course of the life of Jesus or his inner development. We must frankly confess that the character of Jesus as a human personality cannot be recovered by us."[107] Second, characterizations of Jesus derived from historical reconstructions are exercises in Christ "after the flesh." In light of 2 Corinthians 5:16, such projects become anachronistic at best

---

106. Schubert M. Ogden, "Rudolf Bultmann and the Future of Revisionary Christology," in Hobbs, *Bultmann, Retrospect and Prospect,* pp. 55-57. Cf. Bultmann: In the kerygma addressed to us, "the historical Jesus is present *in the sense that* his word has been taken up in the kerygma." *GuV* 4:197. My italics.

107. *EaF,* p. 52.

and sinful at worst once the eschatological destiny of Jesus is regarded as decisive for both Christology and soteriology. Bultmann hears Paul saying that Jesus' eschatological destiny cancels or annuls the perdurable significance of his personality for human salvation: "Not the historical Jesus [*Nicht der historische Jesus*], but Jesus Christ, the One who is preached, is the Lord."[108] For these reasons, one stemming from the results of form criticism and the other from an interpretation of eschatology, Bultmann strips JC-3 of all character traits, and, hence, of any personal identity with JC-2.

Can Bultmann's critics claim vindication? There appears to be no evident connection between the Jesus of history and the present eschatological event, just as Charles David Barrett argues; and, therefore, recalling J. Louis Martyn's criticism, how can the proclaimed "remain" recognizably the proclaimer? Is the voice announcing, "I love you," only that of an anonymous caller? Shorn of his identity as Jesus of Nazareth, does the *Christus praesens* logically become a naked "x,"[109] a "mythological cipher,"[110] a "spectre," or a "ghost"?[111] If the concept of personal "presence" requires a "who" in order to make any sense at all, then how can Bultmann speak of the *presence* of Jesus Christ without also speaking concretely of his identity and, hence, personality? At the outset of chapter five, we shall return to these issues surrounding the identity (or anonymity) of Bultmann's *Christus praesens*.

Summary

Taking "New Testament and Mythology" as our basic text, we uncovered that "Jesus Christ" denotes three distinct, but related, significations for Bultmann: a mythical character or JC-1, a historical figure or JC-2, and the contemporary locus of God's kerygmatic activity, that is, the *Christus praesens* or JC-3.

In the New Testament there is "a peculiar intertwining" of JC-1 and

108. *GuV* 1:208.

109. Schniewind, "Reply to Bultmann," in *KaM* 1:67.

110. Käsemann, "Blind Alleys in the 'Jesus of History' Controversy," in *NTQT*, p. 44.

111. Ernst Steinbach, "Mythos und Geschichte," in *Mythos und Geschichte, Sammlung Gemeinverständlicher Vorträger und Schriften aus dem Gebiet der Theologie und Religionsgeschichte*, vol. 194 (Tübingen: J. C. B. Mohr [Paul Siebeck], 1951), p. 20.

JC-2. Jesus of Nazareth is attached to the prefabricated narrative of the Christ myth, and associated with such titles of preexistence as "Messiah" and "Son of God." Through such "mythologizing" the New Testament vests Jesus with saving significance. Thus, the question for a modern age shaped by science is how the church can continue to claim and proclaim the saving significance of a mythical-historical figure.

Liberalism answers this question by supplanting the mythological formulations of Christology (JC-1) with historical reconstructions (JC-2). Whereas traditional theology views the saving significance of Jesus Christ in his incarnation and mission as Son or Messiah of God, for liberalism only the historical Jesus (JC-2) and not the mythical Messiah (JC-1) is the bearer of salvation. As the heir of liberalism, and as one who accepts its distinction between history and myth, Bultmann nevertheless rejects the attempt to "read off" soteriological significance from JC-2 as such. This liberal project is not only made suspect by form criticism; it ignores the eschatological character of the New Testament, and, by basing faith on historical science, actually turns faith into a "work" of self-justification.

In contrast to liberalism, Bultmann holds that the saving significance of Jesus Christ is permanently lodged in the mythology of the New Testament, that is, at the level of JC-1. In order to unpack its significance Bultmann advances a general theory of myth that indicates the real referent of JC-1 to be the "Beyond," or nonobjectifiable transcendent God, in relation to human existence. The mythically couched confession of salvation through Jesus Christ refers, in the end, neither to the preexistent Messiah (JC-1) nor to the historical Jesus (JC-2) but rather to him "in whom God acts for us in the present," that is, the *Christus praesens* (JC-3).

Bultmann then proceeds to apply this existentialist interpretation of myth to the cross-resurrection kerygma of Paul. Mythological talk of the judgment "of the rulers of this age" wrought in Christ's cross is interpreted as a judgment on all humankind and as a call to carry out "one's freedom from the world by accepting suffering." Moreover, as "the eschatological event," the cross is "not an event of the past to which one looks back," but an event that is "constantly present," that is, "in time" from "beyond time" whenever proclaimed (and, hence, interpreted) for human existence. Furthermore, by appealing to 2 Corinthians 5:18-19 and 6:2 (read through Johannine lenses), Bultmann transposes the resurrection, from a mythical-historical account of the destiny of Jesus Christ (as in 1 Corinthians

15:3-8), into an eschatological-existentialist account of the *Christus praesens* as the determinative power of the word of the cross.

Similarly, John's theme, "the Word became flesh," is also transposed by Bultmann's existentialist interpretation. Soteriologically speaking, the incarnation is not "a datable event of the past," or the destiny of a preexistent entity alongside God. Rather, the incarnation refers to the *Christus praesens*, that is, "the enfleshment" of the saving Word of God that continually occurs in the event of Christian proclamation. The incarnational identity and reality of Jesus Christ derives from proclamation. For Bultmann, therefore, the basic and essential form of the Word of God is the preaching of the gospel.

Through Bultmann's interpretation of Paul's apocalyptic and John's Gnostic concepts, God's eschatological act in Jesus Christ, the divine condition for salvation, is seen as continuing paradoxically in and through the human and temporal occasion of Christian proclamation. In this way, Bultmann seeks to preserve the transcendence of divine action, and, at the same time, to leave intact the closed continuum of worldly occurrences presupposed by a scientific *Weltbild*.

The soteriological transposition of God's act in Christ to the act of kerygmatic proclamation leads Bultmann to reflections on the language of revelation that anticipate later discussions in analytic philosophy. Since the transcendent God is never an encompassed object, but the Encompasser of every object, we cannot know who or what God is in Godself; we can only know who God is for us in Jesus Christ. Hence, we can never speak authentically of God's act in Christ without simultaneously speaking of ourselves. This means that talk of God's act in Christ properly proceeds by representing it as analogous to a human act and by representing the communion between God and ourselves as analogous to that between one human being and another. Central to this understanding is the model of the kerygma as a word of promise by a self-involving agent constituting in its hearers a new self-understanding. Bultmann thereby construes God's act in Christ as that of a "Thou" who directly addresses each hearer with the demand and promise of authentic existence.

Bultmann's appropriation of the Pauline and Johannine *Christus praesens* amounts to a reformulation of the liberal doctrine of the presence of Jesus. The saving efficacy and contemporary agency that liberals attributed to the personality of the historical Jesus, Bultmann now attributes to Jesus Christ as God's speech act, an act continually occurring in and through the kerygmatic occasion of Christian proclamation. Hence, our examination of Bultmann's theological writings has led us as inescapably to the *Christus praesens* as has our previous study of his exegetical works. Christ is our contemporary, present and acting for us, in and through the proclaimed kerygma. This is Bultmann's claim. Having examined, both exegetically and theologically, Bultmann's teaching on the *Christus praesens,* we can now reconsider its significance for today.

CHAPTER 5

Bultmann's *Christus Praesens:*
The Critics Respond

Introduction

In this chapter, we now proceed to reconsider Bultmann's Christology in debate with Hans W. Frei's *The Identity of Jesus Christ*,[1] Dorothee Sölle's *Political Theology*,[2] and Jürgen Moltmann's *Theology of Hope*.[3] I have chosen these thinkers as Bultmann's conversation partners primarily because each represents one of the more recent and, by now, well-established theologies of narration (Frei), political transformation (Sölle), and eschatological expectation (Moltmann). Moreover, in the works we are examining, Frei, Sölle, and Moltmann construct positions in conscious opposition to Bultmann's *Christus praesens*.[4] We have then in these theologians articulate critics who, in this shared capacity, can help us assess Bultmann's continuing significance for the church and theology today.

The coherence and adequacy of Bultmann's doctrine of the *Christus*

---

1. Subtitled *The Hermeneutical Bases of Dogmatic Theology* (Philadelphia: Fortress Press, 1975; hereafter cited as *IJC*).

2. Trans. with an Introduction by John Shelley (Philadelphia: Fortress, 1974; hereafter cited as *PT*); pub. in Ger. as *Politische Theologie: Auseinandersetzung mit Rudolf Bultmann* (Stuttgart: Kreuz-Verlag, 1971).

3. Subtitled *On the Ground and the Implications of a Christian Eschatology*, trans. James W. Leitch (New York: Harper & Row, 1965; hereafter cited as *TH*); pub. in Ger. as *Theologie der Hoffnung: Untersuchungen zur Begründung und zu den Konsequenzen einer christlichen Eschatologie*, 6th ed. *Beiträge zur evangelischen Theologie*, vol. 38 (München: Chr. Kaiser Verlag, 1966).

4. Frei, Sölle, and Moltmann all later modified, in varying degrees, the positions expressed in the books discussed here. Our aim is not to offer a comprehensive retrospective of their work but to enter into it precisely at the point where it is most critical of Bultmann.

praesens is open to question on a number of grounds, three of which preoccupy our chosen critics.

Since Bultmann regards the New Testament's predications of JC-1 as sheer myth and those of JC-2 as mere history, neither can bestow any identity on JC-3, by way of character traits or patterns of personality, that would be decisive for human salvation. Thus, Bultmann's position forces the issue, prominent in the work of Frei, of the identity of Jesus Christ and the putative role of narrative in rendering him present.

Besides the questions surrounding the identity of Jesus Christ, what are we to make of Bultmann's contention that the kerygmatic presence of Jesus Christ is correlative with the self-understanding of the individual believer and with a faith that detaches the Christian from the world? This raises the further question, prominent in the work of Sölle and Moltmann, whether a kerygmatic *Christus praesens,* by its exclusive correlation of divine transcendence and personal existence, abandons social action and acquiesces to the entrenched political arrangements of a sacralized *status quo.*

Closely related to this concern over Bultmann's alleged existentialist constriction of the scope of salvation is the question whether the *Christus praesens* as the eschatological event adequately honors the apocalyptic significance of the gospel promise. Is the resurrection to be understood as simply the presence of Jesus Christ in proclamation, or is Jesus' resurrection the promise that God's faithfulness toward him will ultimately encompass the creation as a whole? Moltmann resists the Christ who is present in the name of the Christ who is promised.

Therefore, when Bultmann speaks of the *Christus praesens,* or Jesus Christ as God's kerygmatic eschatological salvation event, does he speak coherently and adequately of the identity of Jesus Christ, of the scope of salvation, and of the apocalyptic hope of the New Testament? With these interlocking questions of Christology, soteriology, and eschatology, we now turn to Bultmann's critics.

Hans W. Frei and the Narrative Presence of Christ

At the conclusion of chapter four, we indicated that one of the difficulties with Bultmann's doctrine of the *Christus praesens* is the lack of personal identity that can be attached to this construct. Form criticism eliminates the Gospels as legitimate sources for retrieving or reconstructing either the inner intentions or the outer career of the historical Jesus. Moreover, Jesus' eschatological destiny, as the annulment of the *Christos kata sarka* (2 Cor. 5:16), means that Jesus' personality contributes nothing to his divine election or to the possibility or reality of his contemporaneity. Thus, Bultmann concludes that Jesus' presence to us as the Christ, as the kerygmatic eschatological salvation event, requires only *that* he lived and precludes any saving significance in *how* he lived or in *what* he was like — even if such information were available to the historian.

In the view of Hans W. Frei's extended essay *The Identity of Jesus Christ,* this loss, or lack, of identity in the Christ claimed as present invariably occurs whenever one begins with his *presence,* rather than with his *identity,* or "that which makes him uniquely the person he is in distinction from all others."[5] As long as one accepts the premises or framework that inform a Christology like Bultmann's, the result can only be "endless and inconclusive arguments about the relation of the description of the 'Jesus of history' to that of the 'Christ of faith,' in the vain hope that adding these two abstractions together would somehow provide us with the description of one concrete person."[6] Thus, in reaction to Bultmann, the emerging narrative theology of the 1970s gives renewed attention and priority to the identity of Jesus Christ and the putative role of narrative in rendering him present.

Frei holds that by starting with the identity of Jesus Christ one can then move, logically and coherently, to claims for his presence. He argues that to speak of the "presence" of anyone, whether a contemporary or a person of the past, requires us to recall or describe their "identity." So likewise we cannot speak meaningfully of Jesus' presence to us unless, and until, we can speak of his identity. Precisely by giving us a compelling description of his identity, "the Gospel narrative" brings us into the presence of Jesus Christ. This narrative, by identifying Jesus as risen from the dead, entails his personal presence to us here and now as Christ the Savior. Thus, Frei's argument expresses the conviction, or leads to the conclusion, that knowing the identity of Jesus Christ "is identical with having him present or being in his presence."[7]

5. P. 15.
6. *IJC,* p. 86.
7. *IJC,* p. vii. This thesis is reiterated on pp. ix, 4-7, 13-16, 26, 36-37, and 145.

From "Myth" to "Narrative"

Whereas Bultmann speaks of the presence of Jesus Christ in terms of the cross-resurrection kerygma of Paul (interpreted through John), Frei speaks of it in terms of "the Gospel narrative."[8] Nevertheless, this major shift should not obscure the fact that Frei, like Bultmann, finds soteriological significance for Jesus Christ at the level of JC-1. That is to say, Frei, like Bultmann, recognizes that Jesus Christ is the "chief character" in a soteriological narrative.[9] Frei parts company with Bultmann in rejecting the category of myth as appropriate for either the story line or the chief character of the Gospels. If Bultmann pictures the Synoptics as sharing a common Christ myth, on which all sorts of materials and genres have been strung, including the occasional novelistic motif, Frei imagines the obverse: the Synoptics share a common novelistic story, into which a mythical motif is occasionally slipped.[10] Frei finds the real analogue for "the Gospel narrative" in the modern novel and thereby attempts "to distinguish the Gospel *story* of the Savior from a common savior *myth* of the period."[11]

This distinction between myth and narrative becomes crucial for Frei's argument. The distinction is not that a narrative is a story and a myth is something else. Rather, the distinction lies in the gospel story being a peculiar *kind* of narrative, what Frei, following Erich Auerbach, terms a "realistic narrative."[12] That is to say, the gospel narrative is more akin to "history-

8. See *IJC,* pp. xiii, 46, 48-50, 60, 63, and 124. Among the synonyms Frei employs are "the Gospel story," pp. 49, 51-52, 54, 59-60, 72-73, 82, 87-88, 103, 105-6, 109, 111, 117, 124, 127, 138, 140-41, 154-55; "the Christian story," pp. 57-59, 62; "the New Testament narrative," p. 60; and "the New Testament story," p. 102.

9. *IJC,* p. 46. See also p. 51.

10. For Bultmann see *HST,* pp. 282-83, 306, 310-312 and *TNT* 1:86; for Frei see *IJC,* pp. 49-50 and 133-37. Matters are somewhat blurred when Frei continues to refer to myths as "stories" after binding the gospel narrative so tightly to this term. Cf. p. 50 with pp. 56-57, 60, 62, and 139.

11. *IJC,* p. 52, my italics. See also pp. xiv, 82-83, 136, 139-40, 143, and 151. Frei's preference here for "story" over "myth" parallels Barth's preference for "saga" over "myth" when characterizing the biblical accounts of creation and Jesus' resurrection. See *Church Dogmatics* (hereafter cited as *CD*), ed. G. W. Bromiley and T. F. Torrance (Edinburgh: T. & T. Clark, 1960), vol. 3, pt. 2: *The Doctrine of Creation,* trans. Harold Knight et al., pp. 446-47 and 452; vol. 4, pt. 1: *The Doctrine of Reconciliation* (1956), trans. G. W. Bromiley, pp. 336 and 508.

12. *IJC,* p. xiii. See Erich Auerbach, *Mimesis: The Representation of Reality in Western Culture,* trans. Willard Trask (Garden City, N.Y.: Doubleday & Co., Doubleday Anchor Books, 1957), esp. pp. 35-43 on Mark 14:66-72. For Bultmann's discussion of Auerbach and literary

writing and the traditional novel"[13] than to myth in at least three respects: "its depiction of a common public world . . . , in the close interaction of character and incident, and in the non-symbolic quality of the relation between the story and what the story is about."[14] Frei's contention that the Gospels are more appropriately approached through the genre of "realistic narrative" than through "myth" leads him to rechristen Bultmann's "mythical" JC-1 as "storied."[15] As a character in a story, Jesus achieves his identity in the same way Madame Bovary attains hers, namely, through the techniques of realistic rendering. Thus, for Frei, the identity of JC-1 derives from his depiction by the realistic gospel narrative — and not from an existentialist interpretation of the Christ myth.

Frei's debatable assumption that the Gospels have more in common with the realistic fiction of nineteenth-century France than with the apocalyptic and Hellenistic myths of their own time shows, as perhaps nothing else could, how literary criticism has replaced the history of religions as the established framework for much of academic theology since Bultmann.

Nevertheless, the fact that Bultmann's Gnostic Redeemer myth can no longer be assumed as part of the immediate context of the New Testament does not warrant Frei's counterassumption that the nearest literary analogues of the Gospels are the realistic novels of the last century. Hypotheses regarding the genre of the Gospels must take into account comparative studies in the literature and religion of the Greco-Roman world. Only when relatively proximate historical contexts fail to produce literary parallels does the more removed possibility of the Gospels as realistic novels become plausible. Otherwise, the term "realistic narrative" betrays the apologetic strategy of insulating the New Testament from its environment.[16]

---

realism, see "Das Christentum als orientalische und als abendländische Religionen [1949]," in *GuV* 2:207-8; ET: "Christianity as a Religion of East and West," in *EPT,* pp. 231-32; "Die Bedeutung der alttestamentlich-jüdischen Tradition für das christliche Abendland [1950]," in *GuV* 2:239; ET: "The Significance of Jewish Old Testament Tradition for the Christian West," in *EPT,* pp. 265-66; *NTaM,* p. 80; and *History and Eschatology,* pp. 105-9.

13. *IJC,* p. xiv.

14. *IJC,* pp. xiii-xiv.

15. *IJC,* pp. 106, 114, 142, 143, 144, and 154. On p. 88 Frei does call mythical characters "storied," but the reader must understand them as not "realistically" so.

16. Note Frei's judgment that "the literary structure of the [resurrection] account . . . points in favor of the thesis that the resurrection account (or, better, the passion-resurrection account as an unbroken unity) is a demythologization of the dying-rising savior myth." *IJC,* p. 140. But see pp. ix-x for Frei's later retreat from this position.

Identity Descriptions

Before attempting to show how the gospel narrative renders the identity of Jesus Christ, Frei first proposes a working definition of human identity as "the specific uniqueness of a person . . . quite apart from both comparison and contrast to others," or "the self-referral, or ascription to him, of his physical and personal states, properties, characteristics, and actions."[17] Frei's recognition that identity normally involves "a connection or unbroken relationship between the past and present experience of the same self" recalls Locke's definition of "a person,"[18] while Frei's further characterization of identity "as moral responsibility" likewise recalls Kant's definition of *Persönlichkeit*.[19] Moreover, Frei's view — that identity is not only the product of enacted intentions but the result of responses both to the enacted intentions of others and to other "unintended events" — is reminiscent of Albrecht Ritschl's view that personality emerges as the Ego shapes — and is shaped by — its environment.[20] The connection between Frei's concept of human identity and the liberals' doctrine of personality finds additional confirmation in Frei's elaboration of identity as the self-referral of an individual's total "physical and *personality* characteristics."[21]

Nevertheless, there is an important conceptual difference between Frei's account of identity and the liberals' doctrine of personality. Ritschl, for example, holds that personality emerges from the interaction of an *a priori* Ego with its external environment. By contrast, Frei argues that such a view represents a metaphysical explanation, rather than a description, of human identity or personality. Since Frei seeks to account for the presence of Jesus Christ only by means of identity description, he strictly limits the contours of human identity to an integrated pattern of physical and personality characteristics, without metaphysically positing an integrating agent behind this pattern. In this way, Frei's model of identity preserves the developmental aspect of Ritschl's concept of personality, while bracketing the question of a transcendental Ego or soul.[22] For Frei's purposes, therefore, an identity description only presupposes (1) "that that

17. *IJC*, pp. 37-38.
18. *IJC*, p. 38. Cf. Locke, *Essay Concerning Human Understanding*, p. 188.
19. *IJC*, pp. 40-41. Cf. Hirsch, *Geschichte der Theologie*, 4:299.
20. *IJC*, p. 93. Cf. Ritschl, *Justification and Reconciliation*, 3:218-19, 231-37, and 397.
21. *IJC*, pp. 37-38, my italics.
22. *IJC*, pp. 41-42.

to which changing actions, states, and properties are ascribed or referred is nothing more than they themselves under a certain focus, the focus of self-referral. And when the actions, states, and properties change, their change is the self's change"; and (2) that "no set of changing states, properties, and, in particular, set of actions, exhausts the self in such a way that it cannot also provide the bond of continuity between these distinctive acts, states, and properties which it is."[23] Leaving aside the question of how successfully the substituted term "self" avoids the metaphysical complications of "soul," Frei is saying that descriptions of human identity must consider both continuing *change* and abiding *continuity*.

Accordingly, an identity description that captures a person at any given time, in the interplay between inner self and external circumstances, Frei terms an "intention-action" description. Such a description answers the question "What is he or she like?" by focusing on an external action emerging from an inner intention and thereby constituting a person's unsubstitutable identity.[24] On the other hand, an identity description that captures "the person himself in his ongoing self-continuity" Frei terms "a self-manifestation description." Such a description answers the question "Who is he or she?" by focusing on the self's expression through the public media of its own words and body. Without exhausting the elusiveness or diminishing the uniqueness of the self, these media fitly represent it and are the self as subject. Through language and embodiment, therefore, the identity of a person becomes manifestly describable.[25]

Frei uses these two kinds of formal identity descriptions, one involving "intention-action" and the other "subject-manifestation," to highlight the identity of Jesus Christ as rendered by the gospel narrative. Frei contends that "a good storyteller" is able to describe both the changes in, and the persistence of, a person's character as it acts — and is acted upon — over a period of time.[26] To see how this is so, we turn now to Frei's own reading of the Gospels.

23. *IJC,* p. 43, omitting italics.

24. *IJC,* pp. 43-44 and 91-94. As I have already indicated, Frei recognizes that the self's identity is not only the product of its enacted intentions. The self's identity is also the result of its response, whether to the enacted intentions of others or to unintended occurrences as well.

25. *IJC,* pp. 44 and 94-101. For criticism of Frei's self-manifestation model see Ronald F. Thiemann, *Revelation and Theology: The Gospel as Narrated Promise* (Notre Dame, Ind.: University of Notre Dame Press, 1985), pp. 182-83, n. 1. Thiemann argues that the intention-action model is adequate for describing the self's persistency and needs no supplementing by the self-manifestation model.

26. *IJC,* p. 88.

The point is to see how they render the identity of their chief character —
without which he cannot be present here and now as Christ the Savior.

The Gospel Depiction of Jesus

"Intention-Action" Identity Description

Despite his likening the Gospels to traditional novels, Frei can find only
two places in the entire synoptic narrative where the "inner intention" of
Jesus is made clear, namely, the temptation scene, and, more importantly,
the prayer scene in Gethsemane. Each of these two scenes portrays Jesus'
intention as only a novelist can, that is, from "the inside," an intention
Frei characterizes as "obedience" to God on behalf of human salvation.
Frei comments on the Gethsemane scene:

> Set into the midst of this [passion-crucifixion-resurrection] sequence is
> our second glimpse into Jesus' inner life (within the story) when,
> tempted to plead for a way out of what looms ahead, he confirms his
> obedience: "Yet not what I will, but what thou wilt" (Mark 14:36). . . .
> Here, as nowhere else, the story points "from the inside" to his obedient
> intention. This is its focus. . . . Here, then, is the inner point at which
> Jesus' intention begins to mark his identity.[27]

Just as Jesus' obedience depicted in the temptation scene is immediately
enacted in his preaching at the Nazareth synagogue (Luke 4:16-30), so his
obedience to God depicted in the Gethsemane scene is subsequently
enacted in giving up his life on behalf of humankind. Therefore, in his
passion and death Jesus enacts his inner intention, thereby constituting
his identity as "the man completely obedient to God."[28]

---

27. *IJC*, pp. 109-10, omitting italics. See also pp. 82-83, 103, 108, 115, 127, and
144-45. Bultmann notes that John 12:27ff. substitutes a meditation by Jesus "for the
Gethsemane scene of the synoptic tradition." In this regard, Bultmann contrasts John with
Mark: "Whereas in the Gospel of Mark we can recognize the historical process by which
the unmessianic life of Jesus was retrospectively made messianic, in John the inner appro-
priateness of that process is made clear." *TNT* 2:48. Dispensing with Bultmann's form
criticism, Frei argues on literary grounds that Mark also makes clear "the inner appropriate-
ness" of Jesus' mission.

28. *IJC*, p. 111. Frei also calls Jesus' obedience to God "perfect." See pp. 102-3 and
146.

At this point, Frei's methods give us further pause. The more one reads Frei's account of the identity of Jesus Christ as depicted by "the Gospel narrative," the more apparent it becomes that this term refers to no work of literature whatsoever but only to a literary-critical construct imposed on the synoptic Gospels by Frei's imagination. What he presents us with is a postmodern "harmony of the Gospels," which, like its older liberal siblings, still picks and chooses from the three synoptic accounts whatever it needs to construct, in Frei's words, "Jesus' inner life," albeit "within the story."

For example, Frei claims that Jesus' inner intention of obedience to God on behalf of human salvation is revealed in the temptation scene and immediately enacted by Jesus' preaching in the synagogue at Nazareth. Since the Gospel of Mark refers only in passing to the temptation (1:12-13), omitting Jesus' dialogue with the devil, and since both Mark 6:1-6 and Matthew 13:53-58 place Jesus' preaching in the synagogue only later in their Gospels, in stories quite different from Luke's and in contexts removed from the temptation scene, what Frei calls "the Gospel narrative" is really the *Lucan* narrative. Throughout his essay, Frei essentially follows Luke(-Acts), supplemented as needed by Matthew, Mark, and even John.

To return to Frei's exposition, following Jesus' surrender of his will in Gethsemane, the narrative increasingly transfers the power to initiate action from Jesus to his opponents, and above all to God, whose own power to redeem Jesus from death brings the resurrection. Yet "in the resurrection, where the initiative of God is finally and decisively climaxed and he [God] alone is and can be active, the sole identity to mark the presence of that activity is Jesus." Precisely in the resurrection, "when God's supplantation of him is complete," the event is so hidden by the narrative from direct view that only "Jesus of Nazareth, he and none other, marks the presence of the action of God." In other words, the identity of Jesus as God's act and presence becomes manifest at the very point where death denies to Jesus the power to enact his obedience. This state of affairs calls forth from Frei another kind of formal identity description.[29]

29. *IJC*, p. 121.

"Subject-manifestation" Identity Description

The second kind of formal identity description, the "subject (or self-) manifestation" pattern, stresses "the continuity of a person's identity throughout the transitions brought about by his acts and life's events." Here the aim is not to focus narrowly on "a specific sequence of events," by which a person's intention is enacted, but on "the whole scope or stretch of a person's life." Hence, in Jesus' case, a self-manifestation description "involves the full scope of the Gospel story."[30]

Frei argues that, taken as a composite, the Synoptics exhibit three distinct narrative stages, marking step by step, and ever more fully, the identity of Jesus. His identity unfolds beginning with his birth, continuing through his baptism, and culminating in his passion, death, and resurrection.[31]

In stage one the narrative depicts Jesus from birth to baptism. In a variety of forms (prose, liturgical, and poetic), Jesus is identified in a stylized, representative way "wholly in terms of the identity of the people of Israel."[32] Jesus is not an individual but the summing up of the story of Israel, as parallels and references to the Exodus and Exile indicate. At his baptism Jesus begins to emerge "as an individual in his own right."[33] Yet even in this second stage of narrative depiction, Jesus does retain something of the symbolic quality he has in stage one, in that he represents the imminent Kingdom of God (as, e.g., in Luke 4 and 17:19-23).[34]

Only with Jesus' "announcement to his disciples that he and they would now go to Jerusalem" do we reach the third, and most important, stage of Jesus' developing identity. In Frei's view, this is the "part of the story most clearly history-like." By "history-like," Frei means "that it describes an individual and a series of events in connection with him that, whether fictional or real, are what they are in their own right." Hence, in this third stage, Jesus does not simply symbolize some reality, say, that of the Kingdom of God, but becomes himself the center and focus of the narrated pattern of events. Through these events he acquires an unsubstitutable identity and, through him alone, these events acquire an unsub-

30. *IJC,* p. 127.

31. Mark, of course, does not depict the birth of Jesus, nor, if we follow the shorter ending to 16:8, the Risen Lord.

32. *IJC,* p. 128.

33. *IJC,* p. 130. Cf. p. 132.

34. *IJC,* pp. 131-32.

stitutable significance. The earlier connection between Jesus and the Kingdom of God becomes loosened, as the passion story focuses on Jesus "in his unadorned singularity." Then, in the resurrection appearances, notably that of the Emmaus Road (Luke 24:13-31), Jesus himself reappropriates as his own such stylized or mythological titles as "the Christ." He defines them, much more than they him. Thus, the identity of Jesus Christ is manifested preeminently in stage three as the narrative sharpens its focus on him. Who is Jesus? Described by his "self-manifestation" in the narrative, he is "the unsubstitutable Jesus of Nazareth who, as that one man, is the Christ and the presence of God."[35]

The Presence of Jesus Christ

Through these formal identity descriptions, Frei succeeds in extracting or constructing from "the Gospel narrative" the identity of Jesus Christ. More correctly, he succeeds in extracting or constructing the identity of JC-1, the "storied" and "history-like" chief character in the Gospels. Having accomplished this task, he is now in a position to show how knowing the identity of Jesus Christ "is identical with having him present or being in his presence,"[36] for to know *who* Jesus is, "in connection with what took place is to know *that* he is."[37]

Whereas Bultmann argued on form-critical grounds that the Gospels "peculiarly intertwine" the Christ of myth (JC-1) with historical traditions about Jesus of Nazareth (JC-2), Frei argues on literary grounds that the gospel narrative fictionally renders an identity description of Jesus (JC-1) entailing the claim that he factually existed as a historical person (JC-2) and now factually exists as the Risen One (JC-3). Thus, Frei attempts to move from a literary description of Jesus' identity to the affirmation of his factual presence as the Risen Christ.

Frei summarizes his position by speaking in the name of the synoptic writers:

---

35. *IJC*, pp. 133-37. Cf. Hodgson, *Jesus — Word and Presence*, pp. 206-7: "It is simply not the case that the Gospels reach their climax as 'history' in the passion narratives, that here we find the highest degree of concreteness and specificity, that here Jesus' identity is most sharply focused. To the contrary, the whole story of Jesus' death remains — with one exception — highly stylized: it is the death of the suffering, righteous, and innocent Messiah, who will be vindicated by the hand of God."

36. *IJC*, p. vii.

37. *IJC*, p. 145.

"Our argument is that to grasp what this identity, Jesus of Nazareth (which has been made directly accessible to us), is is to believe that he has been, *in fact,* raised from the dead. Someone may reply that in that case the most perfectly depicted character and most nearly lifelike fictional identity ought always in fact to have lived a factual historical life. We answer that the argument holds good only in this one and absolutely unique case, where the described entity (who or what he is, i.e., Jesus Christ, the presence of God) is totally identical with his factual existence. He *is* the resurrection and the life. How can he be conceived as not resurrected?"[38]

Thus, Frei infers the factuality both of the historical Jesus (JC-2) and the *Christus praesens* (JC-3), on the basis of the fictional, but "history-like," identity descriptions of the "storied" Jesus (JC-1).

Here where we were promised such a payoff on "presence," if only we would join Frei in taking his arduous trek of first establishing the "identity" of Jesus Christ, we must confess to disappointment. At the end of the road, we find only a version of Anselm's ontological proof for the existence of God, transposed by Frei onto Jesus Christ.

Anselm, it will be recalled, had argued that God is that than which nothing greater can be conceived. If God existed only in our thought, and not in reality, then God would not be God, that is, nothing greater than that which can be conceived. Therefore, precisely as that than which nothing greater can be conceived, God alone necessarily has real existence. To distill this argument in the language of Frei, just as God's presence is entailed by God's identity, so the presence of Jesus Christ is entailed by his identity as the Risen One. Frei's christological deployment of Anselm's argument assumes with Anselm that we can move from an existent in our thought to that same existent in reality, but, in Frei's case, the existent in our thought is, after all, a literary character.[39]

At least we thought Frei was treating Jesus purely as a literary character; that his descriptions of Jesus' identity or "inner life" were strictly a matter of literary depiction (JC-1) rather than historical report (JC-2):

---

38. *IJC,* pp. 145-46. See also pp. 8, 13-15, 17, 26, 36, 147-52, and 154-55.

39. Cf. Karl Barth's discussion of Anselm's *Proslogion* regarding "quod non possit cogitari non esse" ["that he (God) could not be conceived as not existing"], in *Anselm: Fides Quarens Intellectum, Anselm's Proof of the Existence of God in the Context of his Theological Scheme,* trans. Ian W. Robertson (London: SCM, 1960), esp. pp. 132-61.

But do we actually know that much about Jesus? Certainly not, if we are asking about the "actual" man apart from the story. But that is not our concern. Whether indeed the "historical" Jesus *intended* the crucifixion and in what sense, whether he went freely to his death and with what motives, we cannot infer directly from the available evidence. . . . We are, in fact, thrown back on the story simply as a story, regardless of whether it is well documented.[40]

In contrast to these words, when Frei now claims that "this identity, Jesus of Nazareth . . . has been made directly accessible" to the synoptic writers (as opposed to their *readers*), he appears to switch his presuppositions. Contrary to his previously stated position, in which he imagines the gospel writers more or less as "realistic" novelists, Frei now suggests that they are in fact more akin to biographers or reporters describing a factual "entity" which was "made directly accessible" to them, that is, the historical Jesus. Despite Frei's stated intentions, he, like Bultmann, cannot avoid necessary judgments about "the relation of the description of the 'Jesus of history' to that of the 'Christ of faith.'"[41]

A Reply to Frei

Frei's rendering of Jesus shows the similarity of his christological project to that of Bultmann's teacher, Wilhelm Herrmann, discussed in chapter one. This probably has less to do with the fact that Frei's concept of human identity shares common features with Herrman's doctrine of personality and more with the fact that both Frei and Herrmann read the Gospels as a singular "narrative" (*Erzählung*). This narrative, which each creates out of the diverse synoptic accounts, enables both Frei and Herrmann to speak of Jesus' "inner life" and to characterize its outward course as one of "obedience" to God.

The difference between Frei and Herrmann, with respect to their

40. *IJC*, p. 103. See also pp. 137-38. Cf. p. 159, where Frei confusedly speaks about narrating "the history of Jesus."

41. *IJC*, p. 86. See also pp. 140-41. Cf. p. 48: "About Jesus' intention and his own convictions concerning his identity, one simply has to listen to and weigh specific proposals made by historians, always realizing that they are and will remain speculative and therefore only more or less likely or credible." If the intentions of Jesus are historical reconstructions rather than literary construals, then Frei's overall argument collapses.

descriptions of Jesus, is that Frei does not set out by regarding " 'the inner life of Jesus' as a historical datum present to hand in world history, which can be clearly seen with a little honest effort," as Bultmann once characterized Herrmann's view.[42] Rather, Frei regards "Jesus' inner life" as a *literary datum* "present to hand in world history, which can be clearly seen" with a little help from formal identity descriptions. Hence, Frei takes pains, at least initially, if not finally, to offer his characterizations of the personality of Jesus as purely literary descriptions of JC-1 and not as historical descriptions of JC-2. Thus, even if Frei's Jesus, like that of Hirsch, also leads a life of " 'always prayerful, always obedient surrender,' "[43] Frei intends that this description be understood as falling "within the story" and not, necessarily, within "world history."[44]

Yet inasmuch as Frei attempts to move from literary identity to the presence of Jesus Christ, we see further parallels between his project and that of Herrmann. For Frei's attempted correlation of narrative identity and contemporary presence recalls Herrmann's similar move when he distinguishes the husk of the narrative, that is, "the tradition concerning Jesus," from the kernel of the narrative, that is, "Jesus Himself."[45] Herrmann was convinced, as Frei later would be, that as the narrative was read, the inner life or personality of Jesus was conveyed to the reader. As for Herrmann the inner life of Jesus is the subject matter of the narrative to which the narrative itself only witnesses, so for Frei the narrative renders the identity of Jesus Christ which logically entails his presence to us. Thus, Frei's proposal returns to the liberal category of narrative, refurbishes it in accord with literary realism, and bestows upon it a theological prominence not seen since Bultmann's attacks on liberalism's "lives of Jesus."

Like Herrmann, Frei, too, strains to say that faith can know Jesus Christ as more than the rendered object of a narrative; that faith can know, in Herrmann's words, "Jesus himself." In chapter one, we analyzed why Herrmann's project fails. His historicist presupposition, that all reality claims are subject to the canons of historical science, prevents him from identifying the contemporaneity of Jesus with that of the Risen Lord. By

42. *FaU* 1:137, omitting italics.
43. *FaU* 1:129, where Bultmann quotes Hirsch, *Jesus Christus der Herr*, p. 80.
44. *IJC*, p. 109. Frei's attempt on pp. 106-7 to distance himself from liberalism by claiming that Jesus' "obedience," unlike his alleged "love," "freedom," "authoritativeness," or "faithfulness," is not an "inherent personal characteristic" or "clue to his personality," is specious given Frei's own account of what constitutes a formal identity description.
45. Herrmann, *Communion with God*, p. 66.

contrast, Frei shares no such historicist inhibition. In fact, in the final section of *The Identity of Jesus Christ,* entitled "The Presence of Christ," Frei speaks almost catechetically about "the presence of Jesus Christ now," noting "the gifts of Word and Sacrament" as its "spatial and temporal bases."[46] Unfortunately, these dogmatic affirmations regarding the "how" of Christ's presence appear disconnected from Frei's hermeneutical reflections identifying the "who" that is present.

Why does Frei's attempt to move from the narrative identity to the presence of Jesus Christ fail? Why, at the end of the road, can we *not* claim that knowing the narrative identity of Jesus Christ "is identical with having him present or being in his presence" — at least as the saving subject or acting agent of our salvation?

The answer is that a story, even a "realistic narrative," does not necessarily function as a "performative utterance" by a "self-involving" agent. Admittedly a narrative can render character identities, as good storytellers know, and, arguably, a "realistic narrative" may do this better than a "myth." Indeed, a narrative can depict the identities of putative subjects and agents; but a narrative as a narrative, unlike a promise as a promise, does not render self-involving agency, which is what the *Christus praesens* entails. Short of this kind of "self-involving" presence, a narratively rendered presence of Jesus Christ can only be, at best, the presence of information, of an "entity," or of a literary character. In this case, Bultmann's point is well taken that "I am not at all helped by reading touching stories of how Jesus forgave the sinful woman or Zacchaeus."[47] Help comes only when, in faith, I find myself addressed by Jesus Christ with his word of promise.

Unlike Bultmann, Frei offers no account of how faith finds itself addressed by Jesus Christ, of Jesus Christ as God's speech act, or of Jesus

---

46. *IJC,* pp. 155-56. See also p. 16.

47. *FaU* 1:128. Cf. Philipp Melanchthon, "Faith does not mean merely knowing the story of Christ, for even the devils confess that the Son of God appeared and arose from the dead, and in Judas there was a knowledge of Christ. *True faith* is truly to retain all the words which God has given to us, including the promise of grace. . . . The symbol [i.e., the Apostles' Creed as the summary of the gospel] includes not only the story but also the promises and the fruit of the promise." *Melanchthon on Christian Doctrine: Loci Communes 1555,* ed. and trans. Clyde L. Manschreck, with an Introduction by Hans Engelland (Oxford: Oxford University Press, 1965; reprint ed., Grand Rapids: Baker, 1982), p. 158 (XI). Frei's failure to account for the presence of Christ as agent stems from his preoccupation with "story" to the detriment of "promise."

Christ as the presently acting subject of the proclaimed Word of God. Frei's contention that knowing the narrative identity of Jesus is "identical with having him present or being in his presence" takes the Gospel narrative, as narrative, for the exclusive Word of God. The result, to borrow Barth's language, is to collapse the first and third forms of the Word, namely the incarnate *Logos* and the *Logos* proclaimed, into the second, the scriptural witness to the *Logos,* now redefined as "realistic narrative." Once this hermeneutical move is made, there remains no logical need, or basis, for preaching as interpretive witness; narrative recitation will suffice, and the cantor can replace the preacher, the lectern the pulpit. If narrative presence is all we can have of Jesus Christ, then preaching cannot be regarded as Bultmann finds Paul and John regarding it, namely, as direct address from Jesus Christ himself in and through his heralds' proclamation.[48]

Frei's work does hold heuristic significance by furnishing us with what is absent in Bultmann, namely, an identity description of JC-1, and, hence, of JC-3, beyond the mere "that" of his life and death and destiny. If we are to continue to speak of the presence of Jesus Christ, as Bultmann clearly wants to do, how can we do so meaningfully without referring to his identity as narrated by the New Testament? Identifying the One who enacts his own presence in the proclamation of the kerygma is precisely what realistic narrative can give us, even if it cannot account for that enactment as such.

Nevertheless, the letters of Paul do challenge the essential, perhaps exclusive, role Frei accords to "realistic" narrative in identifying Jesus Christ. As Bultmann observes, "Nowhere . . . does Paul refute claims derived from personal acquaintance with Jesus."[49] To make Bultmann's point in terms more pertinent to today's narrativists than to yesterday's liberals, "The apostle, although clearly a rugged fighter of the theological battlefield, never makes war by appealing to traditions about Jesus' life

---

48. Frei's views prove disastrous for homiletics, at least as executed by Mark Ellingsen in *The Integrity of Biblical Narrative: Story in Theology and Proclamation* (Minneapolis: Fortress, 1990). Frei appears relatively indifferent to Christian proclamation as the divinely instituted means of grace. See *IJC,* p. 8. My criticism of Frei on "narrative presence" is similar to that which Frei himself comes to make of D. Z. Phillips' *Faith and Philosophical Inquiry* (New York: Schocken, 1979), thereby indicating a revision in Frei's position. See Frei, *Types of Christian Theology,* ed. George Hunsinger and William C. Placher (New Haven: Yale University Press, 1992), pp. 46-55.

49. *CC,* p. 156.

and teaching."[50] That is to say, Paul does not draw from synoptic-style traditions in debating or claiming the identity or presence of Jesus Christ. As Bultmann notes, Paul is not interested in "Jesus' manner of life, his ministry, his personality [*Persönlichkeit*], [or] his character."[51]

What does interest Paul about the person of Jesus? According to Bultmann, Jesus' death and resurrection "in the last analysis . . . is the sole thing of importance for him."[52] True, Paul does narrate to the Corinthians the death and resurrection of Jesus Christ as sequential facts in space and time (1 Cor. 15:3-8), if contrary — from Bultmann's perspective — to the Apostle's later and better lights (2 Cor. 5:18–6:2). Yet even when Paul stretches his punctiliar kerygma into a linear narrative, its succinct spareness still lies far from the kind of literary realism Frei finds essential for depicting the identity of Jesus Christ. Indeed, Paul does not concern himself with the lineaments of personal identity which realistic narrative embodies.[53] Yet as we discovered in chapter two, Paul's indifference, or even opposition, to "fleshing out" Christ's identity does not prevent him, as Frei might lead us to suppose, from proclaiming Christ's presence in Christian witness and existence — and doing so through a variety of nonnarrative rhetorical devices.[54]

We cannot leave Frei's essay without noting that his turn from form criticism to literary criticism in pursuing a fuller identity for Jesus Christ

50. J. Louis Martyn, "Attitudes Ancient and Modern toward Tradition about Jesus," *Union Seminary Quarterly Review* 23 (Winter 1968), p. 141.

51. *TNT* 1:294. Cf. *TdNT,* p. 293.

52. *TNT* 1:293.

53. Frei's attempt in *IJC,* pp. 104-5, to enlist Paul as a witness to an earlier tradition attesting to Jesus' obedience (Rom. 5:19; Phil. 2:5-11) ignores Bultmann's exegetical judgment that these passages, as well as 2 Cor. 8:9 and Rom. 15:1-2, are speaking "of the pre-existent Christ" of myth and not a "realistically storied" Jesus. See *FaU* 1:246.

54. On Paul's rhetoric see Bultmann, *Der Stil der paulinischen Predigt und die kynisch-stoische Diatribe,* Forschungen zur Religion und Literatur des Alten und Neuen Testaments, no. 13 (Göttingen: Vandenhoeck & Ruprecht, 1910; reprint ed., 1984).

In *The Faith of Jesus Christ,* Richard B. Hays argues on the basis of Galatians 3:1–4:11 that Paul's theology presupposes a gospel narrative, and he attacks Bultmann's demythologizing as "de-narrativizing," p. 54. In reply, Bultmann is well aware that a story, namely, the Christ myth, is not only presupposed but present in Paul (e.g., 1 Cor. 15; Phil. 2:5-11). The issue is not whether Paul's gospel presupposes a saving narrative centered on Jesus Christ, but whether this narrative is "mythical" or "realistically storied" in genre. For Bultmann the history of religions indicates that this narrative is mythical. The Reformation and the Enlightenment, to which Bultmann is heir, further require that this narrative be "translated" into nonnarrative direct address and interpreted for existence.

results in the loss of any theological significance for the *Sitz-im-Leben* or life situation in which the Gospels arose. If Frei's insulation of the Gospels from Hellenistic and apocalyptic myths is intended to safeguard the real humanity of Jesus Christ, this can only succeed by sacrificing that of the Gospels' first-century authors and readers.

Some seven years after the original serial publication of *The Identity of Jesus Christ,* Frei attempts to compensate for this loss. He urges the supplementing of his original two categories of formal identity description with "the formal analytical devices which sociologists of knowledge and Marxist literary critics use to identify the relation between individual personhood and the contextual social structures."[55] Here we have a tacit admission that there is a world addressed *by* the text that is not identical with the world *of* the text and that the world originally addressed *by* the text has itself an influence on the world *of* the text.

Frei's belated recognition of the importance of the nontextual "situation" for the identity and presence of Jesus Christ brings us to a theme prominent in the "political theology" of Dorothee Sölle. Writing from within the Bultmannian camp, where the existential situation of the hearers of the word was acknowledged, Sölle, too, entered the 1970s urging a turn to Marx. Whereas Frei's nod to Marx was prompted by the need for a more socially textured reading of the Gospels, Sölle's Marxism was prompted by the need for a more critical analysis of those situations of injustice and oppression in which, and to which, the kerygma must be addressed.

Dorothee Sölle and a "Political *coram Christo*"

In her commemorative address in Oldenburg, Germany, on the occasion of Bultmann's centenary, Dorothee Sölle finds "the criticism of Western philosophy by liberation theology" to be "in a way a continuation of what Bultmann did."[56] Sölle's linking of Bultmann to subsequent liberation theology seems initially implausible if she is also correct in her widely

---

55. *IJC,* p. x.

56. "Bultmann und die politische Theologie," in Hartwig Thyen et al., eds., *Rudolf Bultmann 100 Jahre: Oldenburger Vorträge* (Oldenburg: Heinz Holzberg Verlag, 1985), p. 62. Cf. ET: "Rudolf Bultmann and Political Theology," in Sölle, *The Window of Vulnerability: A Political Spirituality,* trans. Linda A. Maloney (Minneapolis: Fortress, 1990), p. 122.

shared earlier judgment that Bultmann's theology "understands itself as essentially apolitical."[57]

Unlike many recent attempts to ground Christian praxis in the revolutionary activity of the historical Jesus, Bultmann holds that Jesus' death resulted "because his activity was misconstrued as a political activity."[58] Indeed, "subversive ideas and revolutionary utterances are lacking in Jesus' preaching."[59] Moreover, "Jesus' attitude toward property cannot be explained from social ideals or from any socialistic and proletarian instincts and motives. . . . The Kingdom is no ideal social order."[60] As far as Jesus is concerned, *"no program for world-reformation is derived from the will of God."*[61] Unlike the prophets who were before him, Jesus does not preach "primarily to the people as a whole, but to *individuals*."[62] The God proclaimed by Jesus "stands precisely beyond world history" and, instead, "meets human beings in their own history, in the daily round with its gift and demand."[63] Likewise, according to Bultmann,

> The new people of God has no real history, for it is the community of the end-time, an eschatological phenomenon. How could it have a history now when the world-time is finished and the end is imminent! The consciousness of being the eschatological community is at the same time the consciousness of being taken out of the still existing world. The world is the sphere of uncleanness and sin, it is a foreign country for the Christians whose commonwealth is in heaven (Phil. 3:20). Therefore neither the Christian community nor the individuals within it have any responsibility for the present world and its orders, for the tasks of society and the state.[64]

Thus, the eschatological *ekklēsia* possesses no divine portfolio for social responsibility or reform.

Similarly, Paul's "negation of worldly differentiations" in 1 Corinthians 7:17-24 "does not mean a sociological program within this world."[65]

---

57. *PT,* p. xix.
58. "The Historical Jesus and the Primitive Christian Kerygma," in *HJKC,* p. 24.
59. *Jesus and the Word,* p. 103.
60. Ibid., omitting italics.
61. Ibid., p. 104.
62. *TNT* 1:25.
63. *TdNT,* p. 26.
64. *History and Eschatology,* p. 36, omitting italics.
65. *TNT* 1:309.

While Bultmann acknowledges that "the social distinctions of freedom and slavery as well as those of sex and race have lost their significance 'in Christ' (Gal. 3:28; 1 Cor. 12:13)," Bultmann takes Paul in a conservative rather than revolutionary way.[66] Paul's injunction, "'do not become slaves of men' (1 Cor. 7:23), applies to all desires for emancipation, for they stem from human evaluations."[67]

Bultmann's "apolitical" interpretation of the New Testament carries over into his preaching. For example, in a sermon on 2 Corinthians 4:6-11 on 17 June 1945, five weeks after Germany's surrender in World War II, Bultmann declares:

> How often have we heard the criticism: what have the Churches done for the life of the people, the life of civilization? As though the meaning of the Church, of faith, were to achieve some practical end within the sphere of the visible world! As though it were not the very essence of religion to be for men an asylum, a sanctuary, to which they might withdraw from the tumult of the visible world in the quest of meditation and devotion, of quiet and prayer! A sanctuary to which man might turn for refuge from the sound and fury of the everyday world, a sanctuary in which God draws near to him, and in whose stillness he derives the power to live in the unseen, eternal world.[68]

Here Bultmann defines the role of religion in quietistic terms. The gospel, it would seem, does not call for social engagement but only for self-examination.

Similarly, Bultmann's concern over pressures to politicize theology and the church in postwar West Germany led him to warn that "the church's task is to proclaim the word of God, not to pronounce political judgments. A political judgment in a concrete political situation is not the word of God. Theology must be sharply on guard against any identification of the Christian faith with a political program."[69]

---

66. *TNT* 1:343.
67. *TNT* 1:343.
68. *Marburg Sermons,* p. 218.
69. "Theology for Freedom and Responsibility," *The Christian Century* 75 (August 27, 1958), p. 969; pub. in Ger. as "Gedanken über die gegenwärtige theologische Situation," in *GuV* 3:195. Bultmann's sharp remarks appear to have been occasioned by the *Kirchliche Bruderschaften* who, under the leadership of Martin Niemöller and Karl Barth, petitioned the Synod of the Evangelical Church in Germany (*EKD*) in March 1958 to oppose preparation for, or participation in, atomic war as a matter of *status confessionis.* For an ET of the

Despite these unequivocal statements of Bultmann, Sölle nevertheless claims "that the move from existentialist theology to political theology
is itself a consequence of the Bultmannian position."[70] Sölle's thesis is that
the historical consciousness which governs Bultmann's exegesis and demythologizing derives from the Enlightenment's calling into question all
received authority — ecclesiastical *and* political.[71] Although she does not
use the term in *Political Theology,* Sölle, in effect, is arguing that the
"hermeneutics of suspicion" which enables the form critic to uncover and
identify the *Sitz-im-Leben* of a New Testament text reflects the same critical
consciousness which enables the social critic to uncover and identify the
sources and structures of class domination behind the contemporary use
of traditional Christian rhetoric.[72] Both mythological *and* ideological criticism are the common, liberating legacy of the Enlightenment.[73] Thus,
from Sölle's perspective, Bultmann's apolitical positions contradict that
comprehensive questioning of tradition presupposed by the very historical
method he champions.[74]

    With respect, therefore, to Bultmann's concept of the *Christus
praesens,* Sölle's political theology poses the question whether such a concept adequately signifies "a political *coram Christo* ['standing before (the
presence of) Christ']"[75] embracing "the liberation of all . . . the oppressed,
the poor, [and] those who mourn."[76] If not, talk of the presence of Christ
amounts to pious jargon behind which, or through which, the powers of
oppression may operate.

    At the outset of her "conversation with Bultmann," Sölle formulates
a criterion by which to test the truth of his theology:

---

petition, together with background commentary, see Clifford Green, ed., *Karl Barth: Theologian of Freedom* (London: Collins, 1989), pp. 319-21.

    70. *PT,* p. 2.
    71. See *PT,* pp. 3-6.
    72. See *PT,* pp. 16-17.
    73. For Sölle's further reflections on this point, see "Dialectics of Enlightenment:
Reflections of a European Theologian," in *Doing Theology in a Divided World: Papers from
the Sixth International Conference of the Ecumenical Association of Third World Theologians,
January 5-13, 1983, Geneva, Switzerland,* ed. Virginia Fabella and Sergio Torres (Maryknoll,
N.Y.: Orbis Books, 1985), pp. 79-84.
    74. Painter notes that "talk of '*the* historical method' is a convention." *Theology as
Hermeneutics,* p. 69. Sölle, following Ernst Troeltsch, sees its "essential features" as "criti-
cism, analogy, and correlation." *PT,* p. 18.
    75. *PT,* p. 92.
    76. *PT,* p. 67, omitting italics to accord with Ger.

The question for Bultmann and for any theology is whether it makes men more capable of love, whether it encourages or obstructs the liberation of the individual and the community. Expressed scientifically, that is the verification principle; expressed biblically, the proof of the Spirit and of power (1 Cor. 2:4).[77]

Sölle goes on to give this formal liberationist criterion of theological truth material content by speaking of "the complete identification with the interests of the poor" which she finds in the message of Jesus (Matt. 19:24; Luke 6:20).[78]

With this overview, both of Bultmann's apolitical pronouncements and of Sölle's remedy for them, we turn to Sölle's discussion of three issues touching on Bultmann's doctrine of the *Christus praesens;* namely, its relation to self-understanding, to the kerygma, and to the historical Jesus.

Self-understanding

As discussed in chapter two, kerygmatic communication, precisely as *Anrede* or direct address, is always directed to the listener's conscience, hence, to his or her self-understanding. Since conscience exists prior to, and not as a result of, the kerygmatic encounter, Bultmann refers to it as "preunderstanding." When the kerygma addresses the hearer's preunderstanding, the result is a new self-understanding, by way of accepting or rejecting the kerygma's claim.

Sölle, too, adopts this "hermeneutic circle," derived by Bultmann from Heidegger, as the formal anthropological framework of kerygmatic communication. But Sölle emphasizes that no aspect of the hermeneutic circle — whether old preunderstanding, new self-understanding, or the content of the kerygma itself, with its own understanding of existence — is ever independent of "social and psychosocial factors."[79]

With respect to preunderstanding, Sölle argues that "being a person first becomes a concrete, tangible reality precisely when one becomes aware of his dependence on society and, conjointly, of the latitude permitted by that society at specific points." Sölle concedes that "Bultmann is certainly

---

77. *PT,* pp. 5-6. Sölle also anchors her love criterion to Kant's moral law. The love command is both "unsurpassable" and "underivable" from the world. See p. 24.

78. *PT,* p. 36.

79. *PT,* p. 15.

aware that man is determined by his past," that is, by "biological, social, and psychological forces, and therefore does not have freedom at his disposal but urgently needs liberation from time to time." Nevertheless, Sölle finds this only a "formal insight which remains unpacked" in Bultmann's thought.[80]

Furthermore, Bultmann's derivation of authentic existence from "the experience of the eschatological moment, which transcends all conditions," really "fails to consider the stamp left upon man by his past, by his origin and place." Thus, Bultmann's "eschatological event" overcomes social forces only by overlooking their ineradicable stamp on personal identity. This atomistic aspect of Bultmann's anthropology leads him to minimize that "even our personal decisions are determined by social behavior patterns that bear the stamp of the classes to which we belong." To remove personality from the constraints of temporality, by means of Bultmann's transcendental "moment," is to regard human identity in a "presociological fashion." Thus, "the conditions of one's own preunderstanding or the condition of the self-understanding constituted by the encounter with the gospel" cannot be withdrawn from the scrutiny of critical consciousness.[81]

In our previous discussion of Frei's *The Identity of Jesus Christ,* we commented on how Bultmann's eschatology, as the annulment of the "flesh," empties the *Christus praesens* of any character traits, even if such were recoverable with respect to the historical Jesus. Thanks to Sölle's analysis, we also see how Bultmann's eschatology empties anthropology and soteriology of sociopolitical content by extracting them from social context. Eschatological existence regards social determinants as "of the flesh" and, therefore, only takes account of them paradoxically, "as if not" [*hōs mē*] (1 Cor. 7:29-31).[82] Thus, for all Bultmann's talk of the subversion of entrenched preunderstanding by the eschatological event of Jesus Christ, and the resulting advent of authentic existence, his sidestepping of all social determinants of human identity actually makes more secure *status quo* social orders and political structures, regardless of their relation to human liberation.[83]

80. *PT,* pp. 45-46.
81. *PT,* pp. 43-45.
82. See *TNT* 1:351-52.
83. One critic of Bultmann has even charged that his "exclusive interest in the individual and the possibility of authentic existence plays indirectly into the hands of Fascism." M. Hermanns, "Wie progressiv sind unsere Progressiven? 3. Rudolf Bultmann," *Kritischer Katholizismus* (July 1969), quoted in *PT,* p. 8. Whatever the truth in this

Furthermore, according to Sölle, the conditions constituting the self-understanding of a text are likewise subject to historical criticism. This includes all texts, not simply those that are overtly "mythological." Bultmann's existentialist interpretation of the cross-resurrection, for example, does not discharge its critical responsibility simply by transposing a mythical-historical event of the past into the existential-eschatological event of present proclamation. For even a "demythologized" account of this event, such as 2 Corinthians 5:18–6:2, may itself reflect, or even reinforce, social views that could conceivably stand as a barrier to human liberation. Until critical consciousness puts the question of social determinants and consequences to all texts functioning in proclamation, the hermeneutical task remains incomplete.

Sölle finds all too often in Bultmannian circles an unfortunate failure to analyze sociologically the factors determining the origin and reception of New Testament texts. This results in the immunization from criticism of certain New Testament concepts, simply because they are deemed nonmythological. For example, recall Romans 10:13-17. In chapter 2 we noted Bultmann's appeal to this text when speaking of "the saving fact" of "the Word as preaching [als Predigt], validated by the person Jesus Christ who is one with it — but in such a way that it, too, is one with him and is encountered only in him."[84] Commenting on this same "oft-cited" text of Paul, Sölle writes that "in this passage Paul traces faith back to hearing, hearing to the sermon, and the sermon to the Word of Christ"; nevertheless, Sölle is disturbed by "ahistorical" appeals to this text in sanctioning the sermon as an "'unalterable structure,'" thereby justifying "existing church practice."[85]

In Sölle's judgment, such appeals to Romans 10:13-17 simply ignore the sociological factors informing Paul's remarks. When the Apostle wrote

---

statement, it should not obscure Bultmann's faithful Christian witness during the Nazi period. See Andreas Lindemann, "Neutestamentler in der Zeit des Nationalsozialismus: Hans von Soden und Rudolf Bultmann in Marburg," Wort und Dienst 20 (1989): 25-52; H. Jackson Forstman, "A Chapter in Theological Resistance to Racism: Rudolf Bultmann and the Beginning of the Third Reich," in Justice and the Holy: Essays in Honor of Walter Harrelson, ed. Douglas A. Knight and Peter J. Paris (Atlanta, Ga.: Scholars Press, 1989), pp. 258-70; and, more recently, under the name Jack Forstman, Christian Faith in Dark Times: Theological Conflicts in the Shadow of Hitler (Louisville, Ky.: Westminster/John Knox, 1992), pp. 203-9 and 222-42.

84. FaU 1:242. Cf. GuV 1:209.

85. PT, p. 15. Sölle's criticism is occasioned by Erich Grässer, "Die politische Herausforderung an die biblische Theologie," Evangelische Theologie 30 (1970): 249.

to the Romans, the New Testament was not even in existence. Hence, Paul is not writing about preaching in the sense of a proclamation based on what we term today "the New Testament." Furthermore, the majority of Paul's hearers, according to Sölle, were illiterate. Hence, the practice of preaching may be more a response to this situation than to God's instituting an invariable structure for faith. Again, Paul was in a situation where information about the Christian movement was more in demand than today. Hence, the urgency and priority of preaching may have been simply a response to this specific and temporary contingency. Sölle goes on to say that "if one neglects these data and translates the Pauline concept of preaching into the present, contending that the church's Sunday sermon is necessary for faith, then the wish may have been the father of the idea."[86]

Sölle's remarks suggest that when textual criticism falls short of sociological analysis, the structures and practices of the contemporary church may too easily be injected into a first-century situation. Thus, a present fixture of Protestant church life — the Sunday sermon — is read into Paul's text and then read back out of it to bolster a practice whose alteration or abandonment now becomes doubly unthinkable. In this way, contemporary church structures, as structures, become insulated from criticism and reformation.

No doubt, Bultmann's doctrine of the *Christus praesens,* or the presence of Jesus Christ in and through the event of church proclamation, takes preaching as essential for the life of the church. Bultmann's frequent and interchangeable use of "preaching" (*Predigt*) and "proclamation" (*Verkündigung*) for kerygmatic communication likewise cements the customary identification of gospel witness with sermonic discourse, and, thus, lends primacy to the Christ of the cult.[87]

Nevertheless, as noted in chapter four, Bultmann does not limit the proclamation of the kerygma to the preaching of the Sunday sermon by an ordained minister:

---

86. *PT,* p. 16. One would have thought that the sociology of early Christian preaching might have something to do with synagogal patterns and parallels, of which Sölle makes no mention.

87. See, e.g., *GuV* 1:267 and 289 and *Exegetica,* pp. 228 and 467, where forms of *Predigt* and *Verkündigung* are used interchangeably. Hodgson charges that "both Bultmann and Barth tended to restrict the word of God and the word of faith to church proclamation, thus losing a sense of the historicity and worldliness of the word by which salvation is mediated." *Jesus — Word and Presence,* p. 262.

The "word" does not at all mean only the word from the pulpit resounding in God's house; it has, of course, taken many different forms, and in them all, the word vexes the world. It can take the form of works of Christian charity; such also is a speaking word, a witnessing act to Jesus.[88]

Bultmann no more limits proclamation to a sermon than he limits the presence of God-in-Christ to the church; that *would* confuse the occasion of revelation with its essential condition!

Yet that does not mean the church can abandon its commission and responsibility to provide for this occasion regularly (cf. 2 Cor. 5:18-19). Openness to new homiletical and liturgical forms can never mean abandoning the witness to Jesus Christ in the form of direct address. To do so would falsely suggest that Christians have God's will and way as their secure possession; that the church, as such, no longer needs to hear "the word of reconciliation"; and that we can live by all sorts of promptings rather than through the kerygmatic occasion where Jesus Christ promises to address us. While we may indeed conclude that "Jesus is present not merely in the word of preaching but wherever and whenever a free, truthful, and salvific word comes to speech,"[89] Christians cannot determine what is "free," "truthful," or "salvific" apart from the gospel of Jesus Christ. If we encounter God everywhere and recognize the presence of Christ in the world, it is because we are already encountering God's Word and discerning its cruciform pattern in and through the church's proclamation of the kerygma.[90]

The Kerygma

In chapter two, in discussing the cross-resurrection kerygma of Paul, we observed that the Greek term *to kērygma* can refer either to the *act* of proclamation (1 Cor. 2:4), an event of direct address, or to the *content* of what is proclaimed (1 Cor. 15:4). We also noted that, according to Bultmann, the content of the Christian kerygma is expressed in "dogmas," that is, in theological statements which are conceptually colored by the

---

88. *Marburger Predigten,* p. 59. In this context Bultmann also mentions the word of Christian witness embodied in art, poetry, music, painting, and sculpture — but not politics!

89. So Hodgson, *Jesus — Word and Presence,* p. 262. See also pp. 280-83.

90. Bultmann shares this conviction with Luther. See *NTaM,* p. 119.

time and place of their formulation. Thus, what is invariable about the Christian kerygma is its form as direct address, that is, the confronting of the hearer with God's claim on conscience. What is variable is not God's claim, as such, but the formulations by which it is expressed.

According to Sölle, this key distinction between "kerygma" and "dogma" has been "suppressed by the entire Bultmannian right." In their hands, the kerygma has become exclusively a matter of dogmatic code words such as " 'incarnation, true manhood, death, resurrection, [and] exaltation.' " These concepts, albeit "demythologized," are no longer correlated with the contemporary "situation" awaiting summoning. Hence, the kerygma resounding from many pulpits today amounts to "a system of propositional truths independent of the situation, a superstructure no longer relevant to praxis, to the situation, to the real questions of life," in short, an "ideology."[91]

Sölle's analysis suggests that when the "situation" that characterizes "hearing" drops out, the kerygma can no longer function as direct address. What remains is simply dogma. In this way, the absoluteness of the kerygma's concrete claim within a specific situation becomes transferred to the claim's original dogmatic formulation. This removes the kerygma, both as act and as content, from "rational control," or, to use Bultmann's term, from "understanding." In this way, Bultmann's insistence that the kerygma calls for a decision made with understanding becomes eclipsed by "a total decisionism" based on submission to christological slogans. Kerygmatic address now becomes an incantation insulated from the human situation requiring liberation.[92]

Sölle's solution to this ideological distortion of the kerygma is to recover Bultmann's distinction between "kerygma" and "dogma," thereby recognizing that "the kerygma necessarily has various situational or relational theological forms."[93] In this regard, Sölle quotes with approval Bultmann's claim that " 'a theological statement is not true because its content expresses something which is timelessly valid. It is true when it gives the answer to the question posed by the concrete situation in time

---

91. *PT,* p. 23. Here Sölle is attacking the summary of the kerygma given in Walter Schmithals, "Kein Streit um des Kaisers Bart: Zur Diskussion über das Bekenntnis zu Jesus Christus," *Evangelische Kommentare* 3 (February 1970): 79.

92. *PT,* pp. 24-25. See also p. 33. Cf. Bultmann, *FaU* 1:301: "The Word of God, although it is subject to no human criterion and is in itself authoritative, is still an *understandable* word. It does not work by magic, nor is it a dogma which demands blind submission or the acceptance of absurdities."

93. *PT,* p. 27.

to which the sentence itself belongs when it is being spoken.'"[94] Sölle
seeks to build upon this statement by a Marxist broadening of "situation"
to include "alienation — in which men are not yet fully conscious of . . .
the burden of suffering brought about by social conditions."[95]

Sölle is surely correct to distinguish Bultmann from a kerygmatic
formalism that neglects the situation of the hearer. She sends a salutary
reminder that the kerygma is essentially an event of encounter that is not
reducible to a printed verse on a page. Yet, in reacting to the church's lack
of seriousness about the situation in which preaching occurs, Sölle so
stresses Bultmann's concern for anthropology that she neglects its eschatological correlate. In so doing, she is led to a conclusion quite opposite
from Bultmann, namely, that "truth is not something we find or by which
we are found, but something that we make true."[96] With this loss of
transcendence and eschatology, Sölle's argument with the "Bultmannian
right" now becomes one with Bultmann himself.

The Historical Jesus

Nowhere is Sölle's conceptual break with Bultmann more clearly evident
than when she strictly correlates the present (Marxist described) "situation"
with the historical Jesus or JC-2, rather than with *Christus praesens* or JC-3.
Sölle claims that only recourse to "the earthly, historical Jesus of Nazareth
[*Jesus von Nazareth, der irdische, der historische*]" can keep "theology from
supplanting the kerygma by reducing it to doctrinal propositions." With
Herbert Braun, she sets her "focus primarily on the historical Jesus himself," understanding "the kerygma as the absoluteness of his claim — not
thereby as an additional content that makes faith possible in the first place,
but as the form in which Jesus encounters us today." The more the contents
of the kerygma are removed from the concreteness of Jesus, the more

---

94. *PT,* p. 22, quoting *FaU* 1:147. Sölle neglects to say that Bultmann's statement
here stands in tension with others such as the following: "[The dialectical theologian]
cannot give meaning and truth (meaning + truth = reality!) to his speaking, because the
presupposition is not at his disposal. His speaking is never anything but a *witness* to God's
truth. . . . This truth is truly the *event* from *God;* it is God's *act.*" "The Question of
'Dialectic' Theology," in *BDT* 1:260. Cf. "Die Frage der 'dialektischen' Theologie," in *AdT*
2:76; italics added to accord with Ger.
95. *PT,* p. 26.
96. *PT,* p. 77.

abstract the rhetoric of "redemption, sin, grace, [and] resurrection" becomes, and the more the kerygma retreats "from the worldliness of Jesus as portrayed in his words and deeds." The result is the "depoliticizing of the gospel."[97]

In Sölle's judgment "the language of Jesus" is both theological and political: "Jesus' call for salvation for the poor (Luke 6:20) and his partiality against the rich (Matt. 19:24 [n.b., omitting v. 26!]) stem from an obvious [*selbstverständlich*] political consciousness." His language, if "ambiguous in its possibilities of application," is "unequivocal only in its concern for liberation." Sölle therefore appeals for "adherence to the language of Jesus" which "would enjoin us to rediscover the political relevance of the gospel." That is to say, if the kerygma is to continue to be characterized as *Anrede,* then it must actually address the concrete social environment and political context as did Jesus' own preaching. Hence, what is required is "a worldly and therefore, in theory at least, a political interpretation of the gospel." Such an interpretation is sanctioned by the utterances of the historical Jesus which reflect "the highest degree of consciousness, the complete identification with the interests of the poor."[98]

Sölle eschews any need to justify biblically "social awareness of transformation." She regards as "useless" or "meaningless" such questions as "whether Jesus would directly intervene to transform social conditions," or whether Jesus was "a revolutionary," or where Jesus stood "on violence, on landed property." Sölle further concedes that "Jesus of Nazareth neither analyzed nor criticized the structural conditions under which tax collectors became tax collectors and prostitutes became prostitutes." Jesus, in her judgment, "could not ask this question, because — in Marxist terminology — the means of production had not developed to the point where the restructuring of society was technically possible." Therefore, Sölle rules out of bounds, as "ahistorical" and "pre-Marxist," the question whether

---

97. *PT,* pp. 27-28, 33, and 36. Cf. *Politische Theologie,* pp. 39-40 and 46-50.

98. *PT,* pp. 36-38. Cf. *Politische Theologie,* pp. 49-52. Bultmann finds "only one passage in the gospel record in which a rich man is declared deserving of hell-fire simply because he is rich, and a poor man simply because he is poor is found worthy to be carried by the angels to Abraham's bosom." In Bultmann's view this story of the rich man and Lazarus (Luke 16:19-26) "is probably not a genuine part of the preaching of Jesus." *Jesus and the Word,* p. 104. Cf. *HST,* pp. 196-97 and 203-4. Bultmann (unlike Käsemann) does assign Luke 6:20 ("Blessed are you poor") to the historical Jesus. See *Jesus and the Word,* p. 204 and *Exegetica,* p. 477.

the New Testament "embraces the conviction that social conditions are transformable."[99]

Given these significant qualifications to Sölle's claim that the historical Jesus is the political Jesus, what significance does the historical Jesus have for the present situation? Sölle abandons any attempt to quote Jesus for specific answers to the questions of violence, revolution, and social transformation. Instead she employs the New Testament to recover "the intention or tendency" of Jesus' "behavior," in order "to realize anew his goals in our world."[100]

Sölle argues that "the manner in which Jesus thought and acted *de facto* broke open and transformed the social structures of the world in which he lived." She cites in this regard Mark 3:31-35 ("Who are my mother and my brothers?"), Matthew 8:22 ("Leave the dead to bury their own dead"), and Matthew 23:8-10 ("You are not to be called rabbi . . . call no man your father on earth . . . neither be called masters"). "Above all, however, the abolition of the hitherto valid horizon of a religiously defined society of achievement has had obvious social ramifications." Here Sölle has in mind Jesus' healings, his associating with women, and his questioning of authority (Matt. 20:25-26).[101]

On Bultmann's form-critical grounds, Sölle's synoptic prooftexts do not necessarily indicate the "thoughts and actions" of the historical Jesus or reflect his attack on "a religiously defined society of achievement," by which Sölle apparently means the Palestinian Judaism of the first century. If Bultmann is correct, only one of the four texts cited in the previous paragraph, Matthew 8:22, is clearly assignable to the historical Jesus himself, and two of the passages, namely, Matthew 23:8-10 and Mark 10:42-43 (the parallel of Matt. 20:25-26), while enshrining rules for the Christian community, may have come directly from Jewish sources other than Jesus.[102] If Sölle aims to construct a Christology of the historical Jesus, then the historical-critical method she endorses must determine the predications that can be assigned to JC-2. Sölle's inconsistency in this regard, perhaps typical of "liberation" Christologies, may reflect her commitment to a Marxist soteriology. If so, her soteriological wishes may be the real source of her Christological ideas.

---

99. *PT,* pp. 64-65.

100. *PT,* p. 64. Sölle's language here has a parallel in Frei's subsequent use of an "intention-action" identity description for the Jesus of the synoptic Gospels. Where Frei seeks to sketch the identity of JC-1, Sölle has in mind JC-2.

101. *PT,* pp. 65-66.

102. See *HST,* pp. 29-31, 77, 81, 143-44, and 147; *Jesus and the Word,* pp. 31, 34, 104, 109-10, and 204; and *EaF,* p. 193.

However we assess her handling of the synoptic materials, Sölle is clearly proposing an alternative to the "apolitical" *Christus praesens* of Bultmann. In effect, she reframes Bultmann's soteriological correlation of anthropology and Christology. Whereas Bultmann accounts for the "I-Thou" encounter of the believer and Christ as the eschatological event which occurs in and through kerygmatic proclamation, Sölle speaks of Jesus as our "contemporary" only in the sense of one whose teachings continue to motivate and instruct us in the present. This contemporaneity with Jesus, Sölle insists, is no different from that which we enjoy "with respect to all historical figures" who have something to teach us.[103] Therefore, Jesus is not our Lord, and the gospel does not exercise an " 'authoritative lordship.' "[104] Rather, Jesus is our "nonauthoritarian" teacher whose message Sölle finds summarized in the Catechism of Isolotto: "Jesus wants us to be friends."[105]

A Reply to Sölle

Sölle's citations of synoptic texts in presenting the historical Jesus as the political Jesus are made independently of perhaps the most important finding of the historical-critical method in the last one hundred years. In Bultmann's words, "the message of Jesus is an *eschatological gospel* — the proclamation that now the fulfillment of the promise is at hand, that now the Kingdom of God begins."[106] Hence, "the poor and hungry are blessed, because the Kingdom of God will end their need (Luke 6:20, 21)";[107] and, hence, what Sölle terms "Jesus' call for salvation for the poor"[108] cannot be divorced from his conviction of the imminent end of this world in which social ills exist. The irony of Sölle's position is that, despite her praise for historical criticism, she virtually ignores its recovery of the eschatology presupposed by Jesus' message.[109]

Even more problematic than Sölle's abandonment of Jesus' eschato-

---

103. *PT,* pp. 30-31.
104. *PT,* p. 30.
105. *PT,* p. 106, quoting from *Die Botschaft Jesu in Isolotto: Der Katechismus des Don Mazzi* (Mainz: Chr. Kaiser, 1969; München: Matthias Grünewald, 1969), p. 41.
106. *Jesus and the Word,* p. 27.
107. Ibid., p. 103.
108. *PT,* p. 36.
109. For Sölle's cursory discussion of eschatology, see *PT,* pp. 50-53.

logical *message*, both its content and its context, is her refusal to reckon with his eschatological *destiny*. Sölle turns exclusively to the historical Jesus. She understands the kerygma "as the absoluteness of his claim," and "not thereby as an additional content that makes faith possible in the first place."[110] Thus, Sölle takes no account that for the New Testament kerygma "faith" is not the faith "of Jesus," or a faith "like Jesus," but faith *in* Jesus Christ, that is, the faith made possible only through the proclamation of Jesus' eschatological destiny.[111] To speak of Jesus of Nazareth, or Jesus apart from his eschatological destiny, as the exclusive criterion for the kerygma's dogmas, simply misreads the Gospels. The Gospels are kerygmatic constructions. As Bultmann points out, they assemble and deposit their traditions around "the kerygma of the death and resurrection of Jesus."[112] Only on the grounds of his eschatological destiny does the New Testament promise or predicate the presence of Jesus. Thus, Sölle's confident talk of the historical Jesus, in terms of the soteriological role she envisions for him as a forerunner of Marx, is itself the casualty of the historical-critical method she lauds as the harbinger of critical consciousness.

All things considered, Sölle's post-Bultmannian political theology represents a remarkable return to the historical Jesus of Bultmann's teachers, albeit partially purged of bourgeois values. The mythical or storied Jesus, that is, JC-1, makes no appearance in Sölle's book, since demythologization in her hands eliminates, rather than interprets, him. Since JC-1 is eliminated, there is no soteriological myth awaiting existentialist interpretation, and thus no remaining grounds for Bultmann's *Christus praesens* or JC-3.

What does remain for Christology is JC-2, an exclusively historical figure. As such, Jesus is neither "above" us nor "before" us, but only "behind" us. His presence, before which we stand, is a lingering posthumous influence that reinforces the absolute demand of love, or the moral law, intrinsic to human existence. Jesus' identification with the poor thus inspires and motivates us to do likewise. Jesus is the evidence that radical social consciousness is indeed a human possibility.[113]

What Sölle overlooks in her *Political Theology* is the key finding of

---

110. *PT*, p. 28.

111. See Bultmann, *FaU* 1:277; *TDNT*, s.v. *"pisteuō* [etc.]"; *TNT* 1:3; and "The Primitive Christian Kerygma and the Historical Jesus," in *HJKC*, p. 34.

112. *TNT* 1:86 and "The Primitive Christian Kerygma and the Historical Jesus," in *HJKC*, p. 42.

113. See *PT*, p. 36. Cf. Herrmann, *Communion with God*, p. 100.

the historical method she celebrates, namely, in the words of Bultmann, "the eschatological position which according to the New Testament Jesus holds as the One who is the crisis (*krisis*), the turning point, of the ages, through whom the human race has won the possibility of being conditioned by love instead of by hate."[114] If Bultmann is right about this "crisis," must the scope of salvation be limited to discrete individuals by an apolitical kerygma? Those who seek with Sölle a reformulation of the kerygma, one that engages human beings in their social and political contexts, must reengage the question, critical not only for the identity but also for the saving scope of Bultmann's *Christus praesens:* the question of Jesus' eschatological destiny.

Jürgen Moltmann and the *"Adventus Christi"*

Moltmann shares Sölle's disquiet over Bultmann's apolitical understanding of Christ and the self. Indeed, even before Sölle challenged the "Old Marburgers" in 1971 with her *Political Theology*, Moltmann had issued a challenge of his own in 1964 in *Theology of Hope*. Moltmann asks, "Is any self-understanding of man conceivable at all which is not determined by his relation to the world, to history, to society?"[115] He answers his own rhetorical question by declaring, "Always man's self-understanding is socially, materially and historically mediated."[116]

Whereas Sölle sees Bultmann's individualism in his neglecting to recognize the social and political implications of his own historical method and in his failing to reclaim for social change the example of the historical Jesus, Moltmann traces Bultmann's constricted anthropology to a "transcendental eschatology," derived from Kant and bequeathed by Herrmann.[117]

In Kant's thought, as summarized by Moltmann, no certain knowledge can be had of the *eschata*, or "last things"; such eternal realities lie "'wholly beyond our field of vision.'" As such, the objective eschatological referents are inaccessible to intellectual investigation and, hence,

114. *FaU* 1:137.
115. *TH*, p. 65.
116. *TH*, p. 67.
117. See *TH*, pp. 45-50 and 58-69. The term "transcendental eschatology" is taken by Moltmann from Jakob Taubes and Hans Urs von Balthasar, p. 46, n. 1.

"completely irrelevant for the knowledge of the world of experience."
Nevertheless, the "last things" can be investigated with respect to their
relation "'to the moral principles concerned with the ultimate goal of all
things.'" In this way, they "form themselves into eternal, transcendental
conditions for the possibility of experiencing oneself in a practical way"
independently of the determinative mechanisms of nature.[118]

Likewise, in this Kantian framework, God, as eternal and transcendent, cannot be an object of theoretical inquiry; hence, Herrmann's dictum
that "we cannot say of God how he is in himself but only what he does
to us."[119] Thus, following Herrmann, Bultmann holds that all proper
speaking of God, including God's act in Christ, is simultaneously a speaking of ourselves. Since all theological statements thereby bear an "exclusive
relation to existence," this entails "the rejection of all objective statements
about God," whether mythical or scientific, "which are not existentially
verifiable."[120]

As noted in chapter three, Bultmann presupposes with Paul and John
that human beings are related to God as creatures to Creator. For Bultmann, as for Augustine, this relation is characterized by the creature's
restless search for God, a search driven "consciously or unconsciously, by
the question about [one's] own personal existence."[121] To seek God, therefore, is simultaneously to seek "authentic existence." Bultmann thus locates
salvation in "the unobservable, hidden correlation of God and the 'self,'"
rather than in the observable and objectifiable "world of things and of
history."[122] One cannot objectively prove a "nonobjectifiable" God. Nevertheless, there is an indirect proof, insofar as the Creator can be confessed
from the self's coming to rest in its own creaturehood.

For Bultmann, the quest for creaturehood, or the question of authentic existence, is resolved in the proclamation of the kerygma. When Bultmann speaks of the "the eschatological event" of Jesus Christ, he means
that in and through "the event of preaching," God's final judgment occurs.

118. *TH,* pp. 47-48, quoting from H. A. Salmony ed., *Kants Schrift: Das Ende aller
Dinge* (1962), p. 44.

119. Cited by Bultmann in *NTaM,* p. 99 (cf. p. 115); *FaU* 1:63; "The Question
of 'Dialectic Theology,'" in *BDT* 1:269; and *JCaM,* pp. 43 and 73.

120. Moltmann, *TH,* pp. 59-60.

121. *JCaM,* pp. 52-53. See also *NTaM,* pp. 87 and 106; and "Reply," in Kegley,
Theology of Bultmann, p. 275. Cf. Bonhoeffer, *Christ the Center,* pp. 30-31: "So the question
of transcendence is the question of existence, and the question of existence is the question
of transcendence. In theological terms: it is only from God that man knows who he is."

122. *TH,* p. 60.

"The active event of revelation is itself the presence of the *eschaton,* for 'to be in the moment' of proclamation and faith is the 'authentic being' of man"; that is, "the restoring of man's original being in the sense of crea-tureliness." Thus, "in the 'moment' of revelation, creation and redemption coincide." For the believer, history comes to an end whenever eschatologi-cal righteousness and reconciliation occur in the preaching of the gospel; there is nothing more to expect in time from Christ other than future re-presentations of the eschatological salvation event, that is, future epipha-nies of the *Christus praesens.*[123]

This existentialist interpretation of revelation leaves "the future as God's future 'empty' as far as mythological, prognosticative pictures of the future are concerned." What can be affirmed, given the search for God inherent in existence, is that God's "future" is nothing other than "'the realization of human life.'" For Bultmann, to speak eschatologically is to speak of "'the goal of the individual human being,'" and not of the "'goal of history'." Hence, according to Moltmann, "the *logos* of the *eschaton* becomes the power of liberation from history, the power of the desecular-ization of existence in the sense of liberating us from understanding ourselves on the basis of the world and of works."[124] Here is the source of Bultmann's blindness to social location as a necessary datum for authen-tic existence. By portraying Bultmann in these Kantian hues, Moltmann clears the way for his own proposal, since he believes that a Christian eschatology "cannot reconcile itself with the Kantian concepts of science and of reality."[125]

In Bultmann's defense, the dualism in Kant between the phenomenal and noumenal worlds and the practical and theoretical reason suggests demythologized analogies with the "two aeons" conceptuality in Paul. Exploration of the possible connections and ramifications would take us too far afield, but "Kant" and "Christian" may be less antithetical than Moltmann allows. The primacy of the practical in Kant may likewise have a parallel in Paul's correlation of Christology and anthropology in relation to justification or reconciliation. Here it suffices to say that Moltmann

123. *TH,* p. 66.
124. *TH,* pp. 61-62, quoting Bultmann, "The Christian Hope and the Problem of Demythologizing," *The Expository Times* 65 (1954): 278 and "History and Eschatology in the New Testament," *NTS* (1954-55): 13.
125. *TH,* p. 69. Moltmann's discussion of the Kantian backdrop for Bultmann's doctrines of eschatology and revelation suggests that Herrmann, more than Heidegger, is the single most formative influence on Bultmann's thought.

pits Hebraic "history" against Greek "ontology," contrasts the coming future of Christ (*adventus Christi*) to the present presence of Christ (*praesentia Christi*), and listens to the letters of Paul while avoiding the Gospel of John and the teaching of Jesus. These hermeneutical decisions render the "Christian eschatology" of *Theology of Hope* far more selective and less comprehensive than that of Bultmann's *Theology of the New Testament*.[126] Insofar as Bultmann and Moltmann both appeal to Paul to frame their respective views on the promise and presence of Christ, we turn now to this apostolic point of contact — and conflict.

Pauline Eschatology: "Present" or "Future"?

Among the many complexities facing interpreters of Paul is what to make of the fact that both "present" and "future" eschatologies are found in his letters. Käsemann speaks of Paul's "compromise" between these two types of eschatology, with the Apostle's distinctive contribution being the "reactionary" one of recovering future eschatology for the purposes of "delimiting" and "anchoring" the present eschatology of the Corinthian enthusiasts.[127] In this latter judgment, Käsemann is followed by Moltmann.[128] Bultmann speaks of the "co-existence" in Paul of present and future eschatologies, but, in contrast and reply to Käsemann, declares that "for Paul the greater weight lies upon present eschatology, so that the future can at times be left behind entirely."[129]

In chapter one we saw that Bultmann follows the outline of early Christianity given in Bousset's study *Kyrios Christos*. Bousset's thesis is that Hellenistic Christianity centers on the cult of Christ as Lord. Jesus is worshiped as the *Kyrios* deity whose sacramental presence is mediated through baptism and the Lord's Supper on the order of a mystery religion. This development is in contrast to Palestinian Jewish piety and practice. Here the *ekklēsia* is essentially an eschatological sect within Judaism that

---

126. For Moltmann's polemics in *TH*, see, e.g., pp. 28-29, 84, 99, and 143 against "Greek" thought and p. 31 against a *praesentia Christi*. Note throughout the absence of references to the Johannine literature, except for 1 John 3:2 ("It does not yet appear what we shall be") on p. 68 — but torn from its accompanying claim, "Beloved, we are God's children now"!

127. "On the Subject of Primitive Christian Apocalyptic," in *NTQT*, pp. 131-33.

128. See *TH*, pp. 154-65.

129. *Exegetica*, p. 479.

organizes its life around the expectation of Jesus as the imminently returning Son of man. As Christianity moves geographically from Palestine to
Syria, it thus moves theologically from anticipating the fulfillment of an
eschatological promise to participating sacramentally in the divine presence. Hope in the coming Son of man gives way to cultic communion
with the *Kyrios*. Therefore, Hellenistic Christianity is the original setting
for what, since Harnack, has come to be termed the *Christus praesens*.

Within the context of Bousset's outline, Bultmann interprets Paul's
theology as a fusion of Palestinian Jewish eschatological expectation and
Hellenistic cultic presentation:

> In the matter of adopting the conceptuality of the Hellenistic mys-
> teries, the conceptuality of Jewish-Christian apocalyptic Christology and
> soteriology fails to express how salvation determines life in the present,
> but rather renders faith as essentially hope. This conceptuality aims at
> indicating that the change of the aeons is imminent and has not yet
> taken place. On the other hand, contemporaneity can be expressed in
> the terminology of the mysteries. What is peculiar to Paul is that he
> understands the presence of salvation as an eschatological phenomenon,
> or that he construes the eschatological event as present.[130]

For Paul, Hellenistic Christianity rightly perceives that salvation is a *present*
reality, while the Palestinian community correctly grasps that salvation is
inseparable from the *eschaton*. Thus, Paul's incomparable contribution was
to fuse kerygmatically these two traditions into a single perspective: in the
proclamation of the kerygma, the *Kyrios* comes, the *eschaton* happens, and
salvation becomes present.

In contrast to this sketch by Bultmann of how present and future
eschatologies coexist in the Apostle's thought to the advantage of the
present, Moltmann interprets Paul's position along Käsemann's revisionist
lines. Käsemann argues that present eschatology is neither the invention
nor the emphasis of Paul but belongs to the pre-Pauline Hellenistic
churches. In Hellenistic Christianity, "the already completed enthrone-
ment of Christ entailed the subordination of powers and principalities."
Ironically, the more the present victory of Christ is emphasized, the more
acutely the question arises "as to what earthly reality corresponds" to his
redeeming reign. The answer, according to Käsemann, emerges anthropologically. Miracles, ecstasy, and the angelic state in which national distinc-

130. *CC,* p. 98.

tions and sexual differentiations are abrogated are taken as visible evidence of the new creation. The enthroned *Kyrios Christos,* with death behind him, bestows his resurrection life on all the baptized. Thus, present eschatology, at the nub of later Corinthian excess, is actually an outgrowth of apocalyptic's "turn of the ages." Moreover, this present eschatology is already on hand when Paul begins his Gentile mission. Present eschatology is Paul's inheritance — both headache and heartache — but not his invention.[131]

Over against Hellenistic Christianity, Paul recovers the apocalyptic "not yet" of "an eschatological reservation." Paul disputes the "basic premise that the Christian participates not only in the Cross, but also in the Resurrection, of his Lord." While baptism conveys participation in the death of Christ, it does not convey the gift of resurrection. This is seen in Paul's use of the future tenses in Romans 6: "For if we have been united with him in a death like his, we *shall* certainly be united with him in a resurrection like his [v. 5]"; and "if we have died with Christ, we believe that we *shall* also live with him [v. 8]." Only Christ — not the Christian — has been raised from death.[132]

Käsemann finds Paul's opposition to Corinthian enthusiasm framed in apocalyptic terms in 1 Corinthians 15:20-28. Here the focus is christological: "Christ must reign [v. 25]," and this grounds Christian hope. More significantly, in indicating that "the lordship of Christ is limited and passing" in relation to God's own (v. 28), "it emerges [*contra* Bultmann] that Paul is absolutely unable and unwilling to speak of any end to history which has already come to pass." Nevertheless, Paul does "discern that the day of the End-time has already broken." To this extent, Käsemann can claim that the "present eschatology of the enthusiasts is therefore picked up but apocalyptically anchored and delimited as it is not with them." Thus, Paul does not fuse Jewish future eschatology with Hellenistic sacramentalism to bring about a present eschatology that is decisive for existence. Rather, Paul's apocalyptic eschatology restrains the present eschatology rampant in Corinth, albeit with implications for anthropology.[133]

131. Käsemann, "On the Subject of Primitive Christian Apocalyptic," in *NTQT,* pp. 125-31. So also Moltmann, *TH,* pp. 155-56 and 158-59.

132. Käsemann, "On the Subject of Primitive Christian Apocalyptic," in *NTQT,* pp. 132-33. So also Moltmann, *TH,* pp. 161-62. Cf. Bultmann: "In a certain sense, i.e. in so far as we belong to Christ, we *are* the resurrected, are the 'first fruits' *(aparchē),* are a 'new creation' *(kainē ktisis),* cf. 2 Cor. 5:14-17." *FaU* 1:93-94.

133. Ibid., pp. 132-34.

In responding to Käsemann, Bultmann defends the primacy of present eschatology in Paul by citing passages where the justification of believers is shown to have already occurred (e.g., Rom. 5:1; 8:3; 1 Cor. 6:11). Moreover, "the *einai en Christō* [to be in Christ] of course signifies for the believers that they are a *kainē ktisis* [new creation], for as 2 Cor. 5:17 says, 'The old is past. . . .'" Thus, when Paul speaks of the new creation he is, *contra* Käsemann, also saying that "history is at the end." In Bultmann's judgment, this does not mean that nothing more will take place in the world or that believers are somehow exempt from trials and sorrows. Hence, Bultmann can agree with Käsemann that present eschatology is anchored and delimited by apocalyptic. Nevertheless, insofar as Paul speaks of the present character of the new creation and its saving, eschatological benefits, Bultmann claims that we must also speak of apocalyptic as being anchored and delimited by present eschatology.[134]

The opposite weighting Bultmann and Käsemann assign to present and future eschatologies in Paul has corresponding implications for both anthropology and Christology. Käsemann stresses that the dominion of Christ over death has not yet ended death's present dominion over the world. Confronted by this seeming contradiction, Paul adapts the apocalyptic "two aeons" to "distinguish sharply between the Church as the redeemed and the world as unredeemed creation." Nevertheless, Christians — between their baptism and their final blessedness — still remain in the body (*sōma*), hence, in the world. Thus found in the body, where the power of the two ages contends, they are called to obedience to Christ the Lord in bodily solidarity with an unredeemed creation "groaning in travail" (Rom. 8:22-23).[135]

In Bultmann's view Paul's real achievement is in removing salvation "from the sphere of speculation and enthusiasm into the sphere of actual human existence." In this regard, Käsemann's contention that Paul transposes the lordship of Christ over the cosmic powers into the realm of anthropology is "only correct if the lordship of Christ is understood as his lordship over me . . . and correspondingly the subjection of the cosmic powers as, indeed, my active participation in this subjection by my obedience." Bultmann does concur with Käsemann that the presence of salvation takes on significance "as life in bodily obedience." But whereas Käsemann emphasizes *sōma* as the human capacity for communication, and, hence, relatedness to the world,

---

134. *Exegetica,* pp. 479-80.

135. "On the Subject of Primitive Christian Apocalyptic," in *NTQT,* pp. 134-36. So also Moltmann, *TH,* pp. 161-62.

Bultmann understands *sōma* primarily as the human being's self-relatedness, which, to be sure, includes an awareness of the world's impingements.[136]

The sharpest disagreement between Bultmann and Käsemann arises over whether Paul's theology and historical understanding is oriented to the salvation of the individual or to that of the creation at large. Käsemann emphatically declares that "Christ's mission and presence was not, and is not, first and foremost to individuals."[137] Bultmann finds this view the unfortunate result of tracing Paul's contribution to a retrieval, rather than to a modification, of apocalyptic eschatology. Such a hypothesis cannot account for Paul's teleological historical understanding (e.g., Gal. 3:19, 24; Rom. 5:20-21), which is never found in apocalyptic thought. As these texts show, the succession of the two ages becomes anthropologically understood, since "the world-time of sin is the appropriate preparation for the world-time of grace." Here, Paul takes the "present-future theme of eschatology" from apocalyptic expectation and transposes it into an existential understanding of sin and grace.[138]

In Moltmann's judgment, such "presentative" formulations of eschatology remove from faith its orientation to God's promise (Rom. 8) and, hence, forget "that faith has itself a goal (1 Peter 1:9) to which it is on the way, that 'it [does] not yet appear what we shall be' (1 John 3:2), and that faith is thus out for something which is promised to it but which is not yet fulfilled."[139] Through his conflict with the Corinthian enthusiasts, Paul is brought to "a new recognition of a truly futurist eschatology" which "becomes a criticism of presentative eschatology as such."[140] Therefore, 1 Corinthians 15 is neither "a relapse into outmoded apocalyptic mythology,"[141] nor is Paul "trying, with the help of the cosmological myth of the Gnostics, to express the contemporaneousness of the fact of salvation."[142] "Rather, the content of the Hellenistic idea of the presence of the eternal is futurized by him and applied to the still outstanding *eschaton*."[143]

---

136. *Exegetica,* pp. 480-81. Cf. Käsemann, "On the Subject of Primitive Christian Apocalyptic," in *NTQT,* p. 135 (on 1 Cor. 6:13).

137. "On the Subject of Primitive Christian Apocalyptic," in *NTQT,* p. 135. See also "New Testament Questions of Today," in *NTQT,* pp. 14-15.

138. *Exegetica,* pp. 481-82. See also *FaU* 1:93: "Christ is not the cosmic ground of a future condition of existence, but the historical foundation of our present life."

139. *TH,* p. 68.

140. *TH,* p. 160.

141. *TH,* p. 163.

142. Bultmann, *FaU* 1:242, n. 17.

143. Moltmann, *TH,* p. 164.

In light of our earlier analysis and reconstruction of the Pauline *Christus praesens,* Moltmann's *Theology of Hope* sharply departs from Bultmann's interpretation. Indeed, if Moltmann is right about Paul's opponents in Corinth, then Bultmann arguably stands closer to them than to the "apocalyptic" Apostle himself. With Moltmann the emphasis for Paul is on the "not-yet" of eschatological expectation; with Bultmann, on the "already" of the kerygmatic eschatological salvation event. With Moltmann orientation to Paul comes largely by way of 1 Corinthians 15 and Romans 8, with their focus on the universal promise made in the resurrection of Jesus Christ; with Bultmann orientation to Paul comes primarily through 2 Corinthians 5 and 6, with their claim for the presence of Christ here and now in the proclaimed word of eschatological reconciliation. The end result of this debate hinges both on research in the history of religions and on judgments as to the subject matter of the New Testament.

Whatever the final outcome, Moltmann's de-emphasizing the presence of Christ, in and through the preached and enacted kerygma, appears motivated by resistance to an epiphanic eschatology of glory.[144] Certainly there is ecclesial danger here — as the history of Christian fanaticism and triumphalism both illustrate. Yet in the *Christus praesens* according to Bultmann, the kerygma is not said to occasion a visible manifestation of the glorified Christ. For Bultmann faith only discerns the glory of Jesus Christ "in, with, and under" the utterly human and temporal forms of the word of the cross. Precisely this paradoxical character of the eschatological event protects Bultmann's kerygmatic expression of the *Christus praesens* from unleashing those experiences of ecstasy which Moltmann, among others, may associate with this formulation.[145]

---

144. *TH,* pp. 158-59. By 1992, Moltmann had come full theological circle, claiming to have "experienced" what he calls "the presence of eternity." *The Spirit of Life: A Universal Affirmation* (Minneapolis: Fortress, 1992), p. x.

145. Noting that "in the Corinthian Gnosticism, Paul battled the illusion that one can experience the glory of the exalted Lord in the present," Wolfhart Pannenberg declares that "the *experience* of the presence of Christ is promised only for the [universal] end of time." *Jesus — God and Man,* 2nd ed., trans. Lewis L. Wilkens and Duane A. Priebe (Philadelphia: Westminster, 1977), p. 28. For criticism of Pannenberg on this point, see Hodgson, *Jesus — Word and Presence,* p. 30 and Cone, *God of the Oppressed,* pp. 121-22.

Promise or Presence?

Throughout *Theology of Hope,* Moltmann frames the issue of Christology in terms of "promise" rather than "presence." For him the Hellenization of the Jewish apocalyptic understanding represents the victory of the Christ who is present over the Christ who is promised:

> The event of promise, which is what the life and teaching, dying and raising of Jesus were held to be, now becomes an event of redemption, which can be subsequently repeated in the cultus in the form of a mystery drama. . . . In place of the eschatological 'not yet' (*noch nicht*) we have a cultic 'now only' (*nur noch*), and this becomes the key-signature of history *post Christum.* . . . When Bultmann interprets Paul by seeing the heart of Pauline theology in Paul's anthropological and existentialist interpretation of the peculiarity of presentative eschatology, then he has undoubtedly discovered an important modification of the theology of the eternal present, but not really a fundamental alternative to it.[146]

In Moltmann's view, the recovery of authentic Christian eschatology can only come by retrieving the theological category of "promise."

Moltmann observes that "the more recent theology of the Old Testament has indeed shown that the words and statements about the 'revealing of God' in the Old Testament are combined throughout with statements about the 'promise of God.'"[147] Hence, unlike "the gods of the epiphanies," Israel's "God of the promise" reveals "himself and his presence" in showing faithfulness to his promises.[148] This pattern of promissory revelation is also that of the New Testament, insofar as the resurrection of Jesus is "an act of the faithfulness of God" that "forms the ground of the promise of the still outstanding future of Jesus Christ."[149]

What does Moltmann mean by "promise"? He gives the following summary:

> A promise is a declaration which announces the coming of a reality that does not yet exist. . . . The promise binds man to the future and

146. *TH,* pp. 158-60.
147. *TH,* p. 42, alluding to the work of Walther Zimmerli, Gerhard von Rad, and Rolf Rendtorff.
148. *TH,* p. 43.
149. *TH,* p. 85.

gives him a sense for history. . . . The history which is initiated and determined by promise does not consist in cyclic recurrence, but has a definite trend towards the promised and outstanding fulfillment. . . . If the word is a word of promise, then that means that this word has not yet found a reality congruous with it, but that on the contrary it stands in contradiction to the reality open to experience now and heretofore. . . . The word of promise therefore always creates an interval of tension between the uttering and the redeeming of the promise. . . . If the promise is not regarded abstractly apart from the God who promises, but its fulfillment is entrusted directly to God in his freedom and faithfulness, then there can be no burning interest in constructing a hard and fast juridical system of historic necessities according to a schema of promise and fulfillment . . . The peculiar character of the Old Testament promises can be seen in the fact that the promises were not liquidated by the history of Israel — neither by disappointment nor by fulfillment — but that on the contrary Israel's experience of history gave them a constantly new and wider interpretation.[150]

These enumerated characteristics of "promise" may be taken as theses for which *Theology of Hope,* with varying success, argues.

For our purposes it is important to note at this juncture that Moltmann's explanations indicate that a promise is indeed a "speech act." That is, a promise not only announces or informs as to a future state of affairs but does so in such a way as to constitute a new state of affairs in the present. For example, a promise, we are told, "initiates" and "determines" history; a promise "binds" its hearers to the future; and a promise "gives" its receivers a sense of history (and destiny and hope) by "creating an interval of tension" between its uttering and its redeeming. The performative power that Moltmann assigns to promise is clearly one of agency.

In chapter two we first noted Bultmann's characterization of the kerygma as "promise," and later in chapter four we observed how his discussion of the kerygma as existential language anticipates subsequent developments in analytic philosophy on the "performative" and "self-involving" status of promissory rhetoric. Nevertheless, "promise" functions very differently in Moltmann than in Bultmann, and this becomes clear with respect to the *Christus praesens.*

---

150. *TH,* pp. 103-4. Moltmann's characterizations here derive from Walther Zimmerli, "Promise and Fulfillment," in Claus Westermann, ed., *Essays on Old Testament Hermeneutics* (Richmond: John Knox, 1963), pp. 89-122.

For example, Moltmann almost always attributes promissory agency to God and not to Jesus Christ. God makes promises to us in the resurrection of Christ, but the Risen Christ, as such, does not address us with the divine word of promise.[151] Jesus Christ is the object rather than the agent of God's promises. In a rare instance in *Theology of Hope* where Moltmann, paraphrasing Barth, speaks of "encounter" with Christ,[152] he does not mean this in terms of, or on analogy with, an "I-Thou" encounter with the believer. Such a formulation, derived from interpersonal communion, falls into the category of the anthropologically given. But Moltmann holds that the Risen Lord cannot be accommodated to analogies taken from present experience: "The expectation of what is to come on the ground of the resurrection of Christ, must then turn all reality that can be experienced . . . into . . . a reality that does not yet contain within it what is held in prospect for it."[153]

Moltmann's transfer of "Christ and his benefits" from an existentially directed kerygma to the horizon of an apocalyptic future proceeds, in part, through his appropriation of the philosophical thought of Ernst Bloch.[154] Bloch contends that the future is the efficacious power transforming the present. While Moltmann, as we have seen, attributes performative power to promissory rhetoric, he later — under Bloch's influence — assigns this same power to the future as such. This confuses categories. The future — unlike a promise — does not entail self-involving agency. This lack of attention to the self-involving conventions of promissory rhetoric leads Moltmann to displace the performative power of promise onto the future as such. This has the twin effect of removing from redemption, now conceived as a temporal process, a personal saving agent and of making biblical promises illustrative, rather than constitutive, of present states of affairs.

151. But see *TH*, p. 325. For Moltmann's polemical remarks against the Christ of the cult, see pp. 161 and 326.

152. "We can therefore say: the risen Lord encounters us as the living Lord, inasmuch as he is in motion, on the march towards his goal." *TH*, p. 87, citing Barth, *CD*, vol. 4, pt. 3: *The Doctrine of Reconciliation* (1961), trans. G. W. Bromiley, pp. 326-27.

153. *TH*, p. 180.

154. See *TH*, esp. pp. 16 and 208. For what follows see Christopher Morse, *The Logic of Promise in Moltmann's Theology* (Philadelphia: Fortress, 1979), pp. 65-66. Morse's analysis of Bloch's influence on *TH* is based on Moltmann's further elaborations in "Theology as Eschatology," in *The Future of Hope*, ed. Frederick Herzog (New York: Harper & Row, 1967), p. 19; and *Religion, Revolution, and the Future*, trans. M. Douglas Meeks (New York: Charles Scribner's Sons, 1969), p. 14.

The Resurrection and the Canons of History

Moltmann argues that the historical character of the resurrection accounts is necessarily raised in that they witness to "a fact and an event whose reality lay for them outside their [authors'] own consciousness and their own faith, whose reality was indeed the origin of their consciousness in remembrance and hope." This is not to say that the accounts, like those "of ancient chroniclers or modern historians," attempt "only to report what happened," for there is clearly a kerygmatic motive at work. Nevertheless, "their statements contain not only existential certainty in the sense of saying, 'I am certain,' but also . . . objective certainty in the sense of saying, 'It is certain.'" That is, the primary referent in the resurrection accounts is the destiny of Jesus and not the faith of the believer. Thus, the resurrection accounts would appear to invite historical inquiry and analysis.[155]

Here arises the problem that "the concept of the historical, of the historically possible and the historically probable [*der Begriff des Historischen, des Historisch-Möglichen und Historisch-Wahrscheinlichen*], has been developed in the modern age on the basis of experiences of history other than the experience of the raising of Jesus from the dead."[156] Modern historical science assumes, as Ernst Troeltsch observes, a basic similarity underlying all events so that we exercise critical judgment in determining the probability of events largely on the basis of analogical correlations with present experiences. Moreover, "in face of the positivistic and mechanistic definition of the nature of history as a self-contained system of cause and effect, the assertion of a raising of Jesus by God appears as a myth concerning a supernatural incursion which is contradicted by all our experience of the world."[157] Indeed, these Enlightenment assumptions, so celebrated by Sölle, prompt Bultmann's own program of demythologization.

Rather than acquiesce, via existentalist interpretation, to the *a priori* dismissal of even the possibility of Jesus' resurrection, that is, as an objective event pertaining to JC-2, Moltmann subjects the Enlightenment's canons of history to eschatological relativization. That is to say, "only when the

---

155. *TH,* pp. 172-73.

156. *TH,* p. 174. Cf. *Theologie der Hoffnung,* p. 157.

157. *TH,* p. 177. In contrast to Frei, Moltmann discusses mythology from the standpoint of the modern *Weltbild* and its historical method, rather than in terms of literary genre.

world can be understood as contingent creation out of the freedom of God and *ex nihilo* . . . does the raising of Christ become intelligible as *nova creatio*."[158] From this vantage point it is the framework of a closed system of causal relations which is irrational. Without relativization by an eschatological perspective, canons, which place all knowable reality within a causal nexus regulated by deterministic laws, lead to a historical framework unconscious of its own contingency.

Moltmann, following Richard R. Niebuhr, suggests that theology construct its own understanding of history on the basis of a theological and eschatological interpretation of the resurrection. The point here is neither to trim theological sails to the winds of a new *Weltbild* (say, that of Einstein instead of Newton), nor to adduce, on the basis of the resurrection, new laws of history for the practicing historian. Rather, it is to see the resurrection of Christ as an "analogy," not "to that which can be experienced any time and anywhere, but as an analogy to what is to come to all." In this sense the resurrection is not a historical occurrence because it can be demonstrated as having occurred in history, but it is historical in the sense of calling into question closed understandings of reality, thereby engendering hope for new, yet unforeseen possibilities in history.[159]

By defining "understanding" and "rationality" on the basis of Enlightenment assumptions, Bultmann severs the resurrection from the world and its history, confining it to the metaphysics and dynamics of subjectivity. "In this form the resurrection faith that makes no assertions of the resurrection fits in exactly with the modern world's view of reality and is in a sense the ultimate religion of our society."[160] Thus, Bultmann's "eschatological event" actually serves to sanction and secure the absoluteness of the *status quo*, precisely through its commitment to the Enlightenment's critical canons. In contrast to Sölle, Moltmann disputes that human liberation or political transformation can result from absolute outlooks based on closed systems of causality.

158. *TH,* p. 179.
159. *TH,* pp. 180-81, citing Niebuhr, *Resurrection and Historical Reason* (New York: Charles Scribner's Sons, 1957).
160. *TH,* p. 181.

A Reply to Moltmann

Like Bultmann, Moltmann operates within a conceptual framework determined by a revelatory understanding of the Word of God. At issue between them is certainly not whether Christian faith can dispense with divine revelation or with the eschatological destiny of Jesus as contexts for Christology. Moreover, both understand the Word of God to be essentially a word of promise. Disagreement arises not over the form of promise but over its material formulation.

In Bultmann's view the eschatological destiny of Jesus as the Glorified of God enables him to be the present, acting agent of the kerygma's word of promise. By contrast, for Moltmann, the eschatological destiny of Jesus is "an act of faithfulness of God" that "forms the ground of the promise of the still outstanding future of Jesus Christ."[161] Can we speak then of the *Christus praesens* or JC-3 with regard to Moltmann? The logic of *Theology of Hope* suggests that Jesus Christ is present only in the sense that he is the object of God's still outstanding promises. Thus, Moltmann supplants faith in the Christ who is present with hope for " 'Christ and his future.' "[162]

The contribution of Moltmann lies in seeing the universality of the promises of God, made known in the resurrection of Jesus Christ, as promises that speak not only to the destiny of individual believers but to that of humanity, and creation, as a whole. The still-outstanding character of these promises underscores that Christians remain in the "body," and, hence, in profound solidarity with a suffering world. This solidarity, the correlative of apocalyptic promise, binds believers to the world and sends them forth into social and political engagement as witnesses for hope and workers for change.

The difficulty with Moltmann's reformulation of the presence of Christ is that it ignores the Gospel of John, with its stress on the presence of the Glorified Son in the paracletic word of the church, and discounts the Apostle Paul's conviction that Jesus Christ speaks in and through the heralds of the gospel. For Paul and John the destiny of Jesus does not remove him from the world, as would be the case if he were simply the object of apocalyptic promise. Rather, the destiny of Jesus enables him to be present in the proclamation of the church, and, in this way, also in the world as its Lord and Savior.

---

161. *TH,* p. 85.

162. *TH,* p. 192, quoting Eduard Thurneysen, "Christus und seine Zukunft: Ein Beitrag zur Eschatologie," *Zwischen den Zeiten* 9 (1931): 187-89.

Moltmann's recovery of the category of "resurrection" is certainly consistent with the fact that the early Christians (leaving aside John) proclaimed the resurrection as a "historical event," insofar as they made factual claims about Jesus on the basis of which they believed him to be the Messiah. Moreover, Moltmann's eschatological relativization of the Enlightenment's canons of reality, itself a foretaste of "postmodern" things to come, reopens the question of "miracle" and supernatural interventionism to which Bultmann's demythologization was an earlier response.

Nevertheless, whatever the reality status of Jesus' resurrection, the credibility of the kerygma, at least for Paul and John, stems from the fact that those to whom it was proclaimed understood themselves as personally addressed by the *Christus praesens*. Bultmann's exegetical and theological perspectives show that no recovery of the resurrection's objective possibility or historical plausibility can offset the absence or postponement of "the speaking of Christ" (Rom. 10:17) by which the church lives but about which *Theology of Hope* is silent.

Conclusion

Through a reexamination of both his exegetical and theological writings, I have established that Rudolf Bultmann consistently holds to a Christology of the *Christus praesens,* the Christ who is present in and through the proclamation of the kerygma. Bultmann's famous dictum, "The proclaimer became the proclaimed," goes together with his often overlooked insistence that "the proclaimed is simultaneously present as the proclaimer." Jesus Christ, as God's kerygmatic eschatological salvation event, is the rendering agent, not simply the rendered object, of Christian proclamation.

The theme of the presence of Christ is mediated to Bultmann through the liberal doctrine of "the personality of Jesus" propounded by his teachers Harnack, Weiss, and, above all, Herrmann. Bultmann overturns the liberal Christology in which he was trained by demonstrating that the synoptic Gospels cannot be taken as documentary sources for the reconstruction of the personality of the historical Jesus. Moreover, in seeking to correlate Jesus' personality with a contemporary piety, liberalism mistakenly assumes that we can have the same first-hand relation to Jesus as with any other of our personal associations. This simply ignores Jesus' death as the end to his personality and overlooks Jesus' Crucified and Risen destiny as the eschatological salvation event.

Bultmann's new interpretation of the presence of Christ occurs through his retrieval of the eschatology of Paul and John as found, especially, in 2 Corinthians 5 and 6 and John 1:14 and 5:24-25. For Paul, Jesus Christ is God's act which puts an end to the determinative status and standards of the old aeon — even with respect to Christology itself. Jesus Christ becomes our contemporary not through the perdurability of his personality but through the continuing proclamation of the kerygma or Christian message of God's act in Christ. The unity between the event of Christ and the office and word proclaiming Christ is one established by God but only encountered by human beings in and through the act of proclamation itself. Likewise, John locates the presence of Jesus Christ in the word of the church proclaimed in the power of the Paraclete. The same soteriological predicates attributed to the Son, or to his word and work, are transferred to the church and the Spirit, principally in relation to their common mission of bearing witness to the Son. In this way, the paradox which is Jesus Christ, namely, the eschatological event in history or the Word of God in human form, continues in and through the coincident witness of the church and the Spirit. Thus, both Paul and John link eschatological salvation directly to preaching.

Bultmann's own interpretation of the *Christus praesens* proceeds by transposing the "mythical-historical" account of the destiny of Jesus, as found in 1 Corinthians 15, into an "eschatological-existentialist" account faithful to John and 2 Corinthians 5 and 6. The resurrection of Jesus Christ becomes understood as the soteriological and performative power of the proclaimed "word of the cross." Moreover, in describing the kerygma as "demand" and "promise" uttered in the "existential language" of "direct address," Bultmann anticipates subsequent discussions in analytic philosophy regarding the performative conventions of "self-involving" promissory rhetoric. In this way, his case that "Jesus is risen in the kerygma," or that Jesus Christ exercises saving agency in and through the proclamation of the church, gains plausibility over against arbitrary appeals bordering on "word magic."

Despite the criticisms directed against Bultmann's *Christus praesens*, any comprehensive christological proposal must take account of Bultmann's three denotations of "Jesus Christ," that is, as mythical (or storied) character (JC-1), as historical figure (JC-2), and as contemporary agent of salvation (JC-3). I have shown that Bultmann's own patterning of these denotations appears incoherent when he both affirms and denies that the *Christus praesens* (JC-3) is the contemporary presence of Jesus of Nazareth (JC-2). The clue to this seeming contradiction lies in Bultmann's operating distinction between "occasion" and "condition." The historical Jesus and the empirical church can occasion but never condition, or causally effect, the saving presence of Christ. While Jesus of Nazareth may be "objectively" present in the kerygma either as a mythical or literary character or as a historical entity, faith arises only in the presence of faith's condition, that is, Jesus Christ as God's present eschatological agent. Bultmann's acknowledgment of all three aspects of Christology — the literary, the historical, and the eschatological — is faithful to the New Testament.

Nevertheless, Bultmann's doctrine of the *Christus praesens* can be legitimately criticized as relatively indifferent to the narrative identity of the Savior (Hans Frei), the social location of the scriptures and their hearers (Dorothee Sölle), and the still-outstanding promise of redemption setting Christians in solidarity with the present sufferings and longings of creation (Jürgen Moltmann).

Frei demonstrates how "realistic narrative" furnishes a character or an agent an identity, but he exaggerates its capacity to render the presence of Jesus Christ. If narrative recital so sovereignly rendered Christ's identity, and, hence, presence, as Frei maintains, then there would be no logical need, or basis, for preaching. But this implication rests on assigning to narrative, as such, properties of "commissive self-involvement" more appropriate to the rhetoric of promise-making.

Sölle highlights Bultmann's inattention to the social determinants affecting the kerygmatic occasion, despite his form-critical method which presupposes just such factors. Yet Sölle's own return to "the historical Jesus" of liberalism itself ignores the one indisputable contribution of the historical-critical method she champions, namely, the recovery of the eschatological content and context of Jesus' message and the primitive community's eschatological understanding of his destiny.

For his part, Moltmann shows how Bultmann's kerygmatic *Christus praesens* as the "presence of eternity" forecloses prematurely on the still-outstanding future promised by God in the resurrection of Jesus from the dead. Nevertheless, Moltmann offers no account in *Theology of Hope* either for the presence of Christ in the proclaimed word or for the implications of the present eschatology known to Paul and dominant in John.

The widespread practice of ignoring Bultmann's exegetical labors in theological discussion has enabled his critics to advance proposals for the presence of Christ divorced from the Gospel of John. Whatever the advantages of future eschatology, the historical Jesus, or the synoptic narratives in framing contemporary Christology, Bultmann's *Christus praesens* is a reminder that any Christology claiming consonance with the New Testament must reckon with the Johannine witness.

As representative of powerful currents of contemporary theology, Frei, Sölle, and Moltmann illustrate the post-Bultmann retrieval of many themes common to the liberalism of Bultmann's teachers. Frei's talk of

Jesus' "inner life" and "the Gospel narrative" echoes that of Herrmann. Sölle's "historical Jesus" reclaims the Christology common to liberalism as a whole. Moltmann's reserve toward a present eschatology of glory recalls the warnings of Herrmann and Albrecht Ritschl against seeking an earthly experience of the exalted Christ. Given Bultmann's convincing and unanswered criticisms of these views, one must conclude that he remains an inescapable conversation partner to the degree that contemporary theology, under a variety of names, represents a revival of emphases common to the older liberalism.

What gives Bultmann's work such perennial prospects is that no other theology in this century provides such a magisterial understanding of preaching as the primary *locus* of Christ's presence in the world. Christ is our contemporary, addressing us with the demand and promise of grace. Christ presides over our time, and every time, from his place in the pulpit. "The *Christus praesens*" is Bultmann's articulation of this claim.

Index of Subjects and Names

Index of Scripture References